D1606032

THE SECRETS OF ARCHITECTURAL COMPOSITION

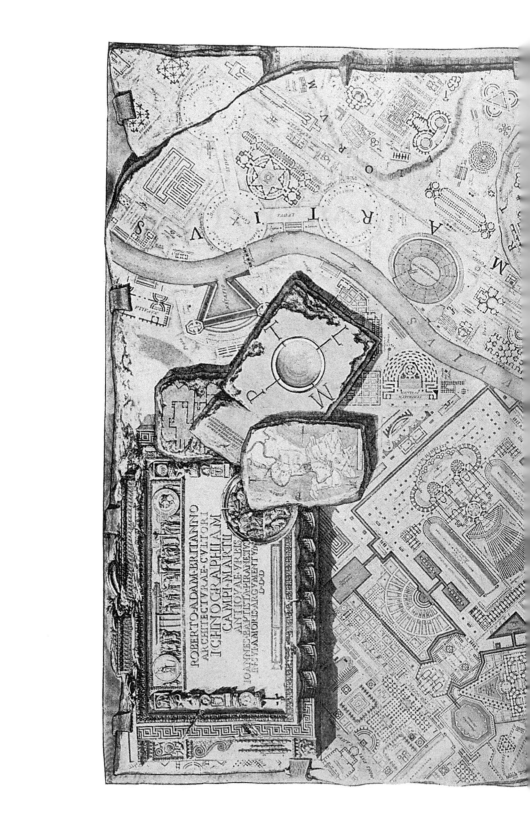

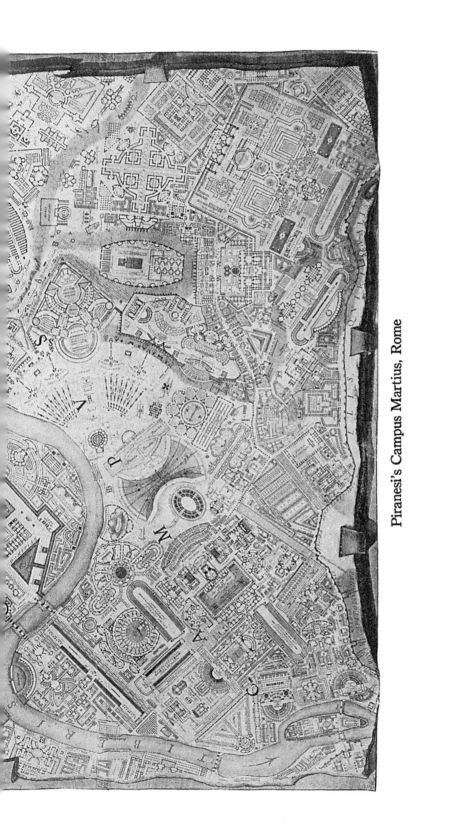

Piranesi's Campus Martius, Rome

Institute of Classical Architecture & Classical America

The Classical America Series in Art and Architecture

DOVER PUBLICATIONS, INC.

Greek and Roman Architecture in Classic Drawings by Hector d'Espouy
Monumental Classic Architecture in Great Britain and Ireland by Albert E. Richardson
The Secrets of Good Design for Artists, Artisans and Craftors by Burl N. Osburn

GUILD FOUNDATION PRESS

The Original Green: Unlocking the Mystery of True Sustainability by Stephen A. Mouzon

W. W. NORTON & CO.

The Golden City by Henry Hope Reed
The American Vignola by William R. Ware (also available as a Dover reprint)
The Library of Congress: Its Architecture and Decoration by Herbert Small
The New York Public Library: Its Architecture and Decoration by Henry Hope Reed
The Elements of Classical Architecture by George Gromort
The Architecture of the Classical Interior by Steven W. Semes
Classical Architecture for the Twenty-First Century: An Introduction to Design by J. François Gabriel
The United States Capitol: Its Architecture and Decoration by Henry Hope Reed
Arthur Brown Jr.: Progressive Classicist by Jeffrey T. Tillman
The Future of the Past: A Conservation Ethic for Architecture, Urbanism, and Historic Preservation by
   Steven W. Semes
Comparative Architectural Details: A Selection from Pencil Points 1932–1937, edited by Milton
   Wilfred Grenfell
The Theory of Mouldings by C. Howard Walker and Richard Sammons
Building Details by Frank M. Snyder, Introduction by Peter Pennoyer and Anne Walker
The Study of Architectural Design by John F. Harbeson, John Blatteau, and Sandra L. Tatman
Edwin Howland Blashfield: Master American Muralist, edited by Mina Rieur Weiner

PRINCETON ARCHITECTURAL PRESS

Antiquities of Athens by James Stuart and Nicholas Revett, Introduction by Frank Salmon
Basilique de Saint Pierre et Le Vaticane by Paul M. Letarouilly, Introduction by Ingrid Rowland

RIZZOLI

Bricks and Brownstone: The New York Row House 1783–1929 by Charles Lockwood

SAN MATEO COUNTY HISTORICAL ASSOCIATION

Carolands: Ernest Sanson, Achille Duchêne, Willis Polk by Michael Middleton Dwyer; produced by
   Charles Davey

STERLING PUBLISHING

Get Your House Right, Architectural Elements to Use & Avoid by Marianne Cusato & Ben Pentreath
   with Richard Sammons and Léon Krier

For a complete list of titles in the Classical America Series, visit www.classicist.org

INSTITUTE OF
CLASSICAL ARCHITECTURE
& CLASSICAL AMERICA

The Institute of Classical Architecture & Classical America (ICA&CA)
is dedicated to the classical tradition in architecture and the allied arts in the United States.
Inquiries about the ICA&CA mission and programs are welcome and should be addressed
to:

The Institute of Classical Architecture & Classical America
www.classicist.org

THE SECRETS OF ARCHITECTURAL COMPOSITION

NATHANIEL CORTLANDT CURTIS

DOVER PUBLICATIONS, INC.
Mineola, New York

IN ASSOCIATION WITH THE INSTITUTE OF
CLASSICAL ARCHITECTURE & CLASSICAL AMERICA

Bibliographical Note

This Dover edition, first published in 2011, is an unabridged republication of *Architectural Composition,* originally published in 1923 by J. H. Jansen, Cleveland.

Curtis, Nathaniel Cortlandt, 1881–1953.
   [Architectural composition]
   The secrets of architectural composition / Nathaniel C. Curtis. —Dover ed.
     p. cm.
   Originally published: Architectural composition. Cleveland [Ohio] : J.H. Hansen, 1923.
   Includes bibliographical references.
   ISBN-13: 978-0-486-48042-8
   ISBN-10: 0-486-48042-9
    1.Architecture—Composition, proportion, etc. I. Title.
NA2760.C8 2011
729'.12—dc22

20010049629

Manufactured in the United States by Courier Corporation
48042901
www.doverpublications.com

PREFACE

In the development of these inquiries into the subject of Architectural Composition the greatest amount of space has been given to the study of the *plan*. This method has been employed because it is believed to be in accord with the opinion of the foremost teachers of Architecture who place the study of the plan at the head of instruction both in theory and practice. In respect to this point of view the reader will note that my study of the subject has led me to a position considerably different from that which has been generally followed by other English and American writers who, while they have not neglected the plan, have at least relegated it to a comparatively subordinate position.

I have therefore purposely avoided a lengthy discussion of those Elements of Composition which have been so well set forth in other books and have sought to direct the reader's attention principally toward the study and analysis of plan-compositions, a direction which, to Architecture at least, is universally conceded to be of prime importance. The plan of a building establishes immediately two of the three dimensions in space and implies the third. It therefore lends itself to thinking in three dimensions. As one distinguished critic of Architecture has well said, "methods of study in plan have been adhered to at all times since the beginning of architecture. . . if the floor plan is well studied, beautiful in proportion, with a proper distribution of piers, thickness of walls, logically disposed and with good circulations, there will be no structural difficulties."

The author does not presume to assert that he has brought to light any new ideas relating to the theory of Architecture; he has not sought to produce an impression of originality but, on the contrary, gratefully acknowledges his indebtedness to the great authorities whose works have been freely consulted. The author wishes to acknowledge in particular his indebtedness to the great work of Guadet, "Eléments et Théorie de l'Architecture."

New Orleans 1923.

Nathaniel Cortlandt Curtis is a member of the American Institute of Architects and was formerly professor of Architecture and head of the School of Architecture in the Tulane University of Louisiana; associate professor of Architectural Design in the University of Illinois; professor of Architecture in the Alabama Polytechnic Institute.

The publisher expresses his appreciation of the assistance on the part of Mr. E. A. Ruggles of the Cleveland Museum of Art for the typographical presentation of this book.

To the Memory

of

WILLIAM R. WARE

*Late Professor of Architecture
in Columbia University,*

and

NATHAN C. RICKER
*Professor of Architecture, Emeritus,
in the University of Illinois,*

In grateful acknowledgment of the
lasting inspiration derived from their
teachings, this book is affectionately
dedicated by the author.

THE SECRETS OF
ARCHITECTURAL COMPOSITION

CONTENTS

PART I

PART II

PART III

PART IV

CONTENTS CONTINUED

LIST OF ILLUSTRATIONS

LIST OF ILLUSTRATIONS—CONTINUED

PART I.

THE NATURE OF ARCHITECTURE

CHAPTER I.

DUAL NATURE OF ARCHITECTURE; FUNDAMENTAL ESTHETIC LAWS OF ARCHITECTURE; ARCHITECTURAL CREATION; BIBLIOGRAPHY.

The nature of architecture is determined by two objects. The first of these objects is the satisfaction of the requirements of use; the second is the satisfaction of the requirements of beauty. Since the purposes of different types of buildings vary greatly, it follows that these two essential characteristics of use and beauty do not exist in the same degree, but alternate in importance within wide limits. Thus in buildings intended solely for use, material necessities dominate; whereas in edifices designed to evoke certain emotions or intellectual impressions through their external form or ornamentation, esthetic qualities would be given the first place. At one extreme, therefore, we have strictly utilitarian edifices, as for example, factories; at the other, monuments and works of sculpture; between, many varying types; all never-the-less, architecture. Throughout the whole range of types of buildings which the manifold requirements of the human race in all epoch and in many climes have called into being, it will be seen that the scope for the expression of character by the treatment of the architecture is practically limitless.

Although the requirements of habitation and the satisfaction of material necessities are the first and earliest objects of architecture, the satisfaction of esthetic needs is that which essentially characterizes it—as architecture. This follows from the fact that a work of architecture, if devoid of the quality of beauty, is not materially different from a work merely of engineering. And while it cannot be denied that stable buildings may be designed and erected without reference to esthetic principles at all, such buildings, although they may in a measure satisfy all the material requirements of man, cannot properly be called works of architecture. Real architecture is only achieved when there is wrought into the composition of the building a certain harmony of form which we call the beauty of the edifice. It is this harmonious combining of elements, then, according to the laws of art, which has been held to differentiate architecture from purely engineering constructions.

In view of these considerations it is proper that the student of architecture should, at the outset grasp clearly the distinction between a work of architecture and a work of engineering.

Broadly speaking any construction possessing one or more of the following characteristics is of the nature of architecture.

First, as to arrangement—A well-composed plan in which the requirements of use and beauty are harmoniously combined. Second, as to form—An external form or configuration in all exterior and interior parts wherein the special requirements of the edifice are expressed in terms of beauty and good proportion. Third, as to finish—By which is meant a due regard for appearance in the selection of materials used in all the visible parts of the structure.

In the light of these distinctions, any edifice even though it is of a nature that would ordinarily be determined by purely structural and utilitarian requirements, such as a lighthouse or a bridge, may properly be classified with the works of architecture, provided a reasonable prominence has been given to external form and appearance. To cite two well-known examples: the Manhattan bridge in New York is certainly a work of architecture; while its neighbor, the Williamsburg bridge is just as certainly a work of engineering.

While the question as to what is engineering and what architecture cannot be settled by reference to a list of positive artistic qualities, it must not be forgotten that magnitude of dimensions alone is often one of the most important and impressive of all artistic qualities.

The nature of architecture is still further affected by many external factors, not strictly speaking inherent, but varying with time and place. Such influences as climate, topography, religious and social customs—the aspirations of the time—are all reflected in architecture, which necessarily therefore environs and adapts itself to the social condition of peoples of every epoch.

There have been theorists who have striven to find in the material side of architecture a sufficient explanation for its esthetic character. They have tried to show that the outward form of a building both in mass and detail is logically and satisfactorily determined by utilitarian requirements alone; their main contention being that no form should be introduced that is not a derivative of a material function. This raises the interesting and pertinent question as to what would be the result should the architect cast aside all striving for effects and give free reign to the mechanical axiom that "form follows function" in architectural design.

Is the principle as stated above sufficient to give to it beauty of form as well as truth of thought and fulfillment of purpose? Before attempting to pass judgment on these questions, let us first analyze somewhat the principle to which we have reference in its application to architecture.

What are the effects or external appearances, for which the architect strives? Naturally these depend on the sort of building he is designing, and there are many sorts between the purely utilitarian and the highly monumental. Generally speaking, it may be said that he strives to produce an impression of a certain definite character which is dependent on the purpose of the edifice. This is particularly that character which we call the beauty of the edifice. As an extreme illustration of this we may be sure if an architect, having for his program the design of a church, evolves a building with the configuration of a box factory then he has missed the primary object of architecture, which in this case was to create the impression of a religious edifice. Effects of this sort are dependent upon many and varying conditions. We may, however, say confidently that they are not dependent upon function solely nor upon materials economically used in construction. The lofty nave of a cathedral has nothing to do with the material function of the building—in fact it rather detracts from the stability of the edifice; yet this is necessary from the consideration that architecture has spiritual meanings, which are expressed in forms having, more than often, nothing to do with material functions.

The effects striven for in all the various works of architecture are like the above; that is the effort is to create a building whose character corresponds to its program, whether this building be a box factory, a church, a residence, a tea house, a monument to the heroes of the Marne, or any other.

In a sense this is a modern conception of the ideal of architecture, for the architecture of antiquity was not strongly characterized. The Propylaea and the Temple of Athena are not essentially different in character, yet one is the portal to a fortress, while the other is a shrine to the goddess of wisdom. The Greeks were not under any necessity for distinguishing between different types of buildings by accentuating their character, since they had only a very few types and these mostly religious. The necessity was the same to a greater degree with the Roman, Gothic and Renaissance architectures, and we must recognize a gradually increasing tendency toward characterization as types of buildings become more numerous and complex. On the other hand the Grecian architecture was closely wedded to the principle that form follows function. All its details and proportions are directly derived from the logical use of materials (limited with them to stone and marble) in construction. Moreover the Greeks were actuated by the search for pure beauty of form above all things.

Is it not more than passing strange, in view of the fact that the most perfect architecture that the world has seen was developed through conformity to the principle of form following function, that the same principle does not seem to be a wholly satisfactory aesthetic guide in modern architectural design? The reply to this query is that we cannot detach ourselves from tradition in the art of architecture any more than we can detach ourselves successfully from tradition in any other art or progressive form of knowledge. We cannot get away from those forms, proportions and meanings which have been established throughout the ages, and it makes little difference if stone architecture was the medium through which those meanings were established. Willful disregard or lack of appreciation of this truth has led, more than anything else, to the confusion which exists in many minds as to what is engineerng and what architecture. Let us hear what Mr. Arthur J. Penty has to say on this point.

"There are," he says, "spiritual differences between architecture and engineering that are not to be ignored. Their aims are different. We may distinguish between them by saying that whereas engineering aims at securing its results with the utmost economy of means, architecture has no such aim. Economy in architecture is invariably a necessity; it is never an aim, for architecture only becomes really impressive when it exhibits an excess of strength, when it is massive, prodigal, and lavish in the use of materials. Reinforced concrete walls four inches thick can never be as im-

pressive as stone or brick walls four feet thick. There is no getting behind the fact that, beyond a certain point, the more scientific construction becomes the less it has to say for itself in terms
of architecture. If, therefore, we disparage esthetics and exalt
utility, we do not encourage architecture but engineering; not art
but mathematics. We exalt construction, which should be the
servant of architecture, into the master; we exalt secondary over
primary considerations, and that brings about confusion, for whereas secondary aims find their place in subordination to primary ones,
primary aims come to be entirely neglected when secondary ones
are stressed."

There is another point that may be noted in this connection.
In antique architecture, actual stability was not sufficient; it had
also to be manifest. Our modern ideas of efficiency and economy
lead us to stress actual stability, and to regard anything added
thereto for the sake of appearances as more or less of a super-
fluity. Let us not forget that in the visual arts appearances count
for everything, after requirement of use and stability have been
properly safeguarded.

In summing up the primary effects which architects strive for,
it seems apparent that these are dependent very largely upon tradition, and if we would apply the formula that "form should follow
function" in its purity, we are compelled to cast aside tradition
altogether and start anew. Now this is the very thing that seems
impossible for the reasons already suggested. Nor is it necessary
to disregard all the accumulated records of the past in order to
achieve a modern architecture which will correctly reflect the spirit
of our own times.

While material functions, such as structure, have great importance in shaping the artistic forms of architecture they are not
sufficient in themselves to give to it the highest expression as a
work of art. A strict adherence to the doctrine expressed by the
phrase "form follows function" is apt to produce edifices which are
sterile creations, devoid of charm and meaning.

CHAPTER II.

Primary Esthetic Laws of Architecture; Architectural Creation.

Theorists agree in defining the basic artistic principles on which the art of achitecture rests. It is generally stated that the impression of beauty depends fundamentally on unity of form; or, in other words, that the plurality of elements that make up a building must be so related and bound together as to make what is termed—a unified composition. In order that this object be attained, it is evident that all these elements should bear, not only a definite relation to each other, but to the composition as a whole.

For example, unity may be secured by having all parts of the composition in the same scale, or of the same stylistic character, or properly proportioned to one another and to the requirements of human needs. These are subtle ideas requiring great knowledge and educated taste for their proper application to any problem of architecture, but such knowledge is nevertheless essential and must be acquired. The ideas of proportion and scale are those which are most closely related to the conception of unity. Unity in architecture can never be realized except through understanding of the principles governing proportion and scale which fix the relation of parts to each other and to the entirety.

To possess unity a thing must be complete in itself. It must have a certain simplicity, easily grasped by the mind, which tends to produce a singleness of impression. The unity of the elementary geometrical solids, spheres, pyramids, cubes, cones and tetrahedrons, is readily comprehended, since nothing can be added to or taken away from any one of them without destroying its form. To these solids of geometry the larger masses of buildings bear a close correspondence since they have in general the same regular stereometric form, yet they differ from them in other essentials affecting their unity. These differences are due, first, to the fact that geometrical solids do not necessarily bear any relation to their surroundings, whereas buildings do bear a necessary relation to their surroundings and particularly to the ground on which they stand.

The singleness of impression which is essential to unity in solid forms is a resultant of the method, system or idea controlling their generation. This produces other differences affecting the unity of the solids of architecture that are not to be found in the solids of geometry. In bodies of regular stereometric form which have no reference to their surroundings this central controlling idea is usually some point, such as the center of gravity, the center of a sphere, or some line like the axis of a pyramid or cone. In the creations of architecture the principles controlling the unity of the composition are much more complicated and difficult of application. Here the singleness of impression results especially from the search for character and the methods employed to make it evident. The importance of character in architecture has already been alluded to. Character here means that every building should have an individual treatment or configuration that is primarily a direct result of the purpose for which it is intended and the materials with which it is built—the use of materials being governed by rational means of construction. In other words the purpose for which a building is intended determines its character, first by determining its plan and outward configuration and second by expressing in it a certain ideal significance which declares in the language of beauty the object and purpose for which it stands.

In buildings of monumental character the impression of unity is realized without effort of the intellect. Such buildings are usually symmetrical with a dominating central portion flanked by wings. The first impression of such an edifice is that of its mass or silhouette as if the building were seen at a distance or through a haze, the eye resting on the central dominating motive. Subsequent impressions of unity are governed by the more detailed qualities of the design, such as equality of scale, uniformity of style, the relative amount of wall and window area, the horizontal lines of cornices, mouldings and string-courses, carved ornament and all minor decorative features.

Up to this point the requirements for unity have been discussed in a very general way. More specifically, then, what are the requirements for unity in architecture? According to the classic statement of Semper there are essentially three. "Symmetry, proportion and direction are collective ideas," says he, "inasmuch as they bind a plurality into a unity." Symmetry or balance in a composition results directly from the force of gravity. In the mind of man there is an innate desire for stability in all objects resting on the ground, and symmetry is that quality in design which renders stability evident. The most stable form is that which tends toward the pyramid. Architecturally this means a structure whose subordinate masses are balanced on either side of a central axis, which has a wide base and general tendency toward set-backs in profile as the walls ascend upward. Historically the Egyptian pyramid is the edifice whose mass expresses stability in perfection. The requirements of space-enclosure, however, demand that walls should be vertical or nearly so, but even here, as has been pointed out, the tendency toward a pyramidal conformation is necessary, although it needs must be slight. It is well-known that the Greeks regarded this as a requirement of architecture, par excellence, so that they did not hesitate to slope all the columns of the Parthenon slightly toward a remote apex.

Certain monumental buildings and groups illustrate forcibly the triangular or pyramidal arrangement demanded by the noblest compositions. The Temple of Scottish Rite in Washington by John Russel Pope is a notable example (Fig. 2).

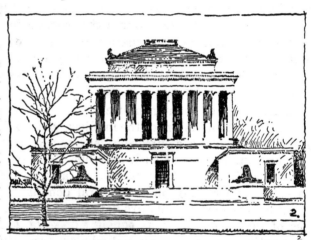

Fig. 2.—Temple of the Scottish Rite; Washington, D. C. John Russell Pope, Architect.

The Perry Memorial (Fig. 3) is composed with a Greek Doric column, the noblest form of the shaft, forming the central dominant. This is flanked by a museum on one side and a statue with its architectural setting on the other, united by a great plateau for ceremonies; the whole forming a perfect triangular composition. Similarly, the Springfield Municipal Buildings compose in triangular fashion. Here the flanking buildings are set quite close to the isolated tower, which like the Doric column springs directly from the ground (Fig. 4). Other examples illustrating this principle are distributed all through this book. See especially Fig. 4-A.

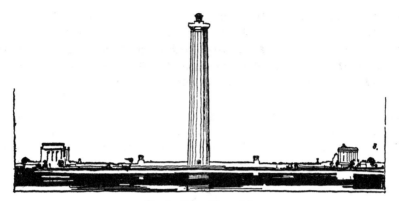

Fig. 3.—Perry Memorial
Friedlander and Seymour, Architects

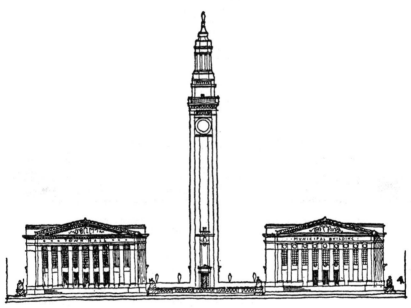

Fig. 4.—Springfield Municipal Buildings
Pell and Corbett, Architects

The primary function of architecture is to provide shelter—the enclosure of space. In buildings this is accomplished in the simplest manner by means of a substructure, walls and a roof. Consequently there results a three-fold division in an upward direction which is, practically speaking, an essential characteristic of architecture in general. All well-articulated architectonic works require fundamentally a base on which to stand, a middle part, wall or shaft, and a protecting cornice representing the eaves of the roof, in order that the impression of completeness may be conveyed and thus satisfy the requirements of unity of form. This three-fold division of membering is the simplest basis for proportion—in a vertical direction at least. Proportions in a horizontal direction are determined by the plan, which establishes the

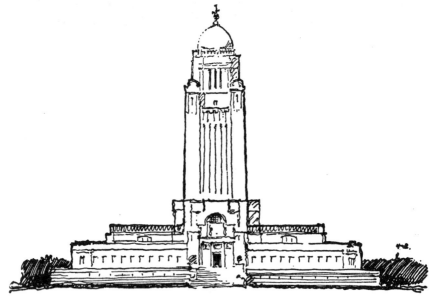

Fig. 4-A.—Design for State Capitol Building, Lincoln, Nebraska.
Bertram G. Goodhue, Architect

location of division walls and the distribution of openings. Proportions are next affected in a broad way by the introduction of intermediate floors, giving buildings of multiple stories. Proportion, as has been said, touches every single detail of the architectural organism, but in the simplest and widest sense proportion means purely the three-fold division necessary to the enclosure of space.

It is in the Orders of Architecture that we find this triple system of membering most clearly, systematically and perfectly expressed. This is why the study of the Orders is given such a prominent place in the preliminary training of the student. When he studies the Orders he is studying proportions, and while acquiring a necessary knowledge of the elements of architecture, at the same time he acquires a still more necessary perception of the relative proportions that exist throughout the whole domain of composition.

Coming now to the third idea essential to unity in architecture, that of direction, as expressed by Semper, we discover this to mean the direction toward which a building may be said to face.

Few architectural structures except the most highly monumental have a vertical, centrally disposed axis of symmetry, with identical elevations on every front. The requirements of planning and location usually necessitate a different treatment of front, sides and rear. Hence the idea of direction is essential to the unity of the composition.

Summing up the elementary requirements for unity in architecture, we find that the singleness of impression produced is dependent on the following conditions.

First there must be a symmetrical disposition of parts so as to convey the impression of equipoise and stability. This is accomplished by the arrangement of corresponding parts with reference to axes and by set-backs in a vertical direction to accentuate stability. Symmetry makes the central, dominating idea of the composition more evident.

Second the three-fold division of membering with respect to vertical proportion must also be evident. There must be a visible relation between burden, support and crowning functions.

Finally a unified architectural structure should show direction; that is a definite front, sides and rear, each of which is composed with regard to the separate conditions that may be imposed upon it.

Such appear to be the conditions on which the beauty of the edifice ultimately depends. It must be remembered, however, that the rules of art are not inflexible. Yet they are necessary for guidance and should not be deviated from without reason.

ARCHITECTURAL CREATION

We have seen that the invariable, underlying, function of architecture is the satisfaction of a definite purpose, which must be made known in two directions—the satisfaction of material and esthetic needs. The satisfaction of its material side is found in the carcass of the building, the satisfaction of its esthetic side is found in beauty of form, proportion and arrangement, qualities which characterize it as architecture. Buildings are the end and aim of all architectural creation, but before buildings can be carried into material effect and creation made manifest, one must first know what he would create. The thing to be created is set forth in what is known as the program of the building, wherein the problem, so to speak, is stated and the principal requirements of the composition explained. Upon the program is brought to bear the process of graphical reasoning, known as architectural designing, which finds its expression in drawings. Designing, thinking and drawing are the essential processes inherent in architectural composition. Finally comes the execution of the building in accordance with the designer's conception and under his direction. Architecture, then, is "the art of planning, designing and drawing buildings, and of directing the execution thereof."

Architectural designing is the process of creative thought, graphically manifested, controlled and ordered by the three ideas summarized in: fulfillment of purpose, truth of thought, and beauty of form. From these primary ideas the theoretical principles of composition are deduced. This theory does not seek to lay down rules with scientific precision, but it establishes certain reasonable limits within which the genius and imagination of the designer may work. Its restrictions are such as belong inherently to architecture, per se; they are part of its nature, they qualify and define it. The artist cannot defy the laws of nature, neither can he defy the laws of art; the first have been formulated by science, the second have been established by tradition, by civilization and environment, and through experience in the use of materials. Considerations of art cannot diminish the safe limits set by science in the use of materials in buildings, but within these there remain almost infinite possibilities for the expression of originality. Variety is made possible chiefly through the study of proportions and the application of the knowledge so derived.

Unlike painters and sculptors, architects do not execute while they conceive. The architect creates the design but the execution of it must be left to many hands, and more than often the direction of the details of the work do not fall under his immediate supervision. The actual work must be done through the medium of an organization, which the architect can do no more than direct and supervise. How much worse is the situation of the mere student of architecture, whose designs for buildings are not conceived with a view to execution at all. This fact makes it very easy for them to fall into the disastrous habit of regarding their problems as merely abstract exercises in artistic expression. The pictorial possibilities inherent in methods of rendering are apt to become more absorbing than the underlying facts of construction. Hence arises the tendency toward what has been aptly characterized as "paper architecture." While there is no denying that the study of a beautiful project not constructible may have had a stimulating effect on the imagination, such practice cannot be considered either rational or wholesome. The student should keep in mind the words of Guadet, "Every architectural composition must be constructible, for every project not so is radically nothing."

Given the program of the building—the statement of what is to be created—it is not out of place at this juncture to inquire briefly as to what the student's attitude of mind should be toward the problem set before him, and what knowledge should be his, that will enable him to arrive at a solution expressed in architectural terms.

The more important of these qualifications are the following:

First—Aptitude; inborn talent and a love of beauty; an earnest impulse toward the creation of artistic things. The earliest and one of the most significant manifestations of aptitude would seem to be capacity to learn to draw readily—especially freehand drawing.

Second—An accurate knowledge of the masterpieces of architecture. It is essential for the designer that he should comprehend thoroughly the nature and historic development of architecture and of the forms of ornament, to be inspired by their perfection and be able to apply his knowledge practically to the problem before him.

Third—A general acquaintance with the nature and properties of building materials; with the fundamental laws of statics and those systematic combinations of structural elements which form the framework of architectural organisms. For the purposes of creation in design it is sufficient that this knowledge be relative rather than absolute. The question here is one purely of proportions as will be more fully indicated later. The function of science in construction is to verify the stability of structural combinations, which must first be created by the art of the designer. Art and imagination are the forces that move one to create; science does not create.

Fourth—Knowledge of the primary laws of composition together with a cultivated sense of proportion and scale. This qualification may be acquired only through unremitting study and practice.

Fifth—Ability in drawing, both freehand and mechanical, but especially the former. Practically speaking, creative thought in architecture cannot be manifested in any visible form except by means of drawing or modeling, which is itself a form of drawing, until the building is erected.

It is apparent that qualifications such as these are not easily acquired but rather form, as severally outlined here, the basis for the study of a lifetime. Because the study is hard many seek to evade it and yet set out to create architecture, believing perhaps, that they have that spark of genius which alone will insure success while permitting them to disregard the trodden paths. Since genius is well-known to be rare, failure, or at least mediocrity, must be the almost inevitable result.

Architectural designing, architectural creation, and architectural composition are in a sense synonymous phrases, although the first has, properly speaking, to do with the practical study of a given program, the second with the realization of architecture as a whole from the study of its nature, while the third is concerned with the theoretical principles governing the planning and embellishment of buildings.

The third distinction, that of architectural composition, is the one to which our attention would naturally be drawn in any written discussion of the theory of architecture. Broadly considered, architectural composition is essentially the art of properly combining proportions. The study of composition is the study of proportion. Proportions, rather than ornament or decoration, determine the individual character of an edifice. The architect must above everything be a master of proportion.

What then is meant by this all-important term? It is not easy to give a definition in a sentence or two. Proportion may be either relative or absolute. In the first sense it is merely the ratio of a certain part to the whole—as, for example, we say a column is eight diameters high, or the entablature is one-fourth the height of the column. In the second sense it is the relation that exists between the different parts of the whole, or the relation of the whole to its separate parts. The unit of comparison or measurement is the factor called "scale". Scale is the relation between the parts of a composition and a certain abstract unit of measurement to which we have become accustomed through everyday use or observation, as, for example, the normal height of the human figure. These factors will be discussed fully in subsequent chapters in their relation to the practical problem.

"The sense of proportion is the chief artistic sense," says Guadet. "Proportions are infinite and delicate in art and are still more so in nature. How do you recognize a friend among all the people you see, even though you see millions pass? A question of proportions alone, for unless your friend be a monster or deformed, his composition does not vary. But proportions are so infinite and variable, that among millions of heads no two are exactly alike. Nothing develops a sense of proportion like practice in drawing. To draw is to perceive and then express those specific proportions that distinguish and identify the model. The best draftsman is the most sensitive to proportions."

Good taste or the educated sense of what looks well is the surest criterion for proportions. Some have sought to substitute for this certain geometrical relations; but while such relations are helpful in some ways, that will be later indicated, they cannot replace artistic judgment and therefore ought not to be seriously considered.

To sum up, we may say—that a good design for a building is one whose elements are combined in such a way as to preserve good proportion throughout and all of whose parts are in scale.

More specifically, the study of proportions includes: First—The study of the relative capacities of materials in construction to resist stress. This knowledge is to be gained rather by practice and study of precedent than by mathematical analysis. It enables us to properly proportion piers and walls so their sections relatively express the material of which they are built, the loads they carry, and the thrusts they resist. The study of the means and results of construction should precede all the rest.

Second—The study of the relative sizes, shapes and distribution of rooms, corridors and all spaces in plan so as to satisfy the requirements of the program in the best manner.

Third—The study of combinations of the elements of architecture and ornament, having consideration for correct proportions and good scale. This means, above all, the study of precedent— of the history of architecture and ornament.

REFERENCES.

Bühlman, Josef. "Die Architektur des Klassischen Altertums und der Renaissance." (text)

Wagner, Heinrich. "Die Architektonische Composition."

Viollet-le-Duc. "Lectures on Architecture."
translated by B. Bucknall.

Guadet, J. "Eléments et Théorie de l'Architecture" Book 1, Chap. VIII. "L'Art et la Science de la Construction."

PART II.

THE ELEMENTS OF ARCHITECTURE.

CHAPTER I.

WALLS; OPENINGS IN WALLS; DOORS AND WINDOWS; BALUSTRADES AND BALCONIES; ROOFS AND DOMES.

In architecture walls may occur either as isolated structures or as connected elements of the building. The isolated wall is a complete composition in itself, while the connected wall—either external or partition wall—is part of a composition and must conform in proportion and scale to the requirements of the edifice as a whole.

The composition of walls results from the materials and method of construction adopted, and from proportion and decoration, and is a powerful means for expressing character. In common with all well-articulated structures, walls usually demand the same triple membering with respect to composition, i. e., base, middle part and crowning part. The base should project in order to give the pyramidal effect satisfying to the eye and required for stability, while moulded sections since they are near the ground and required to resist shock should be strongly accented and heavier to give the impression of strength (Figs. 5 and 6). The cornice crowns and protects the wall and shelters the decoration of the frieze.

Besides the moulded sections of architectural lines and surface ornament carved in relief, the character of walls is dependent upon three elements—the texture given to the stone, the

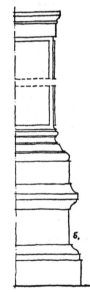

Fig. 5.—Base of the Giraud Palace, Rome.

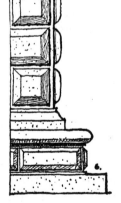

Fig. 6.—Base, Strozzi Palace, Florence.

method of jointing, and the thickness revealed in the openings. Each of these elements must be carefully studied in the light especially of Antique Architecture and that of the Italian Renaissance. The most monumental impression is naturally derived from the use of stone or marble and will be in character with the antique architecture of Greece and Rome.

The thickness of a wall is determined by four considerations. 1 Construction. 2 Climate. 3 Effect desired. 4 Decoration. Of these, construction is the first requirement: for considerations of appearance can never diminish the minimum thickness required for stability. In construction, walls must resist several sorts of stresses—vertical, the result of imposed loads combined with the weight of the wall itself; inclined, due to the thrusts of arches or vaults not counter-abutted, and lastly combinations of forces tending to produce flexure. The two first named are the most important, the former tends to crush, the latter to overturn. Figure 30 gives a diagrammatic representation of how these forces act.

Generally the external walls of buildings, not being in equilibrium, must be thicker than internal walls which are usually subject to balanced loads. Thickness in external walls is also required for protection from heat and cold; this has had a marked effect on the architecture of countries where extremes of temperature prevail and is a source of character in plan as well as elevation.

More often a thick wall is demanded merely for the sake of appearance, the amount of "reveal" in openings always determining the effective thickness, and the consequent impression of strength or richness. The depth of reveal in rectangular and arched openings should be proportioned to the character sought. This is a matter for taste rather than science to determine since mathematical formulas will only be used to establish the minimum thickness.

Walls, especially the basement walls of monumental buildings, are frequently thicker on account of the architectural treatment given to the walls above. Engaged columns, pilasters or other projecting breaks in the upper walls necessitate a corresponding thickening of the substructure. Overhangs in profile are never admissible (Fig. 7).

As regards decoration much might be said, but for our purpose, that is the general scheme of the parti, only the broad essentials need be indicated. First it may be said, that the mode of construction of the wall is in itself a source of decoration. The texture finish given to the masonry and the size and jointing of stonework are important elements of beauty requiring careful study. Bosses and rustications are attributes of powerful, monumental architecture, but the amount of projection should not be so great as to detract from the function of the stone as a supporting feature. Quoins are logically used at angles to strengthen and stabilize. Their number should be odd, beginning and ending with a long quoin. Continuous friezes, bands or panels of carved decoration may be placed along the top of a wall under the cornice, as in the three famous examples of the Parthenon, the Pantheon in

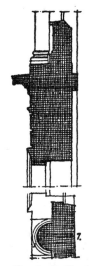

Fig. 7.—Profile of the Exterior Wall of the Ecole des Beaux Arts; Detail

Paris and the Tomb of Cecelia Metella in Rome (Figs. 8, 9 and 9-A) or along the bottom as in Figure 10. Where the mid sections of a wall are decorated with carving, this is usually confined to single courses of stone as in the Roman Pantheon (Fig. 13). Ornament along the lower part of a wall is better placed where the wall comes behind a portico, since

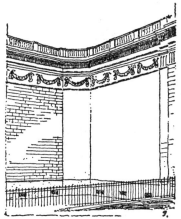

Fig. 9.—Lateral Walls of the Pantheon, Paris

Fig. 8.—Parthenon; Section of Cella Wall and Panthanaic Frieze

protection is afforded. This is especially true if the carving is rather delicate or small in scale.

The varying thickness of walls in plan results mainly from the necessities of construction and the larger features of the archi-

tecture, facts which must be clearly realized and borne in mind while planning. All this will be more clearly brought out under the heading "The Study of Poché" where wall-sections in their varying relations are considered in detail.   Just how much questions of style and appearance should modify the thickness of walls is a matter for supplementary consideration, often also of prime importance in determining the parti.

Undoubtedly the most fruitful source of study for wall treatment is the great body of palaces of the Italian Renaissance, a source to which the student should turn most often for inspiration and suggestion.

Fig. 9-A.—Tomb of Cecelia Metella, Rome

OPENINGS IN WALLS; DOORS AND WINDOWS.

Openings in walls may be either rectangular or arched. Analysis of their legitimate proportions will be reserved for a future chapter; it will suffice to say here that constructively the lintel is for the narrower opening, the arch for the wider, although this principle may be sensibly modified for decorative reasons.

If architecture—*and we are speaking always of masonry architecture*—were restricted to the lintel, great openings could never be attained.   Monumental architecture therefore demands that the lintel be reserved for narrow openings, whose proportions are high rather than wide, for the stone lintel or architrave acts as a beam in construction and even the hardest stone has little transverse

strength. In modern construction wider rectangular openings than
are allowable for stone may be safely carried out by backing the
stone lintel which concealed structural steel members, which really
carry the load, or by jointing the stone as in the flat arch (jointed

Fig. 10.—Base and Portico of the Altar of Zeus at Pergamon
(Restoration by M. Pontremoli and Max Collignon)

platband), thereby seeking to justify the increased span. But
such expedients are dangerous because they tend to encourage
excessive and vicious proportions. The proportions which we
admire and which satisfy the eye are derived from a mode of
construction which centuries of use has taught us to regard as
reasonable and logical. This we find exemplified in antique architecture—the architecture of Greece and Rome and of the Italian
Renaissance.

The invention of the arch is one of the supreme achievements
of human genius, its employment in buildings marvellously extending the scope of design and composition and opening the way to
the development of new types of edifices and new styles of architecture. The arch permits wider spans because the separate stones
of which it is composed (voussoirs) are in compression which is a

natural condition for stone, while it may be subjected to a certain amount of unequal settlement without rupture or sensible deformation.

The stresses which an arch transmits to its supports do not act vertically but along a resultant line inclined to the vertical (Figs. 30 and 31). It must be remembered in designing arches, that the flatter the arch the greater is the horizontal thrust, and since it is a principal condition for stability that the resultant direction of this thrust projected must fall well within the base of the supporting pier, it is evident that the depth of such piers is a corresponding condition for safety (Fig. 30). A pier is further stabilized by its own weight and the load it carries.

In a continuous arcade all the arches are in equilibrium with respect to each other except the end arches, which exert an unbalanced thrust on the last pier. Terminal piers in such compositions must therefore be made wide enough to insure stability, or even wider if the calculated width is not satisfactory to the eye. Here again it is important that the student should familiarize himself with precedent through the study and observation of the proportions exemplified in the great masterpieces of the architecture of past ages.

The rectangular doorway is the simplest and most practical form of entrance that is intended to be closed with hinged leaves. Arched doorways in most cases require a fixed upper part—either in the form of a stone tympanum—or, what is more common in classic architecture, a fixed transom-bar supporting a glazed fanlight. This is necessary not only for the reason that it is usually advisable to bring the height of the doorway down to somewhere near human proportions, but also because there is apt to be difficulty in providing for the opening of the leaves of doors which completely fill an arched opening, unless the soffit of the arch is splayed sufficiently to permit the high point of the door, traveling in a horizontal circle as it is opened, to pass the extreme edge of the arch.

In deciding on the type of opening to use, however, the designer is controlled by the character of the facade. The arched opening with fixed upper part is an entirely practicable motive, capable of beautiful solutions. Artistic expression should govern intention and practical considerations may be properly subordinated in this instance.

An external doorway preceded by steps should always have a landing before the threshold for safety in going out as well as for effect.

It is customary in thick walls to slightly splay the jamb so that the door may open beyond a right angle (Figs. 116, 117).

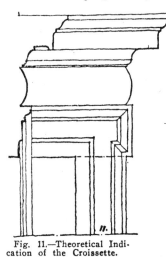

Fig. 11.—Theoretical Indication of the Croissette.

In composition the external doorway and window are almost identical motives. The same treatment of enframement is appropriate to either; the only difference being that the door-opening extends to the floor while the window opening stops at the sill. But the architrave mouldings framing windows are also frequently extended to the floor and in this case the low wall between the jambs which supports the sill is constructed of thinner masonry than the main part of the wall. This seems proper from the consideration that one would wish to approach as close as possible to the outside to enjoy the view, but the arrangement is frequently disregarded in practice. This thinner masonry between the sill and the floor is termed "allege" by the French. If the window sill is very high above the floor then the allege is omitted.

The simplest decoration for a rectangular opening (door or windo) is the enclosing, flat or moulded, architrave. Where the lintel is accented, in principle this accent (croissette) should be on a line with the soffit of the lintel, thus emphasizing construction and insuring economy in stone cutting (Fig. 11).

As the decorative treatment of the opening is further developed, there is first placed above the lintel a cap or cornice to protect the opening from rain water. But with a horizontal capping, rainwater will fall before the opening, although it escapes the sill; consequently triangular or arched pediments came to be added as a decorative feature in order that the drip might be shed laterally

Guadet remarks in this connection that "doubtless from the moment that the use of an architectural form has a motive where it is logical and useful, it escapes all criticism; hence architrave, frieze, cap and pediment form a complete decoration for the external doorway"—thus rejecting the criticism of purists who contend that the pediment is the end of a roof.

The architrave framing an opening is often embellished by flanking columns or pilasters supporting an entablature, as in the beautiful and well known example of the Farnese Palace. This arrangement, especially when employed in connection with the windows of a facade, requires considerable projection for its support.

A very beautiful arrangement and one often used is the motive of the doorway of the Erechtheion—the doorway with consoles supporting an extended cap. It is necessary to understand the logic underlying the design of this motive in order that it may be expressed with classic purity and truth. The following principles should be kept in mind: 1 The console must be far enough from the jamb to allow sufficient support for the lintel. 2 The console should not extend below the soffit of the lintel. 3 The cap should extend little beyond the angle, so as to give equal projection of soffit at front and side of console. 4 Any treatment of bed mouldings or details beneath the cap may stop between the consoles.
5 In general the opening is first enclosed by an architrave, and frequently in addition the width of the console is extended down by another narrower architrave (the "chambranle"). These guiding principles are set forth in Figure 12 which serves to indicate the theoretical scheme. The doorway of the Erechtheion; the Temple of Minerva Polias; the Temple of Jupiter at Cori; the Pantheon; and the doorway at Corneto are examples of great doorways in antique architecture which are particularly valuable for study. (See figures 13 and 14.)

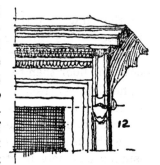

Fig. 12.—Correct indication of the Antique opening with corner consoles according to theory

When we come to the subdivision of the window frame for the support of the glass, little may be learned from the architecture of classic times; we must turn to buildings of our own day. Of the two types of windows—the sliding sash and the casement—the first presents an awkward feature difficult to overcome, namely the heavy division bar which necessarily comes exactly across the middle of the opening. This is an obstacle to the proper subdivision of the space not found in the case of the casement, and for this reason the latter is to be preferred, all other conditions being equal.

Fig. 13.—Doorway of the Pantheon at Rome

ARCHED OPENINGS

The arch has had great influence on the development of architecture and the determination of the styles. One of the fundamental elements of composition, its use imposes certain characteristics upon design which result directly from the function of its parts in construction.

Arches are made up of the following elements:—Vouissoirs, keystones and imposts. These elements, when made evident, determine the decoration of the arch and expression of its function in its simplicity. Since antique architecture was dominated by the theory that construction should be made evident in decoration, only modifying this theory in special cases when the result clearly justified it, we find consequently in that architecture the true decorative scheme of the arch most obviously and beautifully expressed. We find the impost and keystone strongly accented and the archivolt enclosed by continuous mouldings or more or less richly decorated bands, interrupted only by the joints between the vouissoirs, giving to the composition the impression of continuity and stability. Celebrated examples are the gates

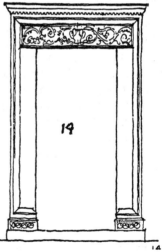

Fig. 14.—Door at Corneto

of Falerii and Perugia, the Roman arcades and Triumphal Arches and the arch of the Fountain at Trevi (Fig. 15).

All arches should be slightly stilted, the center being raised above the top of the impost in order to compensate for the effect of angular perspective.

Fig. 15.—Detail, Fountain of Trevi, Rome

There are beautiful examples of arches where keystone and imposts have been subordinated to the general decorative scheme, such as the arches of the Riccardi Palace and the celebrated arched doorway of the Ecole des Beaux Arts. In the first example the heavily rusticated masonry alone is sufficient to convey the impression of structural adequacy, which requires no further decoration (Fig. 161). In the second example the scheme of decoration centers on the keystone and on the continuous moulded architrave, unbroken by any suggestion of accent at the spring of the arch. These examples are exceptions to the general principles governing the composition of arches, which particularly stress some accent or demarkation at the impost, but they are sufficiently justified by the acknowledged fact that they are beautiful and highly decorative. In general it may be said that when the arch is the motive of an isolated composition, such as a doorway, it may be composed more freely; but when it is linked up with other arches, as in the arcade, it should follow the classic precedents more closely. An arcade without the horizontal tie which the impost mouldings give is apt to appear weak and unsatisfactory.

BALUSTRADES AND BALCONIES

The balustrade is a flexible motive in composition, having many slight variations which, however, become important when we seek to harmonize it exactly with the character of the building. Although primarily a utilitarian element, it has often been used purely as a decorative feature, as above cornices where the roof is steeply pitched behind it, or before windows which do not extend to the floor, or where it has not sufficient projection to permit use as a balcony.

The most monumental balustrades result from the use of turned balusters, whose profiles conform in general to one of three shapes,

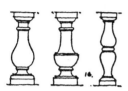

Fig. 16.—Types of Balusters

each having its own determining effect upon the character of the design (Fig. 16). To be in scale a balustrade should rarely exceed four feet in height. Its stability is due to pedestals and plinths, which should not be spaced so far apart that they cannot be spanned satisfactorily by a single stone, as in the top member or rail. Here also the construction clearly establishes the composition.

Support may be given to balconies, by the thickness of the wall below, by the projection of a belt course, or by consoles or brackets.

The most beautiful and instructive examples of the composition of balconies are to be found in the architecture of the Italian Renaissance.

ROOFS AND DOMES

The architecture of our day, residential as well as public and monumental seems committed to the simple roof; that is to the roof composed with simple planes and straight intersections and without useless and unrelated embellishments. In this it acknowledges the guiding spirit of classic times, when buildings were roofed in a straightforward manner which followed and recalled the composition of the plan. In monumental edifices, especially those whose style is derived from the antique architecture of Rome, the roof counts for very little as an external feature. The high roof belongs to picturesque architecture and should be reserved for those styles where informality is the leading motive. But even picturesque roofs should be simply composed; the primary necessity for covering and protection, clearly expressed, properly becoming the ruling consideration, while ornament should be relegated to such accessories as chimney, gables, crestings and minor details.

Roofs as an artistic element have been greatly abused, especially during periods of transition, and the return to simplicity in no way reflects adversely upon the imaginative ability of architects, but is an evidence of a healthy taste.

The architecture of the Renaissance in France displays many superb examples of the accented roof, harmonizing perfectly with the character of the style, but these examples are not adapted to general imitation in our day. The special type of steep and richly decorated roof known as the Mansard is a regal accessory, a relic of monarchies whose emblem was the crown, and which finds no counterpart in the spirit of our age.

Chimney caps should be treated as an element of beauty since they are conspicuous. Tall chimneys are naturally associated with high roofs and their proportions and locations should be carefully studied.

The angle of inclination of a gable is an important consideration, which only a delicate sense of proportion can accurately determine. Geometrical rules are of some value, but the controlling principles must be sought in antique architecture. The pedimented porticos of Greek temples are the models which we should study and follow. The slope of gables varies considerably according to whether the motive is wide or narrow, whether there are many or few columns composing the portico, and the temples should be studied and compared with this fact in mind.

DOMES

Among the conspicuous features of external architecture, the dome, as developed by the architects of the Renaissance takes rank as the most imposing and majestic. The Romans built many domes, but did not make of them a chief feature. As composed the dome of the Romans was always a low, saucer-shaped vault covering a circular hall. It remained for the later architects of Byzantine times to extend the application of the dome, the invention of the pendentive enabling them to vault halls both square and octagonal in plan. Still later during the Renaissance, domes were raised upon high cylindrical drums and crowned with conspicuous lanterns, these features assuming almost as much importance in the composition as the dome itself.

The most celebrated of the antique domes is that of the Pantheon at Rome. This example is typical of the Roman conception of the proper function of the dome. In its perfect state its external effect must have been considerable, but there was no conscious effort to emphasize this. In effect the Roman dome was simply the effect of necessary construction. So also construction alone determines the stupendous effect of the dome of St. Sophia at Constantinople. In both these edifices the dome takes its place as a normally proportioned part of the whole edifice, not drawing undue attention to itself or detracting from other prominent elements of exterior composition.

The saucer-shaped dome may then be said to be a fitting crowning feature for monumental buildings which do not attract or dominate solely by reason of their external configuration—such as art galleries, libraries, museums and the like.

The great domes of the Renaissance, of which St. Peter's is the grandest example, were made to be seen. Effect, whether at a distance or near at hand, is the chief reason for their existence. This form, then, lends itself particularly to edifices whose programs imply ideas of power, dominance or centralization—as the capitol of a nation or of a state. Of St. Peter's dome, Guadet remarks, that "it is less the roof of the greatest of all churches than the covering and sign of this centre to which converges the entire unity of Catholicism." It must not be forgotten, however, that all domes composed like St. Peter's—grand as they may be—are anomalous from the point of view of masonry construction, since their stability depends upon iron bands or girdles built into the masonry at frequent intervals. Such is not the case with domes like the Pantheon's or St. Sophia's, which are sufficiently buttressed.

In profile a large number of domes take the form of a slightly stilted hemisphere. Too much stilting produces the objectionable egg-shaped profile. Many domes are also pointed—notably the domes of St. Peter's, St. Paul's, Florence Cathedral and the Pantheon in Paris.

No high dome is complete without the crowning lantern, usually richly treated and of varying proportions. The composition of the lantern is a subject requiring much study. Often it recalls at a smaller scale the design of the dome itself, with cylindrical drum, colonnade, shell and finial. The low Byzantine or Roman types of domes have also been composed with a lantern; an immensely difficult problem, it would seem, since constructively the flat sum-

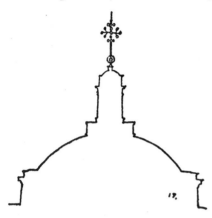

mit of a dome-shell is not adapted to a heavy superimposed load. This problem has been solved with great effect in the dome of the Madison Square Presbyterian Church, New York, by McKim, Mead and White (F i g. 1 7). At the other extreme we have the circular oculus which characterizes the dome of the Roman Pantheon.

Fig. 17.—Madison Square Presbyterian Church; Profile of Dome.—McKim, Mead & White, Architects

In most cases the extrados and intrados of a dome are not concentric, nor is the dome seen from the inside the dome visible from

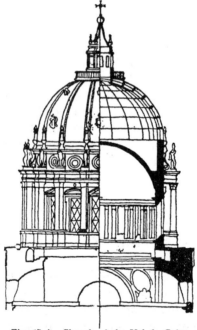

Fig. 17-A.—Church of the Val de Grâce, Paris. Half elevation and half section of Dome

the outside. The construction usually consists of two or more shells, quite widely separated, one designed wholly for interior effect and the other wholly for exterior effect. This requirement of composition in its relation to Renaissance domes is clearly illustrated by the section of the dome of the church of the Val de Grâce, Paris (Fig. 17-A).

Fig. 18.—Profiles of great domes drawn to the same scale; 1 St. Peter's, 2 Florence, 3 St. Paul's, 4 Invalides, 5 Val de Grâce, 6 Pantheon, 7 St. Sophia.

Figure 18 shows the external silhouettes, drawn to the same scale, of a few of the greatest domes of the world. 1 St. Peter's; 2 Florence; 3 St. Paul's; 4 Invalides; 5 Val de Grâce; 6 Pantheon; 7 St. Sophia.

CHAPTER II.

THE ANTIQUE ORDERS; PORTICOS AND ARCADES

The Orders may be reduced to three great families—the Doric; the Ionic and the Corinthian. The Tuscan Order may be considered as a simplified Doric, while the Composite Order is obviously a combination of elements taken from the Ionic and Corinthian. Although the character of each Order is individual and distinctive, it is not of an inflexible nature but is infinitely diverse, due to mutual borrowing and variations in proportions and detail. Any attempt, therefore, to lay down an absolute canon of individual proportions or module unit for the Orders, except perhaps for the purposes of elementary instruction, must necessarily be a fundamentally barren undertaking.

The antique Orders have very properly an important place in the study of architecture, especially in the beginning when the "Analytique" or Order Problem is the chief means for instruction. Closely related is the study of walls, cornices, windows, doorways, and the like elements, involving the application of Orders, all of which are of primary importance.

Orders by nature are powerful means for the expression of character, their individual details and proportions and the way they have been combined in compositions largely distinguishing the different epochs of design. Hence they frequently enter into the study of problems in archaeology, which is the principal means for developing knowledge of variations in the styles. Such studies, however, are necessarily advanced and cannot well come during the period of primary instruction. This is the reason why certain average proportions for the Orders have to be assumed as a basis for instruction in the beginning, since so presented they are readily memorized and applied to problems of varying scale. Thus we have the various systems of "Vignolas" and the diameter of the column or half-diameter (module) as a unit of measurement. The method has its obviously good points but it also has its dangers. Of the latter one of the most serious seems to be, that while the sense of proportion is cultivated, the sense of scale is not. Proportioning the Orders according to a unit diameter tends to give a false impression of size, nor do we find any such constant occurring anywhere in antique architecture. The Greeks and Romans modified the proportions of the Orders in accordance with their positions in the structure and their variations in size, thus seeking to give at once the correct impression of both proportion and scale.

Between monumental architecture and inferior structures are a multitude of variations in proportion, all of which find a direct correspondence in the treatment of Orders. Of these only the most beautiful examples taken from the antique should be the basis for study and inspiration.

The composition of the antique Orders illustrates clearly and forcibly the artistic unity that is a fundamental requirement of every architectonic structure. The Greek Doric order realizes this artistic unity and harmony in absolute perfection. The entasis satisfies the desire of the eye for the slightly pyramidal conformation. Unlike later architecture the shaft was never swelled but tapered uniformly from stylobate to architrave. The cylindrical lower shaft and frequently double entasis became the rule with the Romans and architects of the Renaissance. The double entasis does not seem to be wholly objectionable if used with great restraint. A diminution toward the base was quite common during the Italian Renaissance but was so slight as to be imperceptible unless measured. Such a refinement would appear to be especially appropriate for columns which must be seen at an acute angle from below. Excessive swelling of the shaft produces a coarse and bulbous effect and is to be avoided.

THE GREEK DORIC ORDER

The Doric order belongs particularly to Greek architecture. Its development from Archaic to Attic forms shows how much the Greeks, attached as they were to tradition, slowly and surely perfected the forms of the past, feeling little need for new elements. This restraint gives the idea of perfect mastery of subject and material. The Greek artists were gifted with a refined sense of proportion which has never been equalled and this led them to strive to develop more beautiful forms. Absolute perfection of beauty was their ideal—an ideal reached in the Doric order of the Parthenon.

Concerning the use of the Grecian Doric order, Guadet advises his students as follows: "It requires precise and thorough study—

yet the Grecian Doric order, properly so called, I hope at least will not be employed by you, for less than any other does it lend itself to reproduction; even its perfection making imitations grotesque. But as students nothing better than the Doric order can show you to what degree of perfection the study of architecture may be carried. In that magnificent work of architecture are few elements, but such is their truth and harmony, that no person can with propriety omit or add a single thing. In it is manifested and expressed all the true character of Grecian art."

In the antique Greek colonnades the columns had no bases as this would have proved an inconvenient and obstructive feature for the intercolumniations adopted. It was the same with the early Roman Doric, as for example, the order of the Theatre of Marcellus. The square plinth was a later development evidently required for the completion of the Roman orders.

THE ROMAN DORIC ORDER

The character of Roman civilization was as forcibly impressed upon their artistic works as was Greek civilization upon theirs. The Romans were a composite people, not a single race like the Greeks, and their resultant aspirations were from the beginning totally different. At first, being materially minded, they cared little for art, but as their civilization advanced and conquests of other nations gave them wealth, power, and a desire for luxury, their artistic aspirations found expression in the most magnificent and impressive architecture that the world has seen. An outstanding characteristic of the Romans was the genius for organization—for utilizing and directing the labor of others. This is shown in their employment of Greek architects in all their early architectural works. There were probably no Roman architects for a long time but in spite of this fact, Roman taste—the love of splendor, luxury and magnificence—inevitably fixed and determined the whole trend of their art; a convincing proof of the influence of civilization upon architecture. Through these methods and influences there was developed, as many think, the greatest style of architecture of all, in that, apart from intrinsic excellences, it has been more directly suggestive and has had a more potent influence on the development of later styles. The Renaissance architects found in the Imperial architecture of Rome the models of the orders which they studied and adapted to their own characteristic manner. The great variety and diversity of proportions which the genius of such artists as Bramante, Peruzzi, Delorme and others were able to evolve from Doric prototypes alone is sufficient proof that beauty in the orders does not depend upon any fixed system of modules.

As has been pointed out the Greeks employed columns solely as supports for pediments and other integral parts of buildings, the Romans preferred to use the orders in a decorative sense. This difference was due largely to a different system of construction. Greek architecture was an art of cut stone throughout, usually marble; while the larger Roman buildings were constructed of small materials which could be easily transported, handled, and cemented into a solid mass. Thus the carcass of the Roman edifice was one massive, homogeneous whole, possessing no decorative value except in the larger features of its composition where the surfaces and masses were broken up so as to produce effects of light and shade. The orders were applied after the configuration of the edifice was determined. They formed only one part of a universal system of incrusted decoration. Compared to Grecian architecture, the far greater number, variety, distribution and complexity of Roman buildings made the system adopted by them a necessity.

The Romans changed all the details of the Greek models to suit their own taste and special requirements. They simplified all curves and profiles and adapted them in most cases to circular segments, greatly enriching mouldings and other decorative elements through the use of the acanthus leaf and its derivatives. Rich, carved ornament took the place of sculpture. They made of the Corinthian Order a practically independent and characteristic order of their own.

Proceeding from their point of view of regarding Orders as a decoration, the Romans employed them in the following ways:

1 In the form of free-standing columns and colonnades, carrying either pediments or projecting blocks of entablature, usually as pedestals for statues. Examples are found in the Roman Temples, the Arch of Constantine, The Forum of Nerva. More often, polished monoliths of colored and figured marbles were preferred to plain or fluted stone.

2 As engaged columns, usually in combination with arches, for the exteriors of theatres. amphitheatres, basilicas and the like. The Orders of the Theatre of Marcellus and of the Colosseum are familiar examples.

3 In the form of pilasters, used either behind columns, or in place of engaged columns. The pilaster form was derived from the Greek anta.

In Doric architecture in its purity the spacing of columns is regulated by the triglyph interval. The metope can never be far from an exact square. In the Greek style there is a triglyph at the angle which can never have the same axis as the column below it. This brings the two end columns closer together than those intervening—a logical resultant which both strengthens the corners and gives wider passage where it is required.

THE IONIC ORDER

The Ionic order underwent fewer modifications during successive epochs of design than either the Doric or the Corinthian, the forms perfected by Greek art maintaining their purity through the Roman and Renaissance ages on up to the present day. Even the Scamozzi cap with its four diagonal volutes is plainly foreseen by the angle cap of the antique temple.

The Ionic order may be divided into two classes—the Simple and Decorated, the most beautiful and instructive examples of which are found on the Athenian Acropolis. The former is exemplified by the order of the Temple of Nike Apteros and the interior columns of the Propyleum; the latter by the unsurpassed Order of the Erechtheum. The Decorated cap has more turns in the volutes and an ornamented necking as its principal features of difference. Both types were given a circular base often quite complicated in profile but generally a variant of the Attic base.

The Ionic order is characterized by refined grace and elegance with which is combined a certain stateliness, strength and repose.

THE CORINTHIAN ORDER

Before the other orders the Corinthian lends itself to the expression of magnitudes, richness and majesty of effect. Its decorative possibilities were realized by the Greeks, who nevertheless never appeared to have used it to any great extent, preferring to restrict its application to small buildings, such as the Choragic

Monument of Lysicrates and the Tower of the Winds.   On the other hand its somewhat grandiose character exactly suited the Roman taste for splendor and magnificence, and as developed by them it became the favorite order for all classes of buildings.

The Romans invented an entirely new cornice for the Corinthian order, which was formed by adding a band of modillions to the Ionic cornice.   The modillion, evidently suggested by the console, was one of the most remarkable and fruitful conceptions in the history of architectural ornament.   Having great decorative possibilities its applications soon became numerous and far-reaching. The transformation which the Romans effected in the modeling of the acanthus leaf greatly enriched the Corinthian and Composite capitals, while mouldings and frieze were decorated with an extraordinary variety of beautiful forms, most of them also made up of combinations and elaborations of acanthus elements.

The antique Corinthian order, more than the others, employed monolithic shafts of polished and colored marbles.   Its capital was also invariably of marble, (though not of the figured variety) as this material lent itself to delicate carvings, while at the same time it was most durable and resistant.   When the capital is intended to be executed in a coarser stone as is frequent in modern work, the designer should be inspired rather by the earlier examples which were more robust than by the richer and more highly

developed capitals of the Imperial period. Examples of the former are the Temple of Vesta at Rome and at Tivoli, Palestrina and the Temple of Minerva at Assisi.   Of the latter may be cited the Pantheon, the Temple of Jupiter Stator, the Temple of Antoninus and Faustina and the Temple of Mars the Avenger.   Restorations of all these examples and many others are beautifully shown in the volumes edited by H. D'Espouy, comprising "Fragments d'architecture antique" and "Monuments antiques."

Fig. 19.—Detail of the Temple of Vesta at Tivoli.

The Corinthian order is perhaps furthest of all removed from monotony or fixed proportions (Fig. 19).   The archi-

tecture of the early Renaissance in Italy and France is a witness
to what extraordinary diversity of character the Corinthian type
of capital lends itself, when the artistic genius of master designers is brought to bear upon it. The exquisite examples of the art
of these epochs are coming more and more to dominate the architectural decoration of modern times. This tendency may be particularly noted in o u r
own country where the
masterly work of three
or four leading architects
seems to recall in almost
equal measure the power
of the Italian artists.

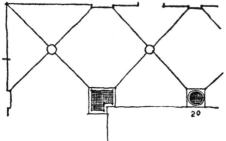

It will not be neces-
sary to consider t h e
Composite order in de-
tail here, although to a
certain degree . it pos-
sesses a character of its
own. With the exception
of its entablature which
is rather a variation of
the Doric, in other re-
spects its details partake
largely of the nature of
the Corinthian. Nor will
it serve our purpose to
give special attention to
the Tuscan order, which
as presented by Vignola
is merely a simplified
form of the Doric. Gua-

Fig. 20.—Angle of the Court Arcade; Cancelleria Palace. det following the characteristics established for the Tuscan order by Leseur recognizes
a certain rustic composition for this order which gives it a definite
place by itself. We see this character chiefly in the translation of
the entablature into wood, omitting both frieze and cornice, and
substituting for the latter far-projecting, visible rafter-ends. This

is also the composition of the pergola so familiar in landscape-gardening.

ARCADES AND PORTICOS

Arcades are of two general types. In one type, which is often called the Florentine arcade, the arches spring from the tops of the supporting columns; in the other, or Roman type, the arches spring from imposts between columns, the orders in this case forming a sort of frame around the opening. The first case is that of the courtyard of the Cancelleria Palace, (Fig. 20) the second is illustrated by the Theatre of Marcellus (Fig. 21) and the Court of the Farnese Palace (Fig. 22).

The Florentine arcade is an exceedingly graceful and pleasing motive but its construc-

Fig. 21.—Portico of the Theatre of Marcellus, Rome.

tion is subject to serious inconveniences. Owing to the thrusts of arches and vaults which cannot be resisted horizontally by the slender supports, it is necessary to employ iron tie-rods in order to insure stability. The purpose of these is so evident that their appearance is not condemned, especially as the great beauty of this form of arcade is a sufficient justification for the use of an extrinsic structural expedient. Narrow imposts and small bed-planes also necessitate the use of hard stone for the bases, shafts and capitals of the columns. The shaft should also be monolithic. Brunneleschi often introduced a section of cornice between the column capitals and the arches, giving the effect of an accented impost. Columns are sometimes doubled either in the direction of the wall or at right angles to it (Fig. 33).

The Roman arcade is a composite arrangement of elements in which arches and piers

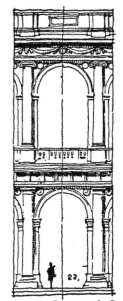

Fig. 22.—Superposed Orders of the Court of the Farnese Palace, Rome.

are combined with engaged columns or pilasters. The general effect produced is one of richness and monumental repose. Its

variations are infinite both as regards proportion and stylistic character. The order is used in this composition rather in a decorative sense, although it also serves the constructive function of a buttress; this is especially true when the thrusts of vaults are concentrated on the supporting piers. The character of the composition depends primarily on whether the arches or the orders are most accented. In this connection it should be remembered that it is logical for the arch to carry the greater part of the superposed load, hence the depth of the arch should always be sensibly greater than the projection of the architrave (Fig. 23). The

Fig. 23.—Detail from the Court of the Farnese Palace.

Theatre of Marcellus (Fig. 21) is an example of accented orders, the court of the Farnese Palace of accented arches (Fig. 22). The Roman arcade motive adapts itself to compositions involving a single arch, as in entrances, either monumental or of ordinary proportions, Triumphal Arches and the like. In such cases the depth of the arch very properly often approaches a shallow barrel-vault, leading the eye through the wall rather than in a horizontal or vertical direction.

The Romans were fond of placing the orders upon pedestals, an arrangement which does not appear to be so much favored in modern uses of the composition. The so-called Palladian Motive, where a small order serves as an impost for the arch, is an illustration of the great variety and richness that the Roman arcade is capable of receiving.

Fig. 24.—Basilica of Palladio, Vincenza.

Two examples are especially well-known—The Basilica of Vincenza

by Palladio (Fig. 24) and the Library of St. Mark in Venice by Sansovino (Fig. 25).

Antique architecture established the principles to be used in designing porticos; hence for free colonnades and pedimented porticos the methods and proportions employed by the ancients should be followed. The horizontal lintel is the only rational system for such cases. On the other hand if the colonnade is not free but included between end pavilions or other massive projections, the arch or jointed platband may be used since the horizontal thrusts at the terminations of the colonnade are counter-abutted.

Where columns are arranged on a circular plan, as in small temples, or the

Fig. 25.—Library of St. Mark, Venice.

Fig. 26.—Rotunda of the Trianon

Fig. 27.—Tivoli. Temple della Sibilia.

colonnade surrounding a dome, all bays are in the same conditions. Here a proportionately narrow spacing of columns is implied owing to the curvature in the lintel horizontally tending to throw it out of balance or to disturb the effect of stability. Historic architecture numbers many correct examples of circular peristyles, among which the little Rotunda of the Trianon is one and the Temple della Sibilia, Tivoli, another (Figs. 26 and 27).

CHAPTER III.

INTERNAL WALL TREATMENT; FLOORS AND CEILINGS

Interior architecture—the decoration of the inner walls of enclosed spaces in a building—depends primarily upon the composition of ceilings. The design of a ceiling directly governs the design of the walls which support it. Just as when studying the composition of a plan it is always necessary to consider the upper parts of the structure—the higher stories and the roof—so in designing the interiors of a building it is essential to think first of all of the ceiling.

Without reference to the external roof, there are three ways of covering an enclosing space—by vaulting, horizontal ceilings, or open timber-trusses. Each of these systems has a determining influence upon the design and construction of the supporting walls; certain forms permitting a uniform and unbroken wall enclosure, while others require the wall to be subdivided into supporting piers.

Whether the wall is to be plain or broken up into a system of bays by pilasters or other projections, its composition must be in harmony with the form and subdivisions of the ceiling. Doors and windows naturally affect a subdivision of the walls in which they occur, and it frequently becomes a difficult matter to adjust the position of openings so that they will harmonize with the natural breaks in the ceiling and at the same time be symmetrically placed with reference to both sides of the wall through which they pass. The four walls of a rectangular room seldom correspond in every respect, although there is usually quite a close correspondence in the treatment of walls that are opposite each other across an axis of symmetry due to the fact that the lines of the ceiling carry the eye across the room. On one side there may be windows while the opposite wall may have no openings at all, or openings of different size, shape or number. A similar disparity may exist in the ends of the rooms.

In spite of the diversity that must frequently occur in the placing and composition of such elements, they cannot be composed without any reference to each other or to the design of the room as a whole. In design the ceiling must be a symmetrical composition and this being the case it is obvious that a break occurring on one wall must in some way have its counterpart on the opposite wall,

This principle also holds for the ends of oblong rooms but not otherwise there would be no connection between walls and ceiling. quite so inflexibly.

It is here that the importance of axes is most strongly felt and there is no getting away from them. We have to think continually of axes in studying interiors—principal and secondary axes, rather than spaces—axes becoming lines of recall for symmetrically placed features (Figs. 105, 120). It is customary to say that this or that feature or point is "recalled" by something already determined. The great importance that must be attached to axes in the study of planning will appear forcibly in connection with the analysis of "partis" to be subsequently considered, but their importance can never be too much emphasized. The effect of interiors may often be more than doubled by the skillful prolongation of an axis through several rooms. Good composition always makes use of a beautiful vista terminated by some feature or view of conspicuous interest.

After the "parti" or provisional plan for a building has been determined upon and in the subsequent development of the design the study of the forms and composition of internal architecture assumes an importance equal to that of the exterior. In the earlier stages of development, the study of the plan—as has been noted—takes precedence over the study of both facades and sections. Later the latter drawings, which may be said to be reciprocal complements of the plan, are more thoroughly studied, often having the effect of modifying to some extent the original parti. But in plan problems it is the common practice, and perhaps rightly, to indicate facades and sections in a very subordinate manner. This practice has the tendency to give the impression that interiors, especially, as shown by section are of comparatively little importance, and hence they are assigned a place of little importance in the "rendu." To make up for this deficiency special problems in the composition of interiors are given. But these studies, though valuable in themselves, are not sufficient, since the greatest value in training results from the study of the section, hence interiors, in direct connection with the plan and the facades.

When we come to the decorative treatment of rooms, after their proportions have been established, we find this to be largely a matter of detail, calling for special study and special methods of presentation.

The following general principles governing the character of room architecture should be borne in mind:

In interiors the forms of architecture are usually seen at a less distance than outside the building. It is therefore proper to treat them with more refinement; giving to proportions more slenderness and to ornament and mouldings greater delicacy. Such forms are also seen more obliquely inside the building, soffits and under surfaces generally assuming greater importance, and due consideration should be given to this relation in designing. On the exteriors the architecture is subjected to bright, direct light from above, whereas in the interiors the light usually comes from side windows, much of the illumination being diffused and frequently of low intensity. There is also the quality of electric lighting to consider. In interiors, then, profiles and other forms require a sharp and highly accented outline, which may be helped out and differentiated by the use of color. Internal architecture must also combine with furniture, draperies and other movables, all of which have their effect on the ultimate appearance of the ensemble. It will also be remembered that the materials suitable for exterior construction do not as a rule lend themselves to interior finish. Rooms require a decorative covering of richer and more plastic materials, which can be modelled and colored in a manner better suited to the special conditions which obtain there. Every treatment of interior walls must have a base connecting them to the floor and, except in very special cases, a cornice at the top to form a transition to the ceiling. Bases are frequently of marble of a darker color than the wall. The crowning members are lightly proportioned for interior design and where the ceiling is horizontal and beamed or coffered its sectional profiles usually member with the upper

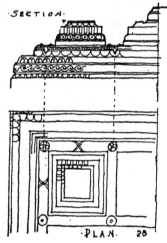

Fig. 28.—From the Farnese Palace showing composition of breaks or mouldings in a coffered or beamed ceiling.

part of the entablature (Fig. 28).

In interior architecture is where close contact with human requirements is found. People are attracted and satisfied by comfort and elegance, by richness and display, by formality or the lack of it. There is a varied program for interior decoration, which must respond as the case may be to intellectual, emotional, spiritual or simply practical needs.

FLOORS AND CEILINGS

Enclosed spaces, as has been said, may be covered either by vaulting, by horizontal ceilings, or by open timber trusses. Vaulting as a rule is restricted to monumental architecture, and since its study is somewhat difficult and complicated, a discussion of vaulted ceilings has been reserved for a separate chapter.

The simplest ceiling is the so-called flat or horizontal ceiling, since constructively it imposes only vertical loads on the supporting walls. The flat ceiling is the form most commonly used for rooms of ordinary height and where there are rooms above, although it may also be adapted to compartments of monumental proportions, as many beautiful examples in Italian and French Renaissance architecture bear witness. Except for the cornice, the treatment of horizontal ceilings is in the best examples independent of the wall-treatment. The composition of ceilings, proceding historically from wood architecture, either emphasizes the equally spaced, parallel rows of structural beams, by making them evident and decorating them, or the ceiling as a whole may be treated as a great panel or frame and be purely decorative without any emphasis on construction. In the first system, particularly if the room is wide, the closely spaced joists are carried by heavier transverse girders. There may even be three sets of beams of different sizes at right angles to each other in rooms of unusual proportions. The decoration is completed by painting the beams or panels in rich colors combined with gilding, the arabesque motives of the Renaissance forming a basis for the ornament. Beautiful examples of this system are the ceilings of the Palazzo Publico in Sienna and of the Galerie des Cerfs at Fontainebleau. In modern American architecture may be mentioned among others, the ceiling of the Delivery Room in the Boston Public Library, the Indianapolis Public Library by Paul Cret, and the San Francisco

Public Library by George Kelham.

The second type, or purely decorative ceiling, is the ceiling ornamented with coffers or divided into great compartments for the reception of paintings or decoration in low relief. The French and Italian Renaissance presents many splendid examples of these compositions; notably, ceilings in the Farnese Palace, the Doges' Palace, S. M. Maggiore and S. John Lateran, the ceilings of Fontainebleau and the Chamber of Henry II in the Louvre. In America the ceiling of the Reading Room in the New York Public Library by Carrere and Hastings is the most notable example.

There is always an impression of flatness to be feared in ceilings of grand dimensions, which must be counteracted by deep sinkages and bold reliefs.

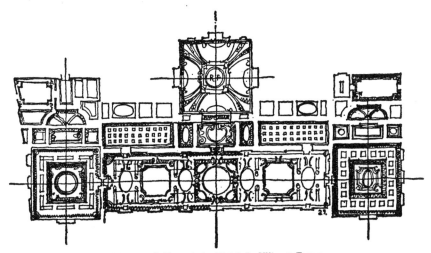

Fig. 29.—Ceiling of the Hotel de Ville at Tours
by Victor Laloux.

Figure 29 is an illustration of the reflected plan of a French classic ceiling in the style of modern Renaissance. The drawing indicates the panel system of the principal ceilings of the Hotel de Ville at Tours, designed by Victor Laloux. At the rear of the building a large coved square covers the grand staircase; the rich central room is the Salle des Fetes; on the right the Council Chambers; on the left the Salle des Mariages. A corridor gives independent circulation. It will be noted how the decoration of the ceilings explains the plan and helps to unify and tie the whole composition together.

Properly speaking, the decorated, visible roof-truss belongs rather to the architecture of the Middle Ages. Classical examples are the framed roofs of San Miniato at Florence and the Cathedral at Monreale.

CHAPTER IV.

VAULTS IN GENERAL; THE DECORATION OF VAULTS

The study of vaulting, as has been said, is difficult and complicated. Yet the subject must be taken up at an early stage in the study of composition and the controlling principles of construction and decoration understood and mastered. This difficulty of comprehension arises largely from the fact that drawings of the different species of vaults can be made readily only in orthographic projection, and such drawings do not serve to represent the actual curvatures and intersections clearly. Consider the simple groined vault, for example. In plan it is a square with diagonals, while the sectional view, taken ordinarily through the horizontal crown element, is in effect a half square enclosing semicircles. Furthermore the usual section through a dome fails very far from explaining the real shape of the pendentives. It is only by taking a special section in a plane at forty-five degrees to the usual one that the pendentive is made to appear somewhat as it really is.

The difficulty of representation is further accentuated by the fact that the plans of several different species of vaults are identical, although they do not actually resemble one another in the least. As examples of this sort of complexity the groined vault and the cloistered vault may be mentioned, each having the same plan.

The nature of vaults may be shown very clearly in perspective and it is very essential for students to practice drawing them this way. It is well also to study vaults by careful scrutiny of the fine perspective drawings that are found in the books, as in "Letarouilly." Such drawings have in many instances been made from actuality with the aid of the camera lucida. Photographs are very instructive, but naturally the observation of vaults actually constructed is the most valuable training of all.

A severe schooling in descriptive geometry is a necessary preliminary to the thorough comprehension of vaulting surfaces and their intersections. Add to this a general knowledge of stresses, thrusts and resultants, and the graphical methods of verification taught by the theory of the stability of vaults, and the designer is then in a position to avoid falling into serious error.

At the end of the next chapter there will be found an indication of a method of studying vaults in actuality by means of easily constructed models, which it is thought will prove to be interesting and productive of good results.

The correct indication of vaulting surfaces, even in the primary drawings for a composition, requires much knowledge which can only be acquired through patience and industry. The study is difficult but its realizations are among the noblest in architecture.

In order to plan vaults intelligently and to provide adequate abutments to take care of the thrusts, it is necessary to understand, as has been said, something about the conditions for equilibrium in vaulting (Fig. 30). These principles may be regarded as supplementary to the study of the design and construction of vaults as they occur in actual architecture.

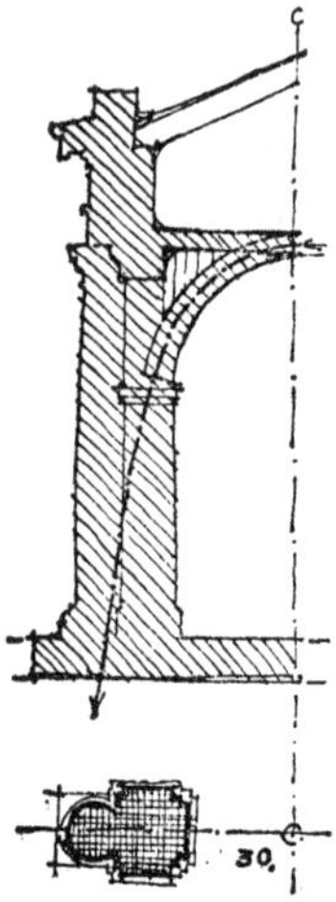

A vault built of cut stones separated by joint planes (stereometric vault) thrusts on account of the mobility of its elements. In cases of rupture the tendency is for the crown to fall in and for the haunches to be pushed out. The arch most frequently exerts its thrust along the length of a wall, whereas the thrust of a vault is usually in a plane at right angles to it, hence the tendency is to push it over.

Fig. 30.—Typical line of pressure and resultant thrust of a semicircular arch ring

It is the counter resistances that hold the elements of an arch or vault immovable, and by their action the natural internal forces that tend to disrupt it are confined and constrained to act along a single resultant, which in turn may be decomposed into two forces, one vertical and one horizontal. The primary condition for equilibrium and stability in vaults is that this resultant line of action should fall within the sectional area of the vault ring and of its abutments (Fig. 30). The stability of the vault is further regarded as doubtful if the foot of this oblique resultant line falls without the middle third of the thickness of the entire section.

A little reflection will make it apparent that resultants in vaults and arches must always act somewheres near perpendicular to the joint planes, which is a proper condition for stone in construction.

The walls and abutments which form part of the composition of vaults must be sufficiently stable to resist overthrow or deformation. These resistances are provided by thickening the piers in the direction of the thrust and by weight due to mass of material

and by top loading. Stability is also directly affected both by the height of the vault and of its abutments (Fig. 31). Like the arch, the vault thrusts more as it becomes flatter. These considerations impose rather massive proportions upon vault construction. The delicacy and grace evinced by the vaulting of the Italian Renaissance are only possible through the use of tie-rods.

Fig. 31. — Stability and instability in the same vault due to heights of abutments.

Beside the vault of cut stone, there are two other traditional systems of vaulting—vaults constructed of concrete and the mediaeval vaults supported by arch ribs. The great Roman Basilicas and Baths had vaults constructed characteristically of concrete. Their immobility is due to their monolithic construction, weighing vertically downward and exerting no side thrusts. The appearance and decorative effect of each of the three systems of vaulting is fundamentally dependent upon the form of its construction. In mediaeval vaults the nature of the constructive means is such that it may be said to be in itself the decoration. These vaults exert many and varying thrusts whose action and counteraction profoundly characterize Gothic architecture.

The vaults of antiquity are by nature heavy and cumbersome. On the other hand lightness in construction is highly desirable, since it is an additional assurance of stability, diminishing the tendency to unequal settlement of the whole mass. This condition was realized by the Roman builders who made use of many expedients for lightening their vaults, such as porous stone, the insertion of hollow tiles into the mass, and so forth. Moreover the traditional systems of vault building are slow and require the use of much wood work for centering. It is not surprising then that modern architects, striving always to gain an effect by the easiest means and in the shortest time, have sought to invent new methods of vault building and to substitute them for the old. Thus we have the suspended plaster vault, the vault of reinforced concrete and the Guastavino vault of flat tiles cemented together. The decoration of the two first named partakes of the nature of the antique Roman or of the Italian Renaissance, the last is often left undecorated by applied ornament.

In America, always fertile in structural expedients, although we can boast a multitude of noble and highly monumental edifices, the number of vaults constructed in cut stone may be counted on the fingers of one hand. The vestibules of the New York Public Library afford the most notable examples of stone vaulting in the United States.

Fig. 32.—Pier sections of a typical Roman Arcade.

The old saying that "the arch never sleeps" is recalled in connection with vaults. Thus the poet phrases the idea of the continual contest that architecture must wage with the concealed forces that are ever tending to destroy it.

Vaults are divided into two groups—those with uniformly distributed thrusts and those whose thrusts are gathered together and concentrated at definite points. To the first class belong barrel or tunnel vaults, the cloister vault, the vault on a polygonal plan, and the annular and spherical vaults. To the second class, which result from the intersection of vaults, belong the groined or cross

Fig. 33.—Plan of the upper arches of the Basilica at Vincenza.

vault, the vault with penetrations and the domical vault on pendentives. Tunnel, spherical and cloistered vaults require walls of uniform thickness, broken only at points where accented arch ribs call for pilasters or other projections. The second class of combined vaults are expressed in the composition of the plan by isolated piers whose form and area supply the necessary resistances (Figs. 32, 33). The study of such pier sections (points of poché) must also be governed by considerations of section, height, materials and method of construction, since each of these factors has a determining influence on the elements of the plan. To this end the most profitable study is that gained from the analysis of existing vaulting constructions.

THE DECORATION OF VAULTS

The natural curvature of a vault is in itself a pleasing form which should always be retained, therefore any system of decoration applied to its surface should not tend to deform or change its character. In principle the opposite is true for large, horizontal ceilings, which are apt to weigh heavily overhead and must be varied and broken up by panels and projecting profiles which enrich the surface and suggest effective support. The principal generating lines must first be emphasized in the decoration of any vault. In a tunnel vault these are the circular arcs which define its surface and the horizontal lines indicating its direction; in a dome they are the horizontal diminishing circles and vertical meridians. In combinations of simple vaults, the lines of intersection between the meeting surfaces must be considered to be the

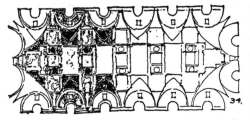

Fig. 34.—Architectural scheme, ceiling of the Sistine Chapel, Rome by Michael Angelo.

principal lines. Such are the primary considerations which apply to the decoration of both modelled and painted vaults. Within the field defined by these limitations the decoration may represent by panels, painted or in relief, possible openings into the vaulted surfaces, which will enclose the subject. Michael Angelo's great ceiling in the Sistine Chapel in Rome (Fig. 34) is a perfect example of decorative painting composed with architecture, where the effect is powerfully accented by the mutual combination of the two systems.

In the decoration of vaults by modelling and relief the following principles should be observed: The decoration should not deform the vaulting surface; the projections should be slight rather than excessive; the ground of the panels should form the surface of the vault itself; sunken compartments or heavy projections are to be avoided. The coffered panel is, then, not the form to use for the decoration of vaults in cut stone, since it cannot be applied to them without violating the principles as stated above. But it is a proper decorative form to apply to vaults in concrete and stucco.

In designing vaults care should be taken to indicate the stone jointing properly, having in mind the effect both of decoration and of correct construction. Constructively it is true for vaults as well as for arches that joint planes should lie as near as possible at right angles to the line of pressure of the stresses, while feather edges should be avoided in the individual stones. The chief difficulties in jointing are encountered at groins and intersections.

The Italian Renaissance produced many beautiful examples of the art of decorating vaults by painting, examples which perhaps offer the most direct inspiration to modern architects. There were two species of decorative painting; one representing conventional ornament of the nature of arabesques, the other subject—painting, depicting allegorical or historical pictures. The method was to plaster the vault first with stucco, which, while fresh, was lightly modelled into delicate forms of relief after designs previously prepared. Painting, done always in fresco or water-colors was also applied to the fresh plaster—a delicacy and easy grace being thereby secured which no other means could accomplish. This art attained its climax with Raphael and Michael Angelo, the Loggias of the Vatican and the vaults of the Villa Madama representing examples which are classed as masterpieces in a period celebrated for beautiful works.

CHAPTER V.

THE DIFFERENT SPECIES OF VAULTS

The Barrel Vault; the Cloister Vault; the Domical Vault; the Cross Vault; the Raised Cross Vault (Ellipsoidal or Conical Penetrations—"Bishop's Cap"); the Raised Annular Vault (Toric or Semi-Toric); the Vault on Pendentives. Construction of Models.

It is the purpose of this chapter to take up the different species of vaults and explain them in a general way, with a view of showing how they should be used and how indicated in the primary drawings of a composition.

As has been said, in order to understand the principles of vaulting thoroughly, serious study is demanded, since in designing them the imagination is controlled by the laws of science as well as art. Even the drawing of vaults calls into play all the resources of descriptive geometry. But precise drawings are somewhat without the limits of our subject, our concern being solely with shorthand methods of representation—with what is technically called "indication."

It will be seen that vaults, whether simple or in combination, in spite of their apparent diversity, reduce finally to the few elementary solids of geometry having regular stereometric form—the cylinder, cone, sphere, and ellipsoid of revolution. A further simplification results from the nature of the generation of these forms, that is either by the movement of straight line elements or of circular meridians. This consideration alone makes practicable the orderly plotting of mutual lines of intersection. On the other hand complication in representation results from the usual necessity for projecting the lines of intersection on planes not parallel to them, consequently their true shape is not shown. But this is one of the limitations of orthographic projection to which we must submit, as there is no easier way.

From the standpoint of indication, vaults are analogous in a sense to architectural shades and shadows, whose typical outlines must be memorized, like the alphabet. So there are typical lines of intersection between the surfaces of all the usual forms of vaults, and these the student must learn to indicate both in plan and section with fair accuracy, so that the part which they play in the explanation of the composition may be intelligently stated.

The simplest vault is the tunnel or barrel vault of cylindrical or cylindroidal surface. Its surface may be either semicircular, semi-elliptical or segmental.

The character and decoration of a barrel vault should emphasize its function, which requires walls of uniform thickness, and its direction, which is generally extended longitudinally. Isolated rooms on a square or nearly square plan are not satisfactorily roofed with a barrel vault unless the tympanums are a source of light; yet such proportions are correct if arranged to combine with a larger area. In the latter arrangement the barrel vaults become in effect deep arches, as when combined with larger barrel vaults or with domes, then playing the part of penetrations which are often pierced for lighting. In decorating the barrel vault the designer must decide whether he wishes to accent its length or its division into bays. The latter case results in a series of transverse arches which will require corresponding offsets in plan, more or less accented, such as pilasters and the like. In the first case projections of this sort will be slight or omitted. In highly decorated vaults it is possible to compromise the two effects by permitting the arches to break against a central compartment enriched with mouldings. Antique architecture characteristically employed coffered pan-

Fig. 35.—Groin of the coffered vault, Pennsylvania Station, New York.—McKim, Mead & White, Architects.

els, usually octagonal, as a decoration for barrel vaults of great dimensions. Usually such halls were lighted through penetrations intersecting the main vault at right angles to its axis, but in such compositions it seldom appears that the resulting groins had a determining effect upon the arrangement of the coffers (Fig. 35). Barrel vaults are also decorated by painting, the composition often including a suggestion of architecture as well as of conventional ornament and subjects purely pictorial (Fig. 34).

THE CLOISTER VAULT

By definition the cloister vault is analogous to the cross vault, since both result from the meeting of two barrel vaults at right angles. There is however no similarity in actuality. The difference results from the parts of the cylindrical surfaces that are taken as forming the vaults; in this respect one vault being the geometrical supplement of the other. The cloister vault has concave groins; the cross vault, convex. Words, however, are insufficient for giving a clear explanation of the nature of these vaults, and it is necessary for the student to refer to drawings or actual vaults in order to grasp clearly the individual characteristics of each.

The perfect cloister vault occurs over a square plan. If the plan is oblong one cylinder must be semi-elliptical, if it is desired that the groins cross at the crown, and in this case for good appearance the oblong cannot be far from a square. But groined vaults are frequently composed with corridors and long rooms,

Fig. 36.—Cloister Vault on a square plan with penetrations.

this arrangement being in effect what is termed the coved ceiling. In combination with panelling and rich ornamentation the cove is adapted to the most beautiful and highly decorative compositions.

Polygonal plans are also naturally covered by cloister vaults. Like the barrel vault, the cloister vault is apt to be insufficiently lighted unless pierced by penetrations, to all varieties of which it easily lends itself (Fig. 36).

In effective internal height the cloister vault over a polygonal plan has much in common with the hemi-spherical vault built over a circular plan (the Dome), but geometrically and constructively there are very great differences. Polygonal vaults are developable surfaces, since they are generated by straight line elements, but this is not the case with the sphere, all of whose sections are circular and therefore cannot be developed. Again the circular horizontal sections of domes give to them the peculiar quality of

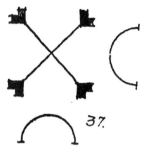

being complete after each horizontal ring of voussoirs is closed. Hence the dome adapts itself to top lighting through a circular opening. This characteristic is identified with all varieties of domes, from the Pantheon with its simple circular oculus to the elaborate lanterns of Florence Cathedral and the later Renaissance churches. Domes may also be combined with penetrations—usually cylindrical. Coffers of varying shapes adapt themselves to the

Fig. 37.—Perfect cross vault on a square plan.

decoration of domes, as do also compartments which accent the meridian circles. If the horizontal circles are too much accented the dome appears flat.

The vaults so far mentioned transmit uniform thrusts. In those to be now considered the thrusts are concentrated on detached piers which naturally form openings.

THE CROSS VAULT

The cross vault on a square plan is a frequently recurring element in monumental and semi-monumental architecture. It is produced by the intersection of two barrel vaults and is characterized by its salient groins rising diagonally from impost to crown in an angle gradually increasing from 90 to 180 degrees (Fig. 37). This type of vault may also cover an oblong plan, in which case the wider vault would be elliptical (Fig. 38). But whether the plan is square or oblong, the true curve of the groin is an ellipse, since it is the diagonal section of a cylinder.

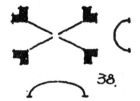

Fig. 38.—Cross vault on an oblong plan.

Accented arch-rings may or may not be part of the design of cross vaults, but, however composed, it is important to remember that the proper effect cannot be secured unless the groin always springs from and is continued by a solid impost. The pier-section in plan must explain this requirement.

Nothing is more disturbing than a groin-spring, from a re-entrant angle, that is from nothing, as often indicated (F i g. 39). If there is a column under the spring, the groin will properly rest upon the entablature. Projecting cross arches require corresponding projections from the p i e r s which s u p p o r t them (Figs. 39, 40, 41).

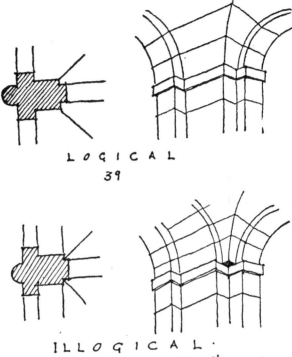

L O G I C A L

39

I L L O G I C A L ·

GROIN SPRINGS FROM NOTHING.

Fig. 39.—Logical and illogical indication of the Groin-Spring.

The cross vault adapts itself t o varying scale and dimensions in architecture — t h e monumental as well as to the average. Its greatest expression is found in the Roman Basilicas and Halls of the Baths, where the simplicity of the means used vastly increases the effect of enormity and power. Other models for study are found in a multitude of diverse buildings of the Italian Renaissance. The arcade treatments of this period are particularly valuable for inspiration.

In regard to the decoration of the cross vaults, this will vary with their scale and dimensions. Coffered panels should be re-

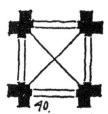

Fig. 40.—Indication of the cross vault on a square plan.

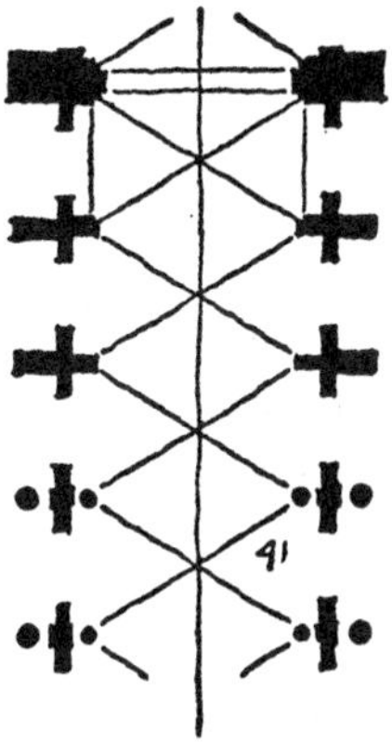

Fig. 41. — Abutments and resistances of cross vaults.

served for the colossal. In vaults of moderate dimensions the most appropriate forms of decoration are by compartments and moulded frames which accent first the groins, or else by the delicate relief and color decoration of the early Renaissance, or by pure decorative painting as in the celebrated Villa Madama.

Vaults of large diameter are frequently pierced by smaller vaults of similar section, called penetrations. The resulting lines of intersection will be wavy curves, which in the case of semicircular vaults are projected horizontally as equilateral hyperbolas (Fig. 42).

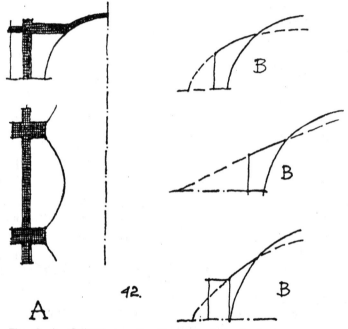

Fig. 42.—A. Cylindrical vault with penetrations; B. Sections of conoidal and ellipsoidal penetrations.

In combinations of this sort the decoration of the main vault should retain the character of the simple barrel vault.

RAISED CROSS AND ANNULAR VAULTS

Up to this point, combinations of vaults having a cylindrical nature only have been considered; the highest element or "ridge" of such vaults being, with the exception of the cloister and dome, a horizontal line. Often it is desirable to raise the crown of vaults above this, defining element, each compartment of a series then assuming in general the form of a shallow inverted saucer (calotte)

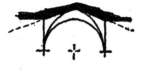

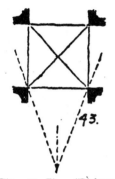

above the crown of the cross arches. Longitudinally the upper section of such a series would be a repeated curve, broken by intervening arches.

On a square plan this species of vaults may be formed by the intersection of either cones or ellipsoids of revolution in two directions. .In both cases the thrusts will be concentrated and the plans analogous to the simple cross vault. These forms are often termed "Bishop's Cap" vaults (Fig. 43). The crown of the double ellipsoidal vault (Fig. 44) is ordinarily less raised than the conoidal, but a still higher vault may be obtained by employing portions of ellipsoids (Fig. 45).

Since meridian sections are in every instance half circles, the groins may be readily

Fig. 43.—The "Bishop's cap" vault.

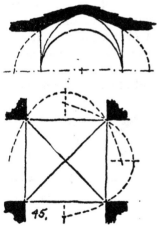

Fig. 45—Raised ellipsoidal cross vault.

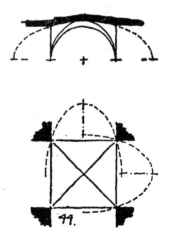

Fig. 44.—Ellipsoidal cross valt.

plotted. For the conoidal vault the groins are elliptical curves, which occur here as rather disagreeable pointed segments. In order that pleasing and flexible curves may result in these combinations, they are designed rather by trial than geometrically. The curve of the groins is first fixed, then the ridge curve, and the rest of the surface made to conform thereto.

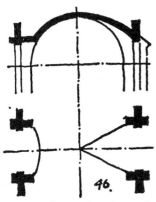

Fig. 46.—Penetrations in an oblong cross vault.

Fig. 47.—Raised conoidal penetrations.

Cross arches are essential to Bishop's Cap vaults w h e n the tympanums are opened, on account of the disagreeable angle at the transition.

For special effects t h e purely cylindrical tunnel or barrel vault may be interrupted b y inclined penetrations

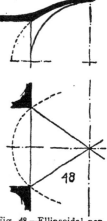

Fig. 48.—Ellipsoidal penetration into a tunnel vault.

analogous to the non-cylindrical forms just discussed. This composition occurs where greater height is sought in the penetrations, together with a more varied decorative scheme. This is accomplished by having the surface of the penetration, part either of a sloping cylinder, cone or an ellipsoid (Figs. 46, 47 and 48).

Hard to conceive, the methodical analysis of raised vaults and of inclined penetrations is a serious task, although results are more satisfactory than when

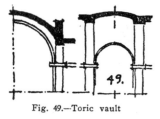

Fig. 49.—Toric vault

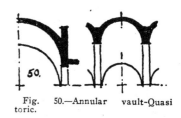

Fig. 50.—Annular vault-Quasi toric.

the surfaces are proportioned by trial.

Finally we have the toric or semi-toric (annular) vaults, a species subject to variations rarely employed. The appearance of this type has little to recommend it over other types similar in appearance and more simply conceived (Figs. 49 and 50).

THE DOMICAL VAULT ON PENDENTIVES

The dome on pendentives, although it appeared toward the end of the Roman epoch, did not become a conspicuous feature of architectural composition until it was taken up and developed by the Byzantines. This singularly beautiful and fruitful invention gave to architecture the unrivalled churches of St. Sophia in Constantinople, St. Mark in Venice and St. Peter in Rome. The pendentive makes possible the covering of a square hall by a spherical vault. It is conceived as follows: Imagine a spherical vault whose

diameter is the diagonal of the square to be covered. Four intersecting planes, perpendicular to its base and coinciding with the sides of the inscribed square, determine the four wall arches, while a horizontal circle tangent to the crowns of the wall arches defines the upper limit of the composition. The parts of the hemisphere remaining within these intersecting planes are the pendentives (Fig. 51). Geometrically they are spherical triangles—that is triangular portions of a spherical surface bounded by arcs of circles.

Fig. 51.—The pendentive in perspective.

In masonry, pendentives are built up in the form of arches which meet at the top in a complete circle. The whole construction is perfectly stable.

The pendentive vault may be covered by one of three species of domes, depending upon the character sought. 1 The upper part of the hemisphere may be replaced, 2 a new dome of greater curvature may be started or 3 a cylindrical drum to support a still higher dome may be interposed.

This method of covering a square plan has numerous analogies to the cross vault among which the following are the most conspicuous. It has tympanums for lighting which may be opened by pendentives, while thrusts are concentrated at the corners. Like the cross vault the pendentive vault may be made the intersection of barrel vaults at right angles. Its height is greater than the Bishop's Cap vault and like it the arch rings must be accented where the penetrations are opened into barrel vaults or shallow arches. Pendentive vaults may be placed in series in a combination of successive bays, but this composition should be reserved for halls of monumental proportions. In general the form is simpler than the groined vault as it has no sharp

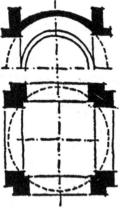

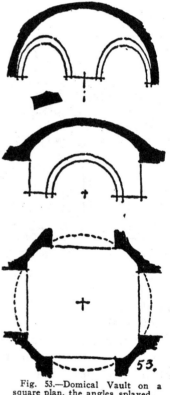

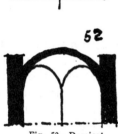

Fig. 52.—Domical Vault on a square plan, not raised.

angles and penetrations intersect in a plane curve.

On a perfect square plan the lower spring of the vault must be a cusp shaped point which may give the impression of inadequate support (Fig. 52). To obviate this the pier is often

Fig. 53.—Domical Vault on a square plan, the angles splayed.

Fig. 54.—Abutment of the splayed pendentive.

widened diagonally, thus giving the splayed pendentive (Fig. 53). Note that although the face of the pier may be a flat plane of varying width the spring line of the pendentive is always a circular arc, which is masked, however, by the projecting mouldings of the impost (Fig. 54).

The pendentive vault may be stopped at the first complete horizontal annular circle, this forming a stable base on which may be raised a higher dome or cylindrical drum. The use of the raised dome and drum is the system characteristic of St. Peter's and other large Renaissance churches. This composition lends itself easily to adequate lighting, since the drum may be arranged with windows, or even the dome shell itself may be pierced, or the source of light may come from an architectural lantern at the summit.

The configuration of the domical vault, whether considered externally or internally is the noblest expression of architectural form. This is particularly true for large monuments, yet the dome adapts itself to the composition of small edifices as well as great. Roman, Byzantine, Renaissance and modern epochs in design have all achieved great masterpieces of domical architecture. Each of these periods offer some distinctive feature of composition peculiarly valuable for instruction, but of all individual monuments, the student may learn the most, perhaps—as M. Guadet declares— from a study of the Invalides in Paris, where the peculiar composition of the pendentive is impressed upon the architecture from the base of the edifice all the way up to the crown of the dome.

The dome of St. Peter's is well known to be the mightiest of all, yet the total effect produced by this great pile can hardly be said to surpass that conveyed by the magnificent church of Hagia Sophia. The reason for this, although it is partly due to the superior handling of scale in the latter edifice, results chiefly from the larger facts of arrangement and composition. In external mass the church of Hagia Sophia is hardly comparable to the magnitude of St. Peter's (see Figs. 18 and 166-A, 166-B) yet its nave measures over 200 by 100 feet. Professor A. D. F. Hamlin describes this marvellous edifice in the following words: "The dome rests upon four mighty arches bounding a square, into two of which open the half domes of semicircular apses. These apses are penetrated and extended each by two smaller niches and a central arch. Thus was secured a noble and unobstructed hall of unrivalled beauty, covered by a combination of half domes increasing in span and height as they lead up successively to the stupendous central vault, which rises 180 feet into the air and fitly crowns the whole. The imposing effect of this low curved but loftily poised dome, resting upon a crown of windows, its summit visible from every point of the nave. . . is not surpassed by an interior ever erected."

Small scale models of all the vaults described in this chapter may be constructed without great difficulty in plaster. This is a very instructive exercise that may be attempted by any student since no particular skill in modelling is required. The chief value of the exercise lies in the fact that a clear conception of the geometry of vaults must be had before the model can be started. Without going into unnecessary detail it will suffice to indicate the suggested method.

As an example, take the case of the raised cross vault formed by the meeting of two semi-ellipsoidal surfaces of revolution. It will first be necessary to model in clay the two solids which define the intersecting surfaces. After describing the directing ellipse on paper, a stiff wire should be bent to the same curve. Form an eye at each end of the wire, so that it may be swung around a nail or other pivot at each side of the partially formed clay. In this way the two solids may be accurately struck. Since the intersectings coincide with vertical planes mitering along the diagonals, these and also the four wall arches may be easily sliced. The whole combination should finally be placed in a box, within which it exactly fits, and covered with liquid plaster of Paris.

Models of the different combinations of vaults thus formed lend themselves very conveniently to demonstrations in the class room, as well as to individual study.

REFERENCES:

Guadet, J.   "Eléments et Théorie de l'Architecture"
                Books III, IV, V
Esquie, P.   "Traité Elémentaire d'Architecture"
Bühlman, J.   "Die Architecture des Classichen Altertums and
                der Renaissance"
Gromort, G.   "Choix d'Eléments Empruntés a l'Architecture
                Classique"

PART III.

THE ELEMENTS OF COMPOSITION

CHAPTER I.

GENERAL CONSIDERATIONS; EXTERNAL VESTIBULES

Very early in the study of planning it becomes necessary to differentiate between areas which are set apart for some special use and those which are necessary merely for access and communication. The former include rooms which are more or less private or which are devoted to some particular purpose; that is areas which are generally called—rooms—the use of which characterizes the general function of the building. The latter, which may be termed—neutral areas—are just as essential to the plan and, in a way, are just as characterizing.

One of the most difficult things in composition is to accurately determine the relative proportion that should exist in area and architectural importance between the first division and the second. The beginner will always magnify the importance of rooms at the expense of circulation; his tendency is to reduce the plan to useful areas alone and it is hard to free the mind from this delusion. No plan can be brought down to this degree of concentration and remain a good plan; there will always be required some sort of neutral areas permitting entrance and exit, circulation throughout the floors, passage from one story to another and courts for light and air.

These neutral areas comprise a multitude of diverse elements always of primary importance which have become increasingly more complicated as architecture has developed and civilization become more complex. Under the general division, then, of the "Elements of Composition" must be included—porticos, peristyles, atriums, porches and entrance motives of various sorts, vestibules, lobbies, galleries and corridors, stairways, ramps and elevators, courts, both large and small, intended for aeration, lighting or circulation. From antiquity to modern times these elements cover a wide field for study—a field which even a lifetime of study would hardly enable one to completely traverse. Our concern here can only be with generalities, leaving for special comment those elements and features which can only be thoroughly considered in connection with special programs.

The development of the human habitation must of necessity keep pace with the advancement of civilization. Always there is a desire for well-being. The search for inventions and devices which will make living more comfortable or luxurious have profoundly modified architecture, and especially modified it in the conception of its essential elements—of rooms and the means of access to them. The question as to whether the simpler life may be or may not be better for the human race is no concern of architectural composition. The social state of the epoch makes the plan and determines its details—the reverse does not hold. It is necessary, then, for us to be of our own times, and one as a designer must know how to adapt the composition of a plan to the mechanical inventions of a mechanical age. It is only necessary to recall the invention of the electric elevator which alone has made the skyscraper adaptable to human needs; mechanical heating and ventilation and artificial lighting have already greatly modified our conceptions of the limitations pertaining to composition and will modify them still more, no doubt. M. Guadet mentions the invention of glass as the one that has contributed much to the development of architecture. "That architecture was transformed by this invention, at least in the composition of edifices, is no exaggeration," says he "and furthermore, if glass had not been invented, civilization and the general history of mankind could not have been what it has been."

Such inventions have rather extended the scope and range of composition than altered our conceptions of its ruling principles. Discoveries which enrich or complicate architecture do not detach it from what has gone before. It is still necessary to study antique compositions, to study them, as M. Guadet further remarks, precisely as one studies the classical tongues, so as the better to speak one's own language.

EXTERNAL VESTIBULES

No matter how simple the edifice may be there is necessary some sort of vestibule at the entrance, even though this be merely a deep portal. From the simplest to the most complex requirements, vestibules as an element of composition show a great diversity in arrangement and architectural design, yet they naturally fall into a certain number of groups according to their use and function. Although the vestibule, according to the ordinary usage of the term, is generally thought of as being a space incorporated within the walls of a building and usually adjacent to the entrance doorway, such external features as porticos and peristyles and the like, which shelter and give importance to the entrance, and which must be traversed in order to pass into the building, are also properly classified with vestibules.

External vestibules, in the above sense, then comprise: Porches —preceding the entrance doorway of an edifice and usually entirely open; this would include a public street into a "court of honor," or from the exterior into an enclosed court or garden; passages of this sort may be for the use of vehicles or simply a footway, or the two uses combined. Internal vestibules, which are entirely enclosed in the edifice—ordinarily either a transitional space from the exterior to the interior, or an area separating one part of a building from another; a case of the latter would be a vestibule between a public lobby or "Salle des pas perdus" and a hall for assembly—for example.

Other special differences result in vestibules from the point of view of their composition in the edifice. Thus a vestibule may be comprised in one story of height only, or it may rise through two or more stories. The architectural character sought, proportions of height and area, method of lighting and character of detail, all produce varieties which are infinite. The architecture of every epoch has produced many beautiful examples of vestibules which for study and inspiration in design are among the most instructive of all the general elements of the plan.

Besides being necessary for use, vestibules may also serve a purely decorative function thereby characterizing and explaining the purpose of the edifice. An entrance portico may have little excuse for its existence except to create an impression—to give monumental character and dignity to a facade. This use when justified by the program takes precedence over purely material necessities. In both cases vestibules are subject to the general principles laid down for proportion and appropriateness of detail.

The entrance vestibule, since it is a transition from exterior to interior architecture, should partake of the nature of both. Its architectural elements should be less monumental than those demanded by external architecture, yet in general not so refined and delicate as the wall-treatment of rooms or halls. Walls of vestibules are often finished in the same materials as for exteriors, but necessarily treated in a more elegant manner and at a smaller scale. For example it is quite proper, as is often done, to treat the vestibule of a monumental stone edifice with all the usual features belonging to exterior stone architecture; such as, jointing, columns,

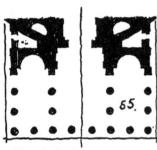

pilasters, vaulting, projecting and receding forms, cornices, niches, carving and the like. Furniture and movable ornaments, unless a highly monumental character is demanded and given to them would obviously be out of place in a vestibule.

Fig. 55.—Portico of the Pantheon, Rome.

Projecting porches or porticos, where the columns are freestanding and include more than one story in height, are essentially the motives of grand architecture, and ought only to be used when considerations of use and beauty imperatively demand it. No other feature can contribute more to the monumental character of an edifice than the portico, properly used. The monumental impression produced appears to be directly proportional to the depth or projection of the portico. All the porticos and peristyles of the highly monu-

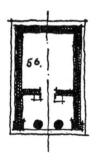

mental architecture of antiquity were deep, see the Pantheon (Fig. 55) and other examples of Roman and Greek architecture.

In these edifices are found three arrangements of the general case of the peristyle. (It will be understood that this term includes colonnades, porches, porticos and the like, either the full height of the facade or only one story in height). In one arrangement the peristyle is exactly equal to the width of the building and is continued down the sides, if at all, by pilasters; in another it is nar-

Fig. 56.—Columns in Antis.

rower and abuts against the facade; and in still another it is wider than the building and comprises the width of lateral colonnades. A special case is that of columns in antis, seen in the smaller Greek temples (Fig. 56).

The first case is that of the lesser antique temples, in general the number of columns being usually four or six. The Propylaea,

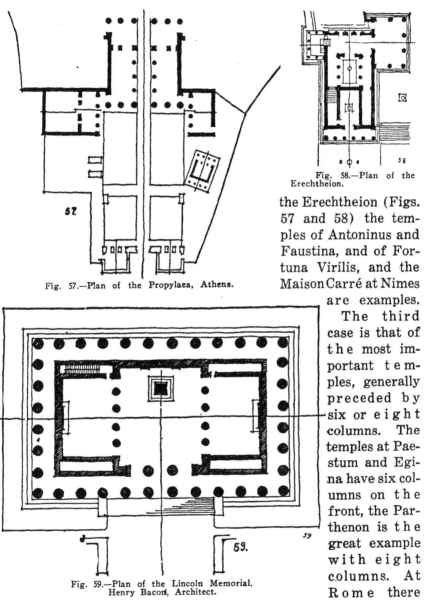

Fig. 58.—Plan of the Erechtheion.

Fig. 57.—Plan of the Propylaea, Athens.

Fig. 59.—Plan of the Lincoln Memorial.
Henry Bacon, Architect.

the Erechtheion (Figs. 57 and 58) the temples of Antoninus and Faustina, and of Fortuna Virilis, and the Maison Carré at Nimes are examples.

The third case is that of the most important temples, generally preceded by six or eight columns. The temples at Paestum and Egina have six columns on the front, the Parthenon is the great example with eight columns. At Rome there are many notable instances—the Temple of Mars Avenger, the temple of Jupiter Stator, also the great temple of Venus and Rome. In modern times, the Lincoln Memorial (Fig. 59).

The second case occurs many times in classic edifices especially the Roman, and has been the motive most frequently recalled in modern work. Guadet, citing the celebrated peristyle of the Pantheon of Agrippa (Fig. 55), makes the following interesting comment, "It appears certain from the labors of M. Chedanne, that the original peristyle must have had ten columns instead of eight, and thus are explained certain anomalies in details, like the exaggerated slope of the pediment and irregular inclination of the ornaments."

The central "court of honor," as has been noted, has found little expression in American public architecture; hence the monumental fence or colonnade barrier separating the court from the public street with its central portal has been a correspondingly seldom occurring motive. This type of composition is rather monarchial in conception, opposed therefore to the democratic ideas of the present day, which hesitate to adopt exclusive motives conceived

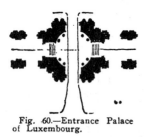

Fig. 60.—Entrance Palace of Luxembourg.

entirely for show, however imposing they may be. The nearest counterparts which we have to this program are found in the monumental entrances to parks, or lodges and entrance gates to private estates, which may or may not be informally conceived. The most celebrated modern examples are naturally found in the French architecture of the aristocratic period which produced the Luxembourg Palace and the Oval Court at Fontainebleau with their entrances (Fig. 60).

This composition has its uses for study, forming a valuable, though occasionally given, exercise in the application of the elements.

If we turn to the architecture of antiquity we shall find the motive of the detached portal frequently treated as an element of the first importance. In Egypt are the colossal pylons before the courts of the temples; the Propylaea at Athens and Eleusis are also in a measure great vestibules and passages leading into templed enclosures, while at Rome there must have been numerous examples of entrances into public places, forums and the precincts of great palaces. Among the latter, the Portico of Octavius (Fig. 150) is a well-preserved example. The Propylaea at Athens (Fig. 57) is the most celebrated example, but its composition is

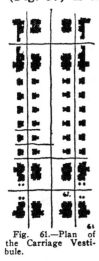

not strongly characterized, since the form of expression in architecture which seeks to give to each different type of edifice its own characteristic design, was not a controlling idea with the Greeks, as it is with us.

There are, of course, many other arrangements of the external or partially included vestibule. The entrance for vehicles, called "porte cochere" is one; the covered driveway into a railroad station or other public building is another arrangement which might be classed among porches (Fig. 61).

Fig. 61.—Plan of the Carriage Vestibule.

CHAPTER II.

INCORPORATED VESTIBULES

The vestibules previously considered do not form an integral part of the building enclosure, although they may be essential to the composition. Incorporated vestibules are considered as being within the external walls of the edifice and as such form an indispensable and integral element of the plan.

The most elementary internal vestibule is a simple passage traversing from the public street to a court (Fig. 62). Such pass-

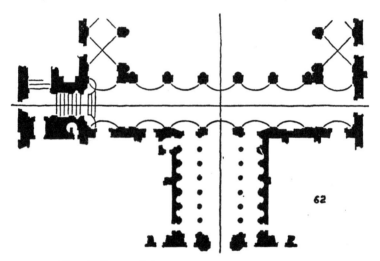

Fig. 62.—Farnese Palace, Interior Vestibule and Arcade.

ages are very common in the architecture of other countries where internal courts are frequently regarded as essential features, but this arrangement is quite rare in contemporary American architecture. Whether simple or monumental then, this form of vestibule is best studied where it occurs most often, that is in Italian Renaissance architecture. Very naturally its direction is usually perpendicular to the facade.

All vestibules have this in common, they cannot be considered apart from the general circulation of the building. Existing primarily for passage and general use, their composition is largely controlled by the arrangement of corridors, by the location of a court, as just stated, or by staircases or elevators.

Passages for carriages with footwalks, treated monumentally, possibly vaulted, are excellent cases for study. They may fre-

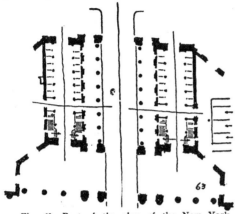

quently be seen in the public and private architecture of France. We have at least one grand example in the United States, where a street is carried through the New York Municipal Building—McKim, M e a d' a n d W h i t e, Architects (Fig. 63).

Fig. 63.—Part of the plan of the New York Municipal Building. McKim, Mead & White, Architects.

Examples of the type of vestibule perpendicular to a facade, often cited, are the two most perfect of the four celebrated vestibules of the Louvre leading to the court—that opening on the Rue de Rivoli (Fig. 64) and that beneath the Pavilion de l'Horloge (Fig. 65). Other beautiful vestibules are that at Versailles adjacent to the Chapel, the vestibule of the Ecole Militaire, and the Vestibule of Hotel de Ville at Rouen. The magnificent vestibule of the Farnese Palace by San Gallo

Fig. 64.—Vestibule of the Court of the Louvre, facing the Tuileries.

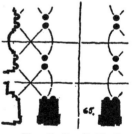

Fig. 65.—Detail, North Vestibule of the Louvre.

(Fig. 62) is particularly instructive. Here the difficulties of connecting the vestibule with the court arcade were considerable on account of t h e non-coincidence of axes, compelling the architect to slightly skew the arches in order to harmonize the composition. So skillfully is this done that it is hardly perceived in reality. The fine works of Letarouilly are full of examples of the splendid vestibules of the Italian masters, most of them simply and largely conceived and full of the finest artistic inspiration for the student.

In American architecture, the case of the elevator lobby in office buildings and hotels is analogous to that of the monumental vestibule perpendicular to a facade. Fine examples of this particular composition are numerous (Fig. 66).

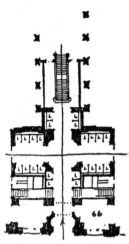

Fig. 66.—Elevator Lobby of the Woolworth Building.

The arrangement of a great vestibule parallel to a facade is less often employed, and on account of its nature should be reserved for the grandest compositions. Great space is required particularly in the direction of length. This is the composition of the great hall, lobby or "salle des pas perdu," very valuable for study, and not seldom occurring in the great public architecture of the United States. Frequently rising in

height through two stories, vestibules of this sort assume great monumental importance, and thus are often com-

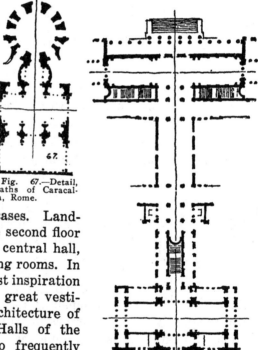

Fig. 67.—Detail, Baths of Caracalla, Rome.

posed with grand staircases. Landings and galleries at the second floor level, opening on to the central hall, give access to surrounding rooms. In classic design the greatest inspiration for this type of hall or great vestibule is found in the architecture of imperial Rome. The Halls of the Baths and Basilicas, so frequently illustrated in books, are the great sources for study and suggestion (Fig. 67). In our own day we may see imposing examples in many

Fig. 68.—Central Portion of the Metropolitan Museum of Art, New York. Richard M. Hunt and McKim, Mead & White, Architects.

American cities. Among others there are the great railway stations of New York City and Washington; the new wing of the Metropolitan Museum of Art (Fig. 68) and the great vaulted vestibules and lobbies of our state capitols.

The great hall for waiting and passage in the modern metropolitan railway station forms, in a sense, the gateway to a city, and thus is conceived perhaps the most monumental expression of the vestibule of all time (Fig. 69).

Sometimes the composition forces the vestibule to be comprised in the ground story only and to have little height (Fig. 70).

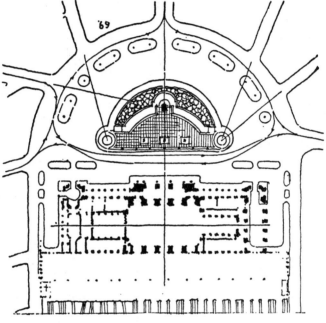

Fig. 69.—Union Station, Washington, D. C.
D. H. Burnham & Co. Architects.

This is frequently the case in theatres where the vestibule is surmounted in most cases by a more imposing foyer. This is a difficult problem, but the designer must know how to make the most of it. Obviously, barrel or other high vaults are out of the question, and segmental or flat vaults, springing from wall colonnades or like projections, are proper to give the effect of reduced span and to obviate a possibility of the effect of crushing or sagging in the ceiling. This composition is also seen in round or polygonal

Fig. 70.—Section through entrance vestibule, Palace Giustiniani.

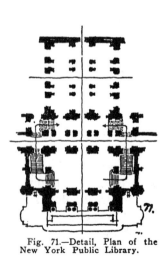

Fig. 71.—Detail, Plan of the
New York Public Library.

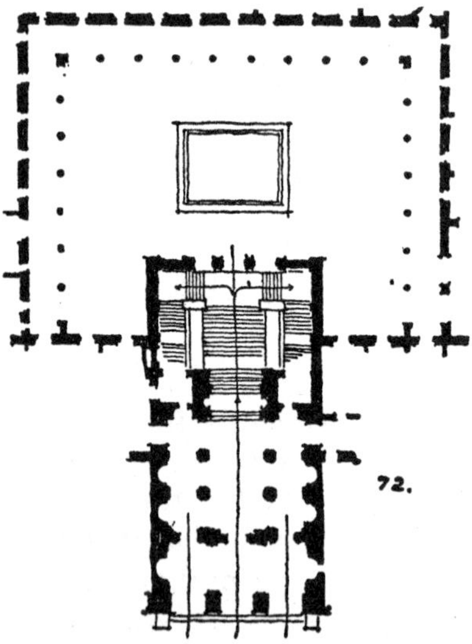

Fig. 72.—Vestibule, Staircase and
Court Arcade, Boston Public Library.
McKim, Mead & White, Architects.

halls as in the celebrated vestibule of the Grand Theatre at Bordeaux by Louis.

Vestibules with an entrance from the street on one side and an access to the circulation on the other are the most frequently occurring of all arrangements. Usually the long axis will be parallel to the facade and lighting will naturally result only from that side. This type of vestibule is analogous to the loggia, the openings in the facade side either being filled-in with a motive of set-in door-ways combined with glazing and iron-work or left entirely open. The latter case has a close resemblance to the portico with arches or rectangular openings, and is simply a monumental case of the loggia (Fig. 71 and 72). This would call for internal architecture corresponding closely with the exterior, and, if in stone, its composition would be fully as monumental. Various arrangements of vaulted ceilings are frequently employed, together with niches, engaged or free columns and other forms of wall-treatment.

In monumental planning it is always imperative that the vestibule be carefully composed with respect to the adjacent circulation and the internal architecture to which it is directly related. This calls for a proper understanding of controlling factors of construction which will invariably require the recall of points of support where they are demanded. A careful and intelligent study of the poché is the only means for accomplishing this. One of the most difficult problems of planning is to transfer the architecture of the facade to the interior of the building by way of the vestibules; yet this is a problem that has numerous and varied solutions, which for instruction are among the most valuable of all (Figs. 62 and 71). In studying compositions of this nature the several factors governing the design of the points of poché should be borne in mind. These are primarily the form and treatment of the ceiling and the wall-treatment of the facade. The problem of the vestibule cannot be separated from the theory of composition as a whole and must be studied in the light of a true understanding of all its relations.

Loggias are typical of the architecture of the Renaissance, but are rather exceptional in our day. We employ them, not so much in the sense of combined elements of the plan, as separate programs, reserving them for the decoration of parts and gardens, where as architectural shelters, open on one side at least to the direct sun and air, they provide beautiful and grateful retreats. The loggias of the Farnesina, Villa Medici and Villa Madama are exquisite examples of the refined art of the Renaissance. In the

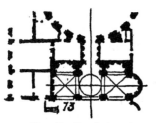

latter, which is celebrated for its decorations in the school of Raphael and Guilio Romano, a central pendentive dome is flanked by two cross vaults and extended in depth by a tunnel vault, while the composition is completed by three large niches (Fig. 73).

Fig. 73.—Vestibule of the Villa Madama.

The composition of vestibules at skew-junctions is a problem of exceptional difficulty, which requires a corresponding degree of skill and ingenuity for its solution. This is the problem of the cut-off angle, familiarly known as "turning the corner." Several examples, to which reference will be made, will be found in various places in this book. The most instructive example of all is undoubtedly the Grand Prix composition of M. Pascal, "Banque et Hotel pour riche Banquier" (Fig. 74, 75 and 76).

It will be seen that the problem reduces itself to the intersection of axes not perpendicular; the vestibule at the junction serving two or more wings of the building. The difficulty is primarily one of connection, the degree of angularity having little to do with it.

In general there are two ways of properly incorporating the skew; by the interposition of a circle or circular segment, or by a triangular or trapezoidal form. The first, which proceeds from the logical deduction that since the circle has an infinite number of radii therefore it will accommodate itself to any axis that is directed toward its center, is much favored because of its simplicity and the obvious grace of the compositions that result. The second —the trapezoidal connection—is apt to be awkward despite a celebrated ancestry. The Octagonal Court of the Belvidere in the Vatican is a famous example of the latter (Fig. 77).

It will be noticed, upon reference to M. Pascal's composition that there are four critical points where several axes join obliquely, and in every case the transition is effected by a circular vestibule. A detail of the plan at a large scale is shown in Figure 76. As previously suggested, this composition will repay the most care-

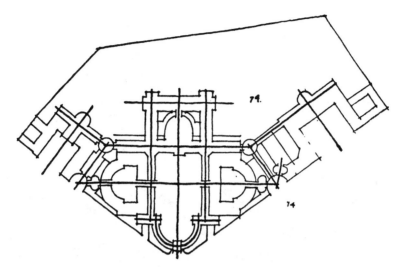

Fig. 74.—Axes of the Grand Prix Plan of M. Pascal.

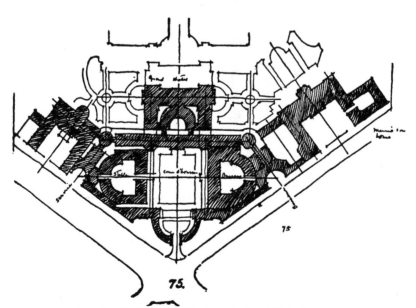

Fig. 75.—Block plan of M. Pascal's Grand Prix Project.

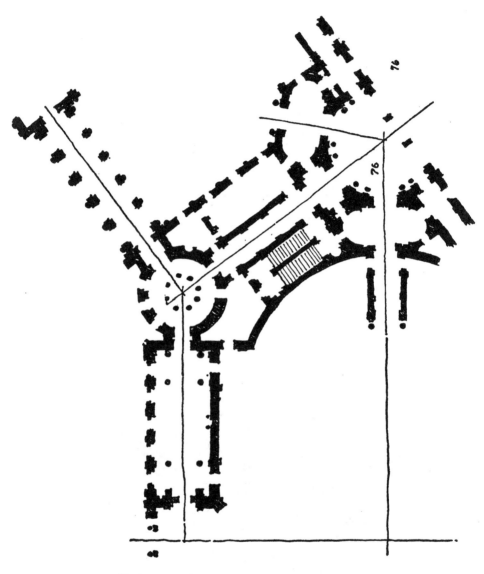

Fig. 76.—Detail from the Grand Prix Plan of M. Pascal.

ful study since practically every typical problem of the skew junction is there beautifully solved. Other examples of varying degrees of axial obliquity are shown in Figures 78, 79, 80 and 81.

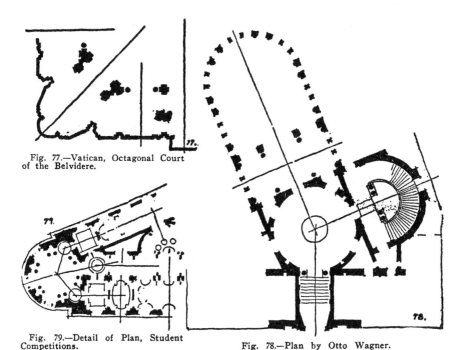

Fig. 77.—Vatican, Octagonal Court of the Belvidere.

Fig. 79.—Detail of Plan, Student Competitions.

Fig. 78.—Plan by Otto Wagner.

In all of these the intersection is characterized by the circle. Figures 82, 82-A, and 83 are characterized b y t h e trapezoidal intersection. As always the chief care in designing the poché should be for the construction and appearance of the ceiling. It is impossible to twist or warp an arch-ring or bend a beam; so that any projection logically called for on one side of the room by the composition of the ceiling must be

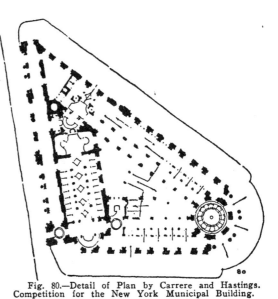

Fig. 80.—Detail of Plan by Carrere and Hastings. Competition for the New York Municipal Building.

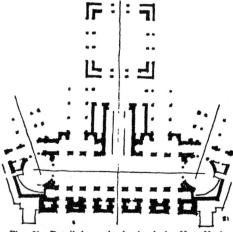

Fig. 81.—Detail from the book of the New York Court House Competition.

inevitably recalled on the other. This is very clearly indicated in Figure 82-A.

Turning to examples less academic, though perhaps more classically conceived, we find in the architecture of the Italian Renaissance many plans on very awkward and irregular sites where nevertheless, the imperatives of symmetrical planning have been admirably expressed. The works of Letarouilly are full of many such examples. The

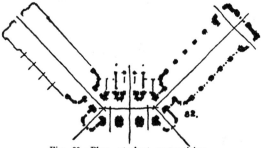

Fig. 82.—Plan, student competition.

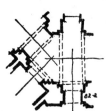

Fig. 82-A.—Detail of the angle, student competition.

Massimi Palaces will be at once recalled as perhaps the most celebrated of this type. Their partis are indicated in Figure 84. The vestibule of the Palace of Pietro Massimi, composed on a bent axis, is a noble composition whose proportions and detail are unexcelled (Fig. 85). Peruzzi was one of those illustrious artists of the Renaissance whose conceptions are of the most distinguished character and therefore most inspiring for study and imitation. He is remarkable, particularly for the great subtlety and beauty of profiles and mouldings.

Finally it may be stated as a general rule, when the angle included between the facades of a building is very acute so as to give an unpleasant appearance of sharpness and weakness at the corner, that the angle should be more or less truncated. This truncation may be either a simple splay or segment of a circle and

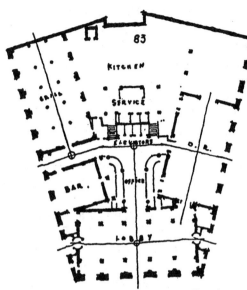

Fig. 83.—Plan of the Hotel Statler, Detroit.
Geo. B. Post & Sons, Architects.

usually it will abut against a slight return in the wall which definitely limits the facade on either side (Fig. 86).

In the composition of vestibules there is this important rule to be followed; often the edifice permits or requires a series of vestibules on the same axis. In this case their design, as expressed by their interior profiles and proportionate heights and widths in section, should be varied in order to increase the effect of the general impression.

Observe how skillfully and beautifully this is done in the section of M. Chaussemiche's Grand Prix composition (Fig. 127-A). See also figures 128-A, and 130-A.

The vestibules so far considered are those which are for the most part contiguous to the facade of the building giving direct access from the exterior. Another class of vestibules are those which are placed wholly within the interior of a building, usually at the end of some circulation already transversed. The function of such a vestibule is often as a center

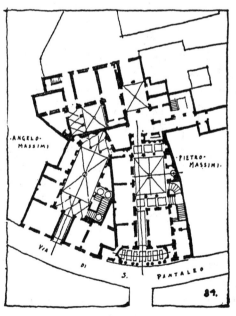

Fig. 84.—Massimi Palaces, Rome. General Plan.

of radiation, providing access to all parts of the building either in horizontal or vertical directions or both combined. There are many examples of this element of composition in antiquity. In domestic architecture, the plans of Greek and Pompeian houses were composed around a central, common court, or atrium, which was reached from the outside street by a passageway. In the ancient house, the atrium—although lighted from above and open

Fig. 85.—Entrance Vestibule, Palace of Pietro Massimi.

to the sky—had a more intimate connection with the general plan than the courtyard. It was paved, often partly roofed, and appropriately furnished, so that it formed, in a sense, a common living hall. The atrium had its origin from considerations of use, convenience and comfort. Being surrounded by four walls, there was always shade—grateful in a semi-tropic climate—while a draft of air through the entrance passage, aided by rapid evaporation of water from fountains and dampened flags, insured a pleasant, cool resting place even on a hot summer day. The plan of the Pompeian house is still typical of much of

Fig. 86.—Detail of a cut-off angle, where the inter-section is acute may be either plane or curved.

the domestic architecture of Latin countries. Even in our own country—in New Orleans—many of the older houses were planned about the atrium, or "courtyard" as it is locally known, a feature which must have contributed most delightfully to the domestic and social life of a period long-since passed.

In latter days the atrium is retained in architecture of a more public and monumental nature in various ways. Usually it is glazed over by skylights; but in many instances the character of the internal architecture of classic times, with its arcades and galleries, finds beautiful adaptations. Again as a center of radiation and clearance in buildings of a highly public character, it finds a variety of treatments which are wholly individual and a resultant of the special program of the edifice. The internal vestibules of the Doria Pamphili Palace at Rome, and of the beautiful Royal Hall in the Vatican, serving for access to the

Sistine Chapel, are celebrated examples of halls where a grand, monumental effect was sought.

In modern architecture, the concourse of a railway station is conceived in a sense as an interior vestibule. American architecture numbers many examples of this division of planning, varying in scale and magnitude. Most important of all is the great concourse of the Pennsylvania Station in New York, treated throughout with architecture in structural iron and glass. The premiated design by Guy Lowell in the New York Courthouse Competition exhibits a striking conception of the design and function of an internal vestibule (Fig. 87). Here the program calls for a building of great size and importance on an irregular site, where large numbers of people will be continually coming and going on business, congestion reaching its peak during certain definite hours. The architect adopted a circular form of building, highly monumental in character and recalling in general style many of the old Roman buildings, particularly the Colosseum. From whatever direction the building is approached there is a passage leading directly to the large, circular lobby at its center, around which the elevators are arranged in an annular ring. The way in which the difficulties inherent in a circular composition are solved is admirable and will repay careful study.

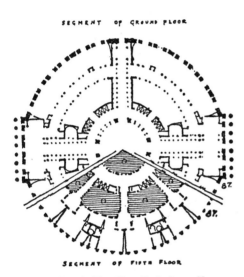

SEGMENT OF GROUND FLOOR

SEGMENT OF FIFTH FLOOR

Fig. 87.—Sketch Plan New York Court House. Guy Lowell, Architect.

A beautiful and well-known example of the atrium, conceived in the classic spirit, is that in the building for the Pan American Union at Washington by Albert Kelsey and Paul Cret. Here owing to certain Spanish or Latin-American traditions, the name "patio" has been retained (Fig. 88).

In vestibules, and in a less accented way, in corridors, the design of the pavement may have great importance. Appropriate treatments range from simple flags to elaborate patterns in marble and mosaic. This subject will be more fully treated under the head of the decoration of the plan.

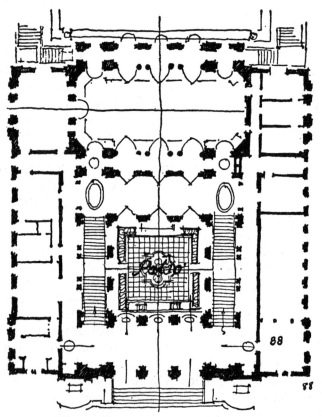

Fig. 88.—First floor plan of the Pan American Union Building. Albert Kelsey and Paul Cret, Architects.

CHAPTER III.

VERTICAL COMMUNICATIONS

EXTERNAL STAIRWAYS; INTERIOR STAIRWAYS. THEIR LOCATION AND ARRANGEMENT. ELEVATORS.

In antiquity the building of one story was the prevailing type for highly monumental edifices; in modern times, on the other hand, multiple story buildings are the rule, while the single story edifice is reserved only for occasional programs. Hence arises the necessity, particularly in interiors, for means of communication vertically throughout the different floor levels. For a long time this has been accomplished by means of staircases and in recent times by the added agency of the elevator.

Large, complex edifices, of only one story, comprising masses of different area and height, are very instructive as academic problems in parti; hence it is the rule, rather than the exception, to find programs written around such types of buildings. In these instances, the staircase is often reserved for study as an element by itself; or in connection with the halls, lobbies, vestibules or other parts which it immediately serves.

Practically the only form of staircase known to the ancients was the external flight of steps, and this we find all through classic times. Many different arrangements are met with in Greek and Roman architecture, although it may be said that antiquity preferred the straight flight before the edifice as being simpler and more impressive.

Staircases are then either external or internal. In studying their arrangement in the general composition let us consider external staircases first. As is the case with all other elements of the plan, it is clear that staircases may be subject to proportions which emphasize, on the one hand simple use, and on the other purely monumental effect. The latter corresponds to the case of the flight of steps before a monument. Here an impressive effect is naturally the prime consideration, and if the design is in the classic manner the staircase will preferably be wide and straight, the monumental idea of the edifice being accentuated by the monumental access to it. The elevation of a monumental edifice above the general level of the ground is a chief contributing factor toward an imposing appearance, and this effect may be said to be largely strengthened through the contrast of scale effected by a repeated element (the steps), whose subdivisions are in human proportions.

The impression produced by a great flight of steps is that it is to be set apart for occasional use—for crowds and ceremonies—

Fig. 89.—Robert Fulton Memorial, Project. H. Van B. Magonigle, Architect.

therefore it will be proper to find beside the main flight additional flights of less pretentious proportions for daily use. Such great flights may be terminated laterally by stepped or raking walls parallel to the slope. These are often designed as pedestals for statuary. Landings must be numerous and it is particularly essential to have wide landings at top and bottom. The steps should be easy and gentle, and it is usual where the amplitude is great, to divide the width by stepped motives for reassuring effect at points distant from the side walls.

The arrangement of the flight perpendicular to the edifice may be seen in all the ancient temples; before the Capitol at Washington, and in many projects such as the well-known competition for the Hudson-Fulton Memorial at New York (Fig. 89).

Fig. 90.—Cour du Cheval Blanc, Fontainebleau.

Two other arrangements present themselves—the straight flight parallel to the facade, as before the Capitol at Rome; finally curved flights of steps, like that of the great Cour du Cheval Blanc at Fontainebleau (Fig. 90).

The arrangement of flights parallel to the building which they serve may be composed in two ways. Two flights may leave the ground at opposite ends of the facade, approaching and meeting at a common landing before the principal entrance on the central axis, as at the Capitol at Rome. Or from a central point on the ground they may rise in a divergent direction, serving independent entrances in the wings, as at the Court of the Fountains at Fontainebleau. The question of what arrangement to adopt depends on the general composition of the plan and the needs of the circulation.

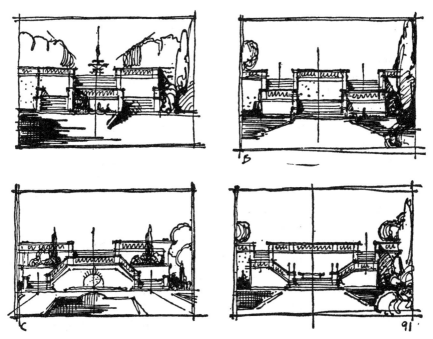

Fig. 91.—Monumental Stairways in landscape architecture.

Sometimes it is necessary to arrange a doubled flight, which is a combination of the two just mentioned. Here two flights diverge from the central axis to two landings midway the height, from which two other flights return again to a common central landing at the top level. In order to tie the composition together, divergent flights should always be connected by two or three steps parallel to the facade.

Beside the simpler schemes mentioned above, many other elegant combinations of straight flights may be conceived. Such are particularly the picturesque and varied arrangements of cruciform steps so applicable to the field of landscape architecture. Some of the more usual of these schemes are indicated in figure 91 A, B, C, D. It will be noticed that little grass plots may in many cases be laid out on a level with the intermediate landings. Curved flights are also adapted to numerous graceful combinations. For elliptical curves it is usual to substitute three- or four-centered curves which are easier to construct and equally effective in appearance.

INTERIOR STAIRWAYS

It will be recalled that the treatment of staircases as a conspicuous element of beauty in the composition is a comparatively modern conception. Even Renaissance architecture, prolific as it was in the invention of novel and varied motives, conceived few combinations of stairs beyond those enclosed between walls with end-supported steps; while classic architecture seems to have employed only the purely useful stair. The development of the so-called suspended stair-case, where open strings support the steps, began with the 16th century. Particularly with the architects of France has this type found favor and their artistic genius has made of it a feature of remarkable beauty and variety. As conceived by them, the stair assumed great importance in composition—an importance which is still maintained in practically every type of monumental building. The public stairway must of necessity be placed where it may be seen by everyone and when treated monumentally it is frequently the focal point of the entrance vestibules. Hence its design presents an unusual opportunity for an expression of the character and importance of the edifice.

From the point of view of use, it is essential that stairs be located with great care for ease and directness of circulation. Transitional as they are between two floors of a building and primarily only a means of circulation, it is imperative that any arrangement of stairs should be conceived simultaneously with the floors which are served and with the corridors to which direct access is given.

The proper location of a stairway is always one of the chief difficulties of composition. It is necessary first, for it to be readily found. Secondly, it is essential to place it so that long distances do not have to be traversed in order to reach different parts of the building. This will probably necessitate several stairways, judiciously distributed, in plans of large extent. Thirdly, it is important that the flights of stairs from the bottom to the top of a building should be placed as near as possible over one another in the same vertical. After ascending to one floor of a building, not to readily find the means to ascend higher is disturbing and inconvenient and an evidence of poor planning. The principal stairway of the New York Public Library is an instructive and beautiful example of a principal stairway ascending through several floors. Here the problem was to provide ascent from the main entrance at the front of the building to the great reading room on the top floor at the rear. Although it is necessary to traverse almost the entire depth of the building in ascending to the top, yet the ascent is skillfully managed by monumental flights which fit naturally and easily into the proper circulation (See Fig. 71).

On account of its importance and decorative possibilities there is always a strong tendency to place a stairway on the principal axis opposite the entrance. This is only justified when the most important rooms are on the second floor, as in an Opera House, Theatre or State Capitol; otherwise, the location is illogical and obstructive.

Classified according to their use, stairways may be separated into three groups: Grand stairways, designed principally for show or monumental effect, which as a rule rise only from the ground to the first story. Obviously, the first story here means the second above the basement or ground story, this method of counting being usual for building of monumental character. In addition to grand stairways, which correspond in purpose to ceremonial occasions there must also be provided stairways for ordinary use. These are classed among the principal stairways, but they vary in importance according to the program and their purpose in the general composition is, to direct the circulation. Lastly, there are secondary or service stairways not ordinarily communicating directly with a public passageway. Of the one or more staircases required in a building, almost always one of them will be a principal staircase.

Although exact locations in plan result from study of the composition as a whole, particularly in respect to arrangement of the corridors, yet it is essential to bear in mind that staircases should be placed in positions where they will be well lighted. For grand

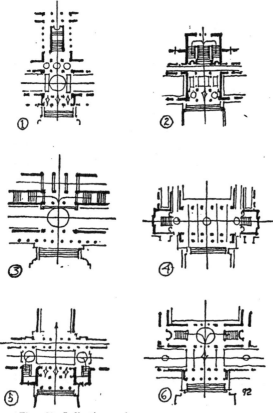

stairways ascending only one story, overhead lighting through decorative skylights may be used; but where there is a succession of flights, windows must be employed. The composition of such windows, externally, presents some difficulties, since they do not come on the same sill-level as the other windows. It is best to compose them with reference to the landing in the bay in which they occur. Windows cut by sloping strings are not a happy solution.

It is necessary to provide landings at the start and ending of a stair which are separate and distinct

Fig. 92.—Indications of common arrangements of principal Stairways in Plan Composition.

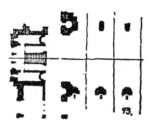

Fig. 93.—Detail of a lobby with end stairways.

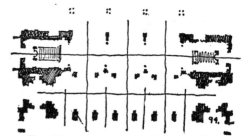

Fig. 94.—Arrangement of Entrance Vestibule and Stair Hall.

from the corridors and vestibules. Staircases ordinarily occur in halls by themselves, called stair-halls or "cages", which although connected to the circulation are at the same time removed from it (Figs. 92, 93, 94, and 95). This is the proper indication for the location of the staircase even in the preliminary sketch. The properly composed stair will then show, a landing at the start adjacent to the hall or corridor served, and a landing at the top similarly placed. This

Fig. 95.—Entrance Lobby and stair arrangement. New York Court House Competition.

arrangement is clearly explained by the illustrations. The only exception to this rule is where stairs are placed in halls large enough to contain, not only the staircase but the necessary circulation around it as well. The Waiting Hall of the Palace of Justice in Paris is a well-known case in point. Returning to the stair-hall proper, the ceiling of the enclosure will always be at the level of the ceiling of the floor reached by the stair. Thus the hall for a stair which reaches from the ground floor to the first floor will comprise this height and one story in addition, and so on.

Internal stairways permit many varied combinations. As to direction, stairways most frequently lead from starting landings to superposed landings immediately over them. From one landing to the next is termed a revolution of the stair-way. This is the most compact arrangement. If the composition calls for a landing at a point distant from the starting point, we have the case of the straight flight, which, again, is also subject to many combinations.

Stairways may be separated into two great divisions, according to the mode of construction. One group will include steps supported on both sides by walls, either solid or open; the other, stairs borne on one side by a wall, on the other by a string, or borne on both sides by strings. The first, as has been said, is the usual case of the Renaissance stair; the second, the so-called suspended stairs of the 16th century and later periods.

Let us now consider the location of stairways in their relation to other elements of the composition, particularly bearing in mind the usually close connection that exists between the stairways and the entrance vestibules (Figs. 92, 93, 94 and 95). These relations are especially important in the planning of monumental edifices where the stairway frequently ascends only one story.

First as to straight stairways of one flight, landing on the second floor at a point distant from the starting point. Their arrangement will be either perpendicular or parallel to the facade (See Fig. 92). In highly monumental stairways of this type where the

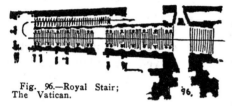

Fig. 96.—Royal Stair; The Vatican.

distance between the floors is considerable, it is inevitable that the upper landing be at a great distance from the lower, and especially will it be far from the entrance after the necessary vestibules have been provided. Thus a straight stairway on the principal axis is possible only when it leads to important rooms at the rear of the second story. This arrangement lends itself to noble and impressive effect, but it is necessarily rare owing to the great depth of building

ing called for combined with certain special requirements in the program. The length of a straight stairway makes it appear narrow and to correct this it should be made wider than the requirements of use ordinarily demand. The whole composition is visible to the eye at one time while the effects produced by perspective are particularly marked. The greatest example of the straight stairway is the Triumphal Stairway of the Vatican (Fig. 96), where it has been sought to accentuate the appearance of height and length by perspective illusions worked into the architecture. Several fine examples may be seen in the United States, notably the staircase of the San Francisco Library by George W. Kelham, Architect, (Fig. 97)

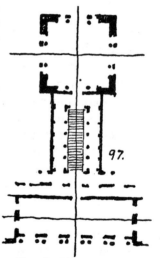

Fig. 97.—Monumental Stairway in the San Francisco Public Library. Geo. W. Kelham, Architect.

and that of the central link of the Metropolitan Museum of art in New York by R. M. Hunt (See Fig. 68). The majority of great staircase halls are vaulted, the interior treatment being closely in scale with exterior architecture.

Stairways parallel to the principal facade are usually double; but may be single if the composition is unsymmetrical and the entrance not in the middle. Their usual location is in a narrow hall adja-

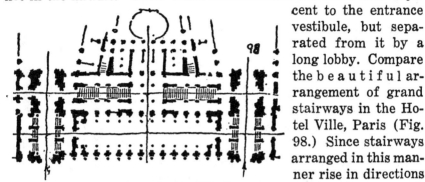

cent to the entrance vestibule, but separated from it by a long lobby. Compare the b e a u t i f u l ar-rangement of grand stairways in the Ho-tel Ville, Paris (Fig. 98.) Since stairways arranged in this man-ner rise in directions o p p o s i t e to each

Fig. 98.—Detail of Plan; Hotel de Ville, Paris.

other along the same axis, the effect will be much enhanced if they are covered by a single vault open to the ceiling of the upper story; thus both stairways are reciprocally visible from their top landings.

STAIRWAYS IN TWO DIRECTIONS

Stairways in one direction, leading to one story only, are exceptional and reserved pri-marily for monumental architecture. By far

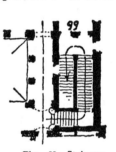

Fig. 99.—Stairway in the Palace Negro-ni, Rome.

the greater number of cases are stairs which turn, leading to a landing directly over the starting point. This is the usual arrangement where sev-eral stories are served. The Italian Renaissance, as has been noted, presents numerous examples of this type of stairway, without exception placed within enclosing walls (Fig. 99). Particularly cel-ebrated is that of the Farnese Palace, monumen-tal in its proportions and with a very gentle rise (See Fig. 62). Another noted example is the Scala d'Oro in the Doge's Palace, Venice (Fig. 100). The method of lighting is usually by windows at the landings with its accompanying problem of com-position in the exterior bay. In modern American architecture

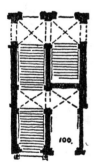

Fig. 100.—Golden Stairway, D o g e's Palace, Venice.

the stairway between enclosing walls has been occasionally employed, always with fine effect. The stairway at the 42nd Street entrance of the New York Public Library is a notable example.

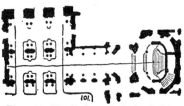

Fig. 101.—Vestibule and Stair, Palais Royal, Paris.

The stairway with three flights also composes between party walls; necessarily more symmetrical and monumental than the arrangement

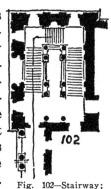

Fig. 102—Stairway; Colonnade of the Louvre.

mentioned above. This stairway nevertheless adapts itself to simple programs, especially where it serves to direct and divide the circulation. There are two arrangements possible. Two separated flights on either side lead to an intermediate landing and a third from the landing leads to the floor above at a point on the central axis; or the lower flight may be in the middle and the two upper flights separated. The first case emphasizes a through passage on the axis at the first floor level; the second case emphasizes the ascent and often the window treatment at the landing level. Either arrangement results from conditions imposed by the program. The single flight must always be wider than the lateral flights, but not double their width. A strikingly beautiful example of the stairway with three flights is found in the Boston Public Library (See Fig. 72). Celebrated examples in European architecture are the magnificent stairway of the Palais Royal on a curved plan (Fig. 101), the demolished stairway of Percier at the Louvre, and the splendid stairway of the

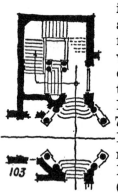

Fig. 103—Stairway; Hotel de Beauvais, Paris.

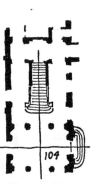

Fig. 104—Stairway; Hotel Salle, Paris.

Palace of Caserta at Naples. The vestibule of the Palais Royal leads by a gallery to the magnificent stairway of the architect

Constant d'Ivry, declared by Guadet to be the most beautiful of all stairways of mansions or palaces existing in France.

Analogous to stairways between solid enclosing walls are those where the walls are pierced by openings (Figs. 102, 103 and 104). Thus result many beautiful and varied conceptions, the architecture frequently taking the form of rampant porticos or inclined arcades. Many examples of such treatments may be seen in the palaces of Genoa. Specifically may be mentioned the stairway of the Braschi Palace in Rome and the grand stairway of the Opera in Paris, the latter a magnificent example of monumental architecture perfectly adapted to the highly decorative and theatrical requirements of its program.

The constantly changing direction in curvature is the most conspicuous element of beauty in circular and elliptical staircases. This type lends itself to curved walls and occasionally to free-standing constructions where the staircase is self-supporting. It is particularly effective when developed in wood or metal, and is adapted to the requirements of mansions and houses both great and small. But the curved form of stairway does not correspond so well to the solemn repose of character demanded by monumental interiors.

SELF-SUPPORTING STAIRWAYS

The monumental free-standing stairway in stone presents great difficulties in design and construction. Few examples exist in America, where the tendency has been to employ forms which are easier to build besides being at the same time equally as effective. In France, on the other hand, where the art of stereotomy is a favorite tradition, there are numerous beautiful and highly ingenious cut stone stairways without intermediate points of support. The principles of vaulting are employed. Generally an arch or elliptical vault supports the corner landings; the string is also jointed and supported by half vaults springing from the side walls. A simpler mode of construction, requiring less theoretical knowledge, is where the landings are of a single stone slab resting on the walls; the steps are also of one stone, tied into the wall at the ends and resting on each other by a narrow margin. Curved as well as straight stairs may be built this way. But if these strictly monumental types are rare, the self-supporting stairway in wood, metal, or combined with plaster finish, is by far the most common arrangement of all. Here the external character is determined by the openness of the construction which permits a horizontal ceiling under the landings and a sloping ceiling under the steps. In general there are two types; one where the ends of the steps are concealed by the strings—called closed strings, and the other where the ends of the steps show—called open strings. Each type has a characterizing effect upon the design. These are the stairways most used for domestic architecture, adapted as they are to every straight or curved arrangement. It is to be remembered that in every stairway of importance, or where grace and beauty are a consideration, that the start of the flight should be enlarged and accented by widening the steps and by treating the newel so that it becomes a point of interest. A beautiful example in point, among many others, is the celebrated stairway of the Ecole Militaire in Paris.

While the stairway is a conspicuous and interesting feature of interior architecture, care should be taken not to exaggerate its importance beyond the reasonable requirements, esthetic and purely useful, of the program. If, as often happens, a single stairway will serve the purpose, this fact does not force it to be placed on the principal axis. It may well be placed at the end of a hall to one side, although in this case the hall should be so open that a person entering the building will not start in the wrong direction.

In studying the plan ample space should be allowed for staircases in order that they may be easy and gradual in slope, and since they are a part of the circulation of a building, they should be considered in conjunction with the floors, corridors, and lobbies which they serve. Too often as indicated in preliminary studies, the staircase becomes an obstruction rather than a help to free circulation. Often it is indicated in an improper or impossible location, as where the whole flight is placed in a space insufficient to contain it, or a passage indicated under or over a landing where there can be no headroom, or other fault due to lack of study or prevision.

In monumental architecture is where gentle inclinations are sought, and in general it may be said that external stairs and stone architecture call for a more gradual slope than interior stairs or stairs built of wood. Landings should be placed at intervals where they seem to be demanded for rest or considerations of appearance, and there should always be a landing before an external door.

For curved flights the width of the treads is applied along the travel line—that is about eighteen inches from the handrail. It is usually possible to pass under a staircase at the fourteenth step from the bottom and over it at the same number from the top.

ELEVATORS

Vertical communications are completed by elevators. The program of the elevator is the same as for the stairway. Its locations are governed by the same considerations; hence elevators will commonly be near stairways (Figs. 105, 106, 107). In any case the elevator is only a kind of stairway, a stairway in which the ascent is accomplished by the aid of mechanical force instead of by the power of the muscles. If the extension of the application of structural steel to architecture made possible the multi-

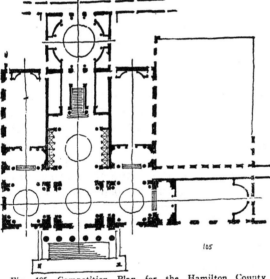

Fig. 105.—Competition Plan for the Hamilton County Court House, Cincinnati, Carrere and Hastings, Architects.

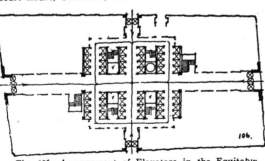

Fig. 106.—Arrangement of Elevators in the Equitable Building, New York.

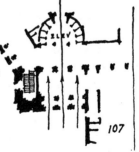

Fig. 107.—Elevator and stair locations in a public building.

storied building, from the standpoint of construction—the invention of the elevator made it possible from the standpoint of utility. Moreover many changes in buildings themselves and in the architecture of cities have been introduced through the extended use of elevators. Among other things the elevator has in general tended to destroy the established order of preference of the stories, since it is no more fatiguing to ascend to the top of a building than to the second floor, which is traditionally the important floor of a building. But the elevator will never come to be the sole means of ascent, nor will it destroy the importance of the stairway as an ornamental and necessary feature of compositions.

Elevators naturally assume their greatest importance in large office buildings, hotels, apartment houses, factories, loft buildings and other commercial establishments. They are located in halls and vestibules and contiguous to lobbies. Of equal importance to passenger elevators are freight lifts and elevators for service (Fig. 108). Elevator grilles, doors and enclosures are important features of design in the internal wall treatment of the halls where they occur.

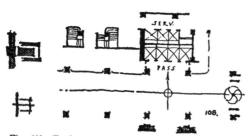

Fig. 108.—Typical elevator arrangement in a hotel.

In establishing the plan the designer has to provide the enclosure for each elevator, which means a free shaft from the bottom to the top of the building. Furthermore, the sizes and number of elevators have to be accurately proportioned to certain standards based on the use to which the building is to be put. One class of buildings will require elevator installations different from other classes, while the motive power will invariably be electric.

Many factors must be taken into consideration in the design of elevator installations, such as the character of the building, the height, the rentable area, the time intervals between the departure of cars, the number of stories to be served, the average number and length of stops per trip, the speed of the elevators and the type used. In hotels the problem is further complicated by the introduction of banquet halls, roof gardens and ball rooms—to and from which a large volume of passengers has to be handled during short periods; also there are ordinarily required separate elevators for passenger, baggage and meal service to bed room floors (Fig. 108).

In an office building the average area of the car will be 40 square feet, which corresponds to 20,000 square feet of rentable space. The number of stories served by any group of cars, excluding all stop local cars, should not be over fourteen. No shafts should extend above the usable limits of service. The maximum speed for cars approximate 450 feet per minute for local cars and 650 feet for express service. Batteries of elevators are limited to four cars. This makes the alcove arrangement of cars advantageous in large buildings. Compare the Equitable Building plan (Fig. 106) also other examples (Figs. 107 and 108).

In apartment houses, one elevator for 24 apartments or less, two for over 24, gives satisfactory results. Twenty-six square feet of platform area is the average, corresponding to 12 passengers. Where there is only one elevator for a building 8 stories or more in height, there should also be a service lift which can be used for passenger service in emergencies.

Loft buildings, factories and warehouses require special elevators designed to take care of the specific kinds of business to be carried on in the building. Usually the freight lifts are used by operatives also.

The arrangement of stairways and elevators together in the same shaft is to be condemned as a fire hazard. Iron fire escapes built against the outside of high buildings have also proven to be hazardous to human life in many instances. The best modern practice seems to be to place fire escape stairways in isolated shafts, so enclosed and ventilated by natural cross drafts as to prevent any possibility of their serving as flues for smoke in case of fire.

CHAPTER IV.

GENERAL FORM AND DESIGN OF THE ROOM IN PLAN; CORRIDORS AND PASSAGEWAYS; COURTS

The primary aim of architecture is the enclosure of space; therefore the simplest form of building will be a single room. The room is the nucleus and starting point of architectural composition. Whether rooms exist singly or in combination with others, their arrangement anticipates the composition of all other elements of the plan. Arrangement of rooms in logical sequence and order may be said, then, to be the first object of architectural composition. Their harmonious combination with the necessary vestibules, circulations, courts or other elements into a unified whole is the

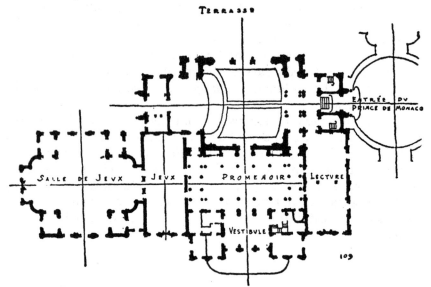

Fig. 109.—Plan of the Casino at Monte Carlo; Ch. Garnier, Architect.

ultimate end and aim of composition. To design is to combine the elements, of which the room is one.

Merely the general form and shape of the room will concern us here; the use to which it may be put is properly a resultant of the special program of the building.

Rooms may be classified into two groups according to whether they are formed by the space-enclosing or space-dividing parts of the building. Space-enclosing parts are the external walls and roof; space-dividing parts are the partitions, floors and ceilings.

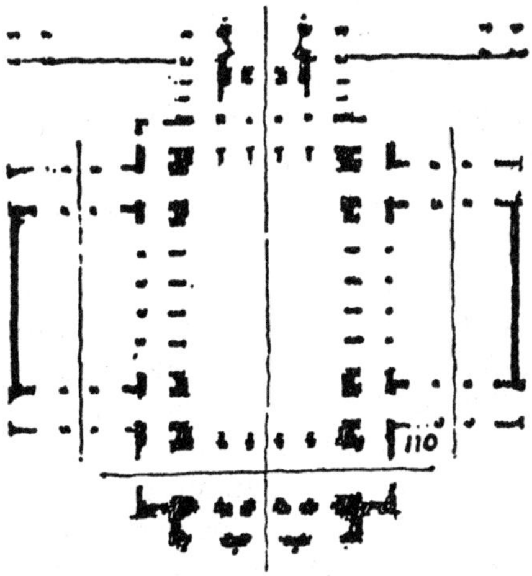

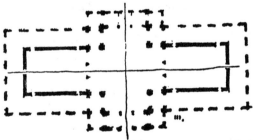

Fig. 110.—Detail of a plan with dividing elements reduced to "points".

Rooms are not always isolated from other parts of the building by solid walls; frequently they are connected in a more or less open manner. The space-dividing parts may, then, be simply a row of columns or series of arches. Many cases occur in planning where it is a nice problem to decide just how much connection or separation is desirable between two contiguous compartments (Figs. 109, 110, 111).

Generally speaking the different forms of rooms which ordinarily may be employed in planning are very few. Forms other than the

Fig. 111.—Detail of a plan opened along the principal axes.

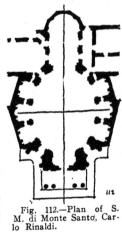

Fig. 112.—Plan of S. M. di Monte Santo, Carlo Rinaldi.

square, circle and half-circle, rectangle or octagon, and to less degree the oval and ellipse (Fig. 112), and their combinations are exceptional, and usually where seen they are evidence of bad planning. This statement, of course, only refers to those areas which are of primary importance in determining the parti, and not to small spaces of irregular shape which inevitably occur in problems of oblique connection (See Figs. 76, 78).

The rectangle is the usual and preferred elementary form of the room. It makes construction simpler, it is pleasing in proportion, while rooms of this shape are easier to furnish. Forms with equal axes, such as squares and circles, are rather reserved for the more monumental parts of an edifice—for vestibules, halls and lobbies. This usage naturally results from the obvious connection of vaulting with the square plan. The theoretical advantage that square and circular forms have over the rectangle, in that they require less wall-surface to enclose a given area, is of little importance in architecture. Theorists have also sought to establish an ideal form for the rectangle, such as the proportion of the side of a square to its diagonal. Undoubtedly this is a symmetrical form for the oblong considered by itself, but in planning other factors of greater importance usually combine to neutralize it. Actually it makes little difference in the appearance of a rectangular room, whether its proportion is a square and a half (50 to 75) ; or

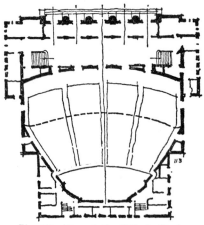

Fig. 113.—Plan of the Hill Auditorium, University of Michigan. Albert Kahn Architect.

that referred to above (about 50 to 70).

It is well to remember in planning that the square is the normal unit of measurement in proportioning areas. We habitually speak of rooms as being a square and a half, or two or three squares in proportion.

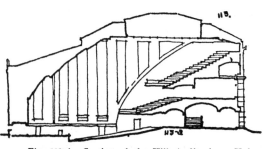

Fig. 113-A.—Section of the Hill Auditorium, University of Michigan, Albert Kahn, Archtect.

In many respects the circular and octagonal forms of rooms have close analogy to the square. This relation is especially seen in vaulted ceilings where, as has been previously indicated, the domical vault may serve to cover either the square or the octagon. The elliptical form is exceptional and is often replaced by a figure composed of circular arcs. Towers are usually built over square plans.

In respect to the application of various types of programs to special room-forms, large lecture or audience halls lend themselves logically to the ellipse, hemi-cycle, or so-called acoustic form of the oval, in fact an adaptation of the paraboloid (Compare the Hill Auditorium, Figs. 113, 113-A). The latter form has manifest disadvantages from the standpoint of appearance although conforming to theory.

Combinations and extensions of the elementary forms of the room are of frequent occurrence; as the square or oblong extended by the semicircle, or extension through repetition of the same or similar forms (See Figs. 109, 110, 111, 121, 166-B). Effect is accentuated by contrast with the ordinary form, but in simple or frequently repeated rooms the unusual form is unjustifiable. Rooms in combination as well as in extension are at the same time connected and separated by their space-dividing and space-enclosing parts. The study of these elements is the study of wall-section, of poché, the analysis of which is reserved for a later chapter.

CORRIDORS AND PASSAGEWAYS

Historically considered, there are two conditions imposed on the circulations by the requirements of composition as a whole. The circulations may be either open on the side, as in the case of colonnades, porticos and arcades; or closed, which is the usual case of passages, corridors and galleries within the external walls of the building.

Before the use of glass became general for closing openings, the open passage, usually treated as an arcade, was the chief means of circulation from one part of a plan to another. This was true even in the grand, palatial architecture of Italy, and if architecture was the gainer through the opportunities for beautiful conceptions which the open gallery afforded, there must have been, at the same time, in these edifices a surprising lack of privacy and comfort. Except in the tropics, the open gallery no longer serves as a means of communication between rooms. Practically the sole function which it has today is that of decoration or show. This statement is to be taken, of course, as without reference to its domestic counterpart—the veranda. Public buildings are given a stately and highly monumental expression by the use of free-standing colonnades, which may rest on the ground or on a high basement, but the passage which results is rather an incident to architectural effect than the conscious effort to provide circulation. Notable examples of the use of the colonnade are the colonnade of the Louvre, Place de la Concorde, the lateral porticos of the Madeleine, the peristyle surrounding the dome of the Pantheon, and in numbers of modern American public buildings among which may be mentioned the Congressional office buildings in Washington.

But if the arcade, strictly speaking as a passageway, has little place in modern compositions, the innumerable examples of this element in the Architecture of the Italian Renaissance furnish an inexhaustible patrimony of beautiful suggestions. Conspicuous among these may be mentioned the arcades of the Farnese Palace, the Cancelleria and S. M. della Pace. The courtyard of the Boston Public Library is an admirable modern example (See Figs. 22, 62, 154). Among documentary sources of study, the great work of Letarouilly takes the first place.

Where the portico or arcade exists by itself, the point of view is very different. Here it is in no sense a passage, but a shelter and resting place. Such were the detached loggias of the old Italian cities, often recalled by us in decorative architecture with the belvidere, exedra, residential porch or other variant of the Renaissance loggia.

The corridor is primarily an element of use rather than of beauty. It is necessary to reach all parts of the plan, and the principle is fixed that this penetration must be by the simplest and most direct means. Complicated circulations should be avoided.

In width, corridors in buildings are more often too narrow than too wide. The rule for all cases is to proportion corridors to the maximum number of persons traversing them at one time, but these proportions are not the result so much of theoretical considerations as of experience and repeated use.

Ordinarily corridors are only intended for passage, therefore obstructing projections are omitted. In studying the poché of a plan it is well to remember this in order that the character of this element may be properly indicated.

Corridors may occur in the composition of the plan in two ways, either centrally, with rooms on both sides; or along an external wall, with access to only a single row of rooms. Questions of concentration and limited area make the first arrangement the usual and ordinary one. But in the enclosed corridors, light is frequently lacking—not to speak of ventilation. It is true that some light may be admitted through end windows or windows on stair landings and some through transoms and glazed doors, but the fact, supported by ordinary observation, still holds that the central or enclosed corridor is often dark insofar as daylight is concerned.

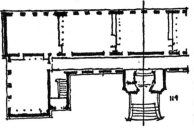

Fig. 114.—Plan with a lateral corridor.

In respect to lighting and aeration, at least, the lateral corridor has every advantage over the corridor centrally placed. For certain species of plans the former arrangement is particularly desirable—notably in school buildings of one or more stories, and where the site is not restricted (Figs. 114, 114-A). It is proper to place the corridor on the side least favorable to comfort, when a building is composed with a lateral corridor; yet other conditions of the program may require the opposite scheme. For example, the necessity of avoiding noise may dictate that the occupied rooms may be placed on a court rather than on a street facade.

In monumental buildings or public architecture corridors often assume importance as waiting halls or Salles des Pas Perdu, in which case they merge into galleries or great vestibules and thus are placed ordinarily lengthwise the facade. A corridor wide enough to permit decorative wall treatment involving projections becomes a gallery. Galleries although partly conceived for passage are primarily circulations intended for use on such occasions as receptions or other formal or festive entertainments. Monumental and decorative character is here appropriately

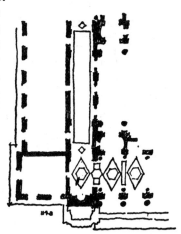

Fig. 114-A.—Junction of a lateral corridor with a principal vestibule.

introduced, as in the grand salon or foyer. Examples are numerous, but it will suffice to recall the grand galleries of Versailles and Fontainebleau.

COURTS

In large compositions involving buildings of extended area and in the planning of groups it is necessary to introduce courts so that all parts of the interiors may be adequately lighted. The location, form and size of courts are then factors of general composition. As an element, taken by itself, the court is subject to an immense variety of architectural treatments, some reference to which has been made under the heading of atriums and arcades.

Courts are either open or closed, the latter being, historically, the usual case of the Italian courts, and the former the case of the French court in front of a facade—the Court of Honor. Courts of Honor were much favored in the architecture of the seventeenth and eighteenth centuries, as the volumes of Blondel, treating of that epoch, show. This is the great work entitled "Architecture Francaise". Letarouilly in "Les Edifices de Rome Moderne" has recorded for us the many beautiful compositions and details of the internal court architecture of the great Roman palaces.

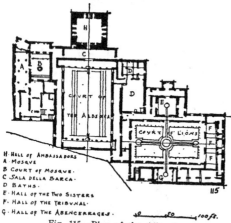

H · HALL OF AMBASSADORS
A · MOSQVE
B · COVRT OF MOSQVE
C · SALA DELLA BARCA ·
D · BATHS ·
E · HALL OF THE TWO SISTERS
F · HALL OF THE TRIBVNAL ·
G · HALL OF THE ABENCERRAGES ·

Fig. 115.—Plan of the Alhambra.

The Italian courts although based in plan primarily on the regular quadrilateral, were occasionally of irregular shape. Such were the courts of the Massimi palaces, already noticed, where the site was exceedingly restricted and difficult (See Fig. 84). Precedent combined with simplicity of planning as a rule fix the square form as that best adapted to the internal court, other forms being regarded as exceptional. Apart from the question of mechanical ventilation of dead and torpid spaces, it may be said that the court closed in on all sides is a bad necessity, when of small area and the building high. On the other hand we must not fail to recognize those circumstances which often make this element of planning not merely necessary but a feature of great beauty. Such were the courts of the Italian palaces which, although primarily required for circulation, gave opportunity for the design of some of the greatest masterpieces of the Renaissance. The enclosed court of the Alhambra in Spain is an example of great beauty—of considerable area, it is true, and surrounded by low buildings (Fig. 115). Other notable examples are the court of the Boston Public Library and of the American Academy in Rome (See Fig. 137-A).

The Court of Honor is merely a recession of the facade of an edifice for greater effect. Here the designer has perhaps the greatest opportunity to be monumental, for the greater scale of a central motive is particularly justified by the greater distance at which it must be viewed. Except for the open courts which necessarily occur in group planning, the American architect has little opportunity for developing a Court of Honor. Only in the plans of great "World Fairs" has this been possible. The Court of Versailles is the most imposing example of a Court of Honor in existence. Here the perspective effect of depth is greatly enhanced by the successive recessions of the lateral facades (See Fig. 234).

INDICATION OF POCHE AND MOSAIC

Poché is the familiar term for the horizontal sections of walls and piers appearing in plan, which are ordinarily blacked-in with India ink. Naturally poché cannot be studied by itself, for every break that occurs in the silhouette of a pier is inseparably connected with other elements of plan, section and facade—in fact with the entire composition. The study of poché, then, is very nearly the study of everything else in architecture. But if the actual size and shape of a piece of poché are primarily the result of such factors as material, mode of construction, style and character of architecture, they may also be said secondarily to be the result of an artistic feeling for relative scale and proportion. This is true because this special artistic instinct is cultivated only through the study of architecture as a whole—the study of scale and proportion comprising practically everything with which we have to do. Therefore the often heard phrase "a feeling for scale in poché" assumes a real and unmistakable importance.

The design of poché is first an art and afterwards a science; for it is the part of art to arrange the silhouette of a pier—to compose it; it is then the part of science to verify its area with respect to loads and thrusts and factors of safety, and it should not be forgotten that science can tell us nothing about the former, whereas art can say a great deal about the latter.

The general principles which are used to determine the relative sizes or weights of varying points of poché will be considered more fully in the discussion of scale and proportion. Questions of the outline or silhouette of pieces of poché may properly engage our attention at this time. This is reasonable since breaks in plan are directly due, first to wall treatment, which in turn is connected

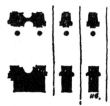

Fig. 116.—Versailles; Garden side projection, detail.

with the form of the ceiling—arches, vaults, beams and all the rest—second to the connection of differing forms and shapes of rooms, rather than to questions of material or structure. Thus arise such problems as the joining of a circular to a rectangular area, or of two circular areas. Only through the judicious composition of the poché can this be accomplished properly.

From the point of view indicated, poché must be either space-enclosing by nature—as outside of court-walls or space-dividing—as interior points of support or partitions, between contiguous rooms.

Apart from special considerations, such as the inclined thrusts of vaulting or other modifying factors, the outside enclosing walls of a building would usually be thicker than internal walls. This results from the nature of the design which only a reference to vertical sections can determine with accuracy (See Fig. 7). When the walls are quite thick, as in a basement supporting orders, the door jambs

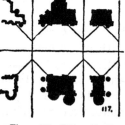

Fig. 117.—Pier Section; Vestibule of St. Peter's, Rome.

are often splayed, which assists in giving to the opening an indication of its purpose and permits the doors themselves to be opened beyond a right angle (Figs. 116, 117). Windows are also frequently characterized by the small bits of poché which indicate the sections through mullions. Openings in general, however, receive their greatest accentuation from the indication carried out in watered ink, which is a part of the convention of "mosaic" to be presently considered.

Interior points of poché seem to show in general a greater variety of difficulties than exterior points. Often, as where a circular

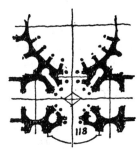

Fig. 118.—Detail of a plan from Chenavard.

form of room joins a rectangular form great skill and imagination are required to solve the problem (Figs. 118, 119). The danger is always present in such cases of exhibiting too much ingenuity; it is hard to be simple when the problem itself is complicated (Fig. 119 is a beautiful and instructive example of how such a problem should be solved). Interior points, however, have this in common—they invariably show a reciprocal treatment across an axis of symmetry. That is, breaks in a piece of poché recall themselves or are reflected by the piece directly opposite. Lines of recall will then be perpendicular to an axis of symmetry (Fig. 120). This evidence of simplicity results naturally enough from the desire to see things balanced as well as from the inherent nature of architecture. In this connection it is well to remember that symmetry is regularity of that which can be seen from a single point of view. There is no reason, therefore, why one side of a solid should be like the other. "The two sides are alike only when the

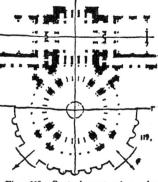

Fig. 119.—Central part of a plan from Chenavard.

Fig. 120.—Corner Pavilion; Colonnade of the Louvre.

motives framed in are alike." The best way to study poché directly is to trace on thin paper from the documents in which the best examples occur. In doing this the effort ought to be for relative proportion—for form and weight, rather than for small details. The value of this training is in the exercise, which gradually establishes correct principles in the mind. It is not essential for the mind to be burdened with the effort to remember the actual forms traced.

From the nature of architecture there inevitably results a certain quality in the indication of poché which is a most forcible means of expressing character. Compare the plan of a Gothic cathedral with the basilica of St. Peter (See Fig. 166-A) or the plan of the Propylaea (See Fig. 57) with the Madeleine (Fig. 121). The character of each is strongly expressed in the poché alone.

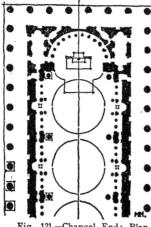

Fig. 121.—Chancel End; Plan of the Madeleine, Paris.

MOSAIC

Like the word Poché, the word mosaic, in the paper representation of architecture, has a special application and meaning quite different from that given in the dictionary. In the vernacular of the atelier, mosaic means rather the decoration of the plan by a conventional system of lines and patterns usually drawn in watered ink. Thus the plan acquires a pleasing combination of values in black, grey and white even before the application of washes.

Although highly decorative possibilities are inherent in poché and mosaic, of course, this is not the primary object of either. The object of poché has already been sufficiently indicated; the object of mosaic is to help to clarify the parti, to explain the program and to enhance the characterizing effect of poché. Hence it serves the artistic purpose of unifying the composition. It is a form and means of expression, a vehicle for stating facts more clearly and at the same time in an artistic manner.

The artistic statement of fact is the logical function of all indication as applied in architecture. It is not to be denied that the highly decorative possibilities of the vehicle tend to focus the attention upon the paper representation—the rendering—as an end in itself, rather than upon the potential actuality—the building. But this is a danger which is latent in every indirect artistic method and is to be guarded against. An analogy to the proper use of mosaic is to be found in the artistically printed book. Pleasing,

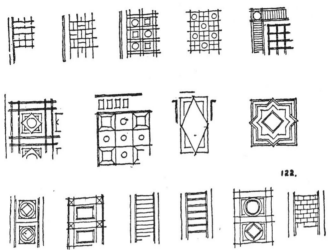

Fig. 122.—Interior and exterior Mosaic patterns.

well-spaced type and wide margins add materially to the enjoyment of reading without detracting anything from the thought.

There are three kinds of mosaic indications which may be employed either separately or in combination. Floor patterns, ceiling decoration, and furniture. The first named finds, perhaps, the most extensive application, the second is used to express a system of vaulting or to indicate very important rooms, which are relatively rich and interesting, while the third is employed where the purpose of a room needs to be more evident and the effect of formal decoration is not so essential.

The judicious indication of mosaic throughout the composition is a question first of broad contrasts and correct feeling for proportion. Since the eye is most attracted by white, this value is ordinarily reserved for the climax. The richest spot of all is probably the white circle with a decorative frame separating it from the jet black of the poché.

It may be said of mosaic in general, that within the plan it should be kept light and the motives should be smaller than in the indication of the entourage.

Besides explaining the purpose and relative importance of rooms, mosaic also defines and carries the eye around the circulations. Where two circulations cross, the pattern of the more important should be carried by, and the lesser circulation interrupted. This device may be seen in many of the Grand Prix plans. It is especially evident in the plan by M. Chaussemiche for "Un Palais des Sociétés Savantes". The indication of important entrances and other accesses is often accented by arrow points or by interrupting the mosaic of a circulation against a narrow strip of white carried through the opening.

Passages are often left white except for the border lines which frame them. When it is preferable to use a pattern, it should be a simple one, after the type shown in (Fig. 122) which is adapted to corridors and courts. Features such as pedestals and statuary, placed with reference to architecture, ordinarily combine with mosaic and form an element of the pattern. Small compartments which are ordinarily dark are given a closely hatched pattern to subordinate them.

For the study of floor mosaic, the original sources are the patterns derived from antique architecture—especially the opus sectile and opus Alexandrinum of the Romans and Byzantines. Naturally the most serviceable academic record of such study is that to be found in the collections of competitions for the Prix de Rome.

In studying a plan composition, even in its elementary stages, it is almost as important to indicate the mosaic as to indicate the proper form and weight of walls and points of poché. It should be remembered that all this can be done in the freehand sketch, although considerable skill, not to mention knowledge, must be acquired before it can be done convincingly and with artistic economy. Progress will only come through practice; by the study of beautiful plans, chiefly through tracing them. The effect secured in a beautifully presented esquisse is the same as that given by carefully rendered project seen at a distance where detail is obliterated and only the essential features of the drawing stand out.

CHAPTER V.

FACADES AND BAYS. FORM OF MASS; WALL TREATMENT; VARIED OR BROKEN FACADES; TOWER-LIKE BUILDINGS

It has been often remarked that a facade cannot be studied by itself, but only in conjunction with the plan and sections. More than this, a facade is particularly the resultant of the plan. The plan determines many of the elements essential to the composition which cannot be fixed by the elevations or facades, and to which the latter must conform. The plan determines, above all, those elements which are the result of division and extension in a horizontal sense. It determines what may be stated as the direction of the building and the side which may be considered the principal front; the location and distance between axes; the amount of projection or recession of various parts, and the placing of doors and windows. Vertical proportions are primarily the result of requirements of construction and of the heights of stories and roofs. These are expressed by the profiles of the sections. Since the purpose of the edifice controls the arrangement of the plan and the mode of construction controls the vertical proportions, it follows that these two essential factors of purpose and construction also control the composition of the facade.

While this is a true statement, it must not be taken in too narrow or literal a sense. This is the essence of the creed of the advocates of functionalism, convincing enough in theory, but a too strict adherence to which easily results in the production of dry and cheerless works. At least it may be said that the purpose of the edifice and the manner of construction establish certain limitations without which the designer is not free to move, and while he cannot ignore the facts of the architectural organism and maintain the unity and harmony of the composition, still they permit him ample latitude for the expression of character. All this depends on the program. In some types of buildings it will be the highest art to accentuate in a visible manner both purpose and construction as much as possible; in other words it will be appropriate to strive to make them less evident.

In the composition of facades the designer should feel, in spite of formulas often dogmatically expressed, that he is an artist who has very great freedom. He should recall that many of those principles which are held to give character to an edifice are of relatively modern conception, and that many of the most remarkable works of external architecture were produced without reference to such principles. This is true to a very great extent of the art of Greece and Rome and of the Italian Renaissance, which have always been the great sources of inspiration.

The plan, as we have seen, is clearly solved when it combines all the requirements of the building in a proper sequence and proportion. It is reasonable to expect that a good elevation will result from a good plan, for one cannot be studied without the other. The study of the plan begins first, but the facades must also be foreseen almost from the beginning.

The variations possible in facades are enormous, consequently it would be futile to attempt to analyze all of them. But leaving out questions of stylistic character there remain certain general features which may be used as a basis for a broad classification. Features such as varying mass, which gives to every edifice a well defined silhouette or configuration, and the treatment of the surface of the facade by horizontal and vertical subdivision. Character and distribution of ornament do not concern us here, but rather the architectural framework of the edifice and the effect resulting therefrom. It will be seen that in external composition as well as in plan, beautiful effects are to be obtained chiefly through the proper handling of the proportions; decoration fulfills its part when it contributes to the effect of the whole through a due subordination.

FORM OF MASS

The first factor upon which the appearance of a building depends is its mass. The silhouette of the mass will be the sole effect observable when a building is seen in reduced light or through a haze. This silhouette will be composed of one or more of the following four elements, depending upon whether the form or grouping is closed or open.

The elements of mass are:

The Principal Mass.

Subordinate Masses.

Links.

Appendages.

The closed form is characteristic of tower-like structures of prismoidal or cylindrical mass, of highly monumental edifices usually of pyramidal form. Such types of buildings are produced by the development of the principal mass, alone or in combination, with subordinate masses.

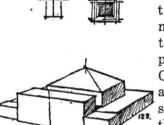

In the open form of grouping the subordinate masses are detached from the principal m a s s. Connections then

Fig. 124.—Typical mass form, analogous to Fig. 160.

assume greater importance because they serve to unite the diverse elements of the composition into a single organic whole.

Fig. 123.—Mass combination characteric of the simple mass plan.

In any case the grouping and annexing of the different parts of the entirety is determined beforehand by the composition of the plan. This principle is clearly illustrated by the following examples of closed and open forms of buildings drawn in block perspective (Figs. 123, 124, 125, 126).

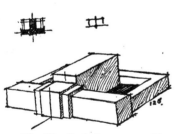

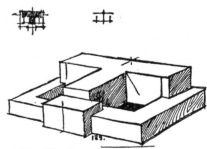

Fig. 125.—Typical mass combination characteristic of the building with two courts.

Fig. 126.—The building with two courts. Type of the New York Public Library.

It is evident that the effect of a building is very largely determined by the amount of care given to the study of the external form alone. A great deal of time should be given to the profile of the silhouette, chiefly by studies in direct elevation. The trained sense of three dimensions teaches how to make due allowances for the effects of distance and foreshortening and it is fairly certain that if the form of the edifice looks well in elevation it will also look well in perspective. We may remark here, that this is also true for the silhouette of ceilings in section (Figures 127-A, 128-A). The eye must be the judge of what is pleasing in form and what otherwise.

Fig. 127-A.—Section of M. Chaussemiche's "Palais des Sociétés Savantes".

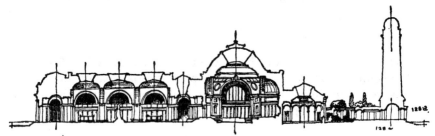

Fig. 128-A.—Section of M. Recoura's "Palais des Sociétés Savantes".

The grouped form of building will ordinarily be horizontally rather than vertically extended (Figures 127, 128, 129, 129-A, 130, 130-A, 131, 131-A). Variations in the effective heights of masses may be produced either by differences in actual height or by variations in the projections of masses horizontally, as at Versailles.

WALL TREATMENT IN FACADES

While the general impression is produced by the entire mass of the building, the particular impression or special artistic effect is produced by the treatment of the vertical surfaces of the masses —by the subdivision and ornamentation of the walls.

The composition of wall surfaces is dependent, first upon their construction, which requires that they shall be vertical, that piers

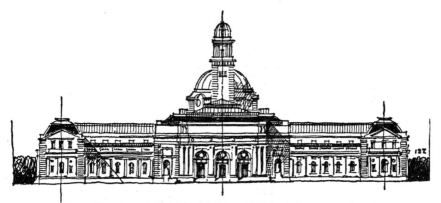

Fig. 127.—Elevation of M. Chaussemiche's "Palais des Sociétés Savantes".

Fig. 128.—Facade of M. Recoura's "Palais des Sociétés Savantes".

Fig. 129.—Elevation of M. Abella's "College de France".

Fig. 129-A.—Section of M. Abella's "College de France".

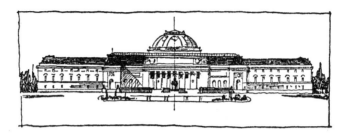

Fig. 130.—Elevation of M. Bonnet's "College de France".

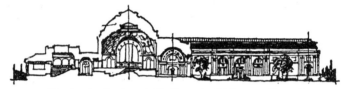

Fig. 130-A.—Section of M. Bonnet's "College de France".

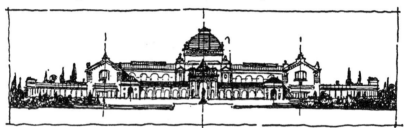

Fig. 131.—Elevation of (M. Chedanne's "Gymnase".

Fig. 131-A.—Section of M. Chedanne's "Gymnase".

shall rest upon the ground, and openings be placed above each other. The impression of stability is further accentuated by the spreading base and diminishing thickness of upper walls, while the impression of permanence is assured through the use of re-sisting materials.

Architecture has been truly declared to be "essentially the art of building with blocks, and its development depends upon a rec-ognition of the limitations that particular materials impose". Antique architecture is in agreement with Nature in decreeing that the material upon which the monumental impression chiefly depends shall be stone.

The artistic subdivision of the wall in a vertical direction logically follows from the desire to produce a stable and permanent construction. Thus results the triple division in membering of firm base, middle enclosing part and projecting cornice, essential to every monumental facade. The degree of emphasis given to the base depends upon the style of architecture and character sought. In general the base will partake of the tripartite division of the pedestal. The Italian Renaissance affords numerous beautiful examples of this feature of wall-treatment (See figures 5, 6).

The division of the facade horizontally into bays and projecting pavilions or other projecting masses results, as has been said, directly from the purpose of the structure. Purpose fixes primarily the arrangement and proportionate areas of rooms, consequently determining the position of external walls and partitions and the location of the principal and subordinate axes of symmetry. It logically follows that these elements be recalled in the horizontal subdivision of the facades. Principal and subordinate axes in plan will therefore coincide with the horizontal traces of planes passing through the principal axes in elevation. Whether the parti be symmetrical or unsymmetrical, the principal axis will be the vertical axis of the principal mass, which thus fixes the focal point of the composition. Depending on the program, this focal "point" may be either a simple portal or a richly treated architectural mass having complete unity by itself. In the extended facade, corresponding to a complex plan, the other elements of mass,—links, subordinate masses and appendages,— will as a rule be tied in to the central mass by horizontal bands, usually the mouldings of the base, water tables, string courses and cornices, and by the recall of certain levels of height, such as imposts and lintels in subordinate features (Figures 127, 128, 129, 129-A, 130, 130-A, 131, 131-A). The terminations of facades of this type may consist of strong piers or pavilions to which is given a character subordinate to the central mass. The term pavilion properly means an isolated structure, but in the extension of the use of the term to apply to the massive terminations of facades, the analogy is quite close, since in both cases the pavilion has unity by itself in common with the principal mass (Figures 127, 129).

One of the most difficult things in design is to secure the necessary connection between the horizontal and vertical subdivisions of a facade so that the whole composition may appear unified. To arrive at this result requires rather the cultivation of taste and imagination than the search for and application of rules. The study of historic buildings and research among the documents is the slow but sure way to arrive at discrimination and feeling for proportion in the composition of facades.

CLASSIFICATION OF FACADES
UNIFORM FACADES

The first group of facades are those in which there are no pronounced recesses or projections.

Two general classes of facades fall within this group.

1 Plane facades, retaining the essential character of the wall surface.

2 Facades treated with orders.

The first system is that of most Italian palaces; the second of antique architecture, with its continuous colonnades and superposed orders, both free standing and engaged. It will be sufficient to briefly describe each system with reference to the requirements of composition.

The statement of Professor Bühlmann that "the harmonious union of wall surfaces, doors, windows and cornices, so as to make entire fronts or facades is preeminently the work of the Italian Renaissance" correctly indicates where we should look for the treatment of uniform facades without columnar orders in its greatest perfection. This species of composition gave little thought in its outward expression to the varied arrangement of spaces, rooms, and halls within the walls of the building, but in its modern adaptations it is found to be almost as conformable to the doctrine of functionalism as the more strictly formal architecture of the Romans.

In the facades without orders the elementary division of the facade vertically into base, shaft and crowning cornice is given its most striking expression. The Riccardi Palace at Florence and the Farnese Palace at Rome are the finest examples of this species of composition (Figures 132, 133). Of facades of analogous character erected in modern times there may be cited the Library of Ste. Genevieve and Ecole de Médecine in Paris (Figures 134, 135);

Fig. 132.—Angle of the Palazzo Riccardi.

Fig. 133.—Facade of the Farnese Palace.

The Boston Public Library, the University Club in New York, both by McKim, Mead and White, and the Brooklyn Trust Company by York and Sawyer. Inspiration for the last named building was drawn from the Gran Guardia Vecchia in Verona (See Fig. 153), an edifice of powerful

Fig. 134.—Facade of the Library of Ste. Genevieve, Paris.

character. Gromort remarked of the Gran Guardia, that if not unknown, it was certainly little appreciated; but modern American architecture has several notable examples which go to prove that architects of the present have known how to look to it for inspiration.

The character of composition based on the plane facade is capable of producing the most imposing effects (Fig. 136), but it risks being monotonous unless

Fig. 135.—Ecole de Médecine, Paris.

studied with great care as to detail and the proper proportioning of voids and solids. Its resources for variety are found in the details of the composition and in the diversity in proportions of minor features.

Fig. 136.—Bryant Park Elevation of the New York Public Library. Carrere and Hastings, Architects.

Little needs to be said here concerning the use of colonnades in uniform facades, as these combinations of the elements have already been sufficiently discussed in other chapters. The colonnade is the medium par excellence for producing the grandest effects. Its great resource is in the repetition of motives, thereby multiplying the effect of elements which even when taken singly are among the most impressive in architecture.

VARIED OR BROKEN FACADES

Facades with a marked subdivision of masses into projections, recessions and varied heights are held to clearly express the arrangement of the plan (See Figs. 127, 129, 131). This characteristic above all may be said to distinguish them from uniform facades. Varied facades create effects first by the play of perspective, second by the diverse proportions of their masses; means which are lacking in the composition of uniform facades. Furthermore this variety is a powerful means for expressing character—for the visual interpretation of program and type. Essentially this is what is meant by the term "functionalism", already alluded to. Academically at least, functionalism has come to be one of the most potent tendencies in the architecture of modern times. As summed up by Kimball: "The conscious endeavors in modern architecture to make the forms of individual members correspond to their structural duties, to make the aspect of buildings characteristic of their use and purpose, to make the style of the time expressive of the distinguishing elements in contemporary and national culture, may thus be inclusively designated by the name "functionalism". Whether the nature of this philosophy is justified by results or not, it has come to be the solid foundation for all criticism in design in most contemporary schools of architecture.

In the plan, then, according to the rational theory of composition, will be found the key to the design of the facades. From this relation the assurance so often stated that a good plan will give good facades, logically results. Or as Guadet more accurately puts it, "a plan truly merits being called a good plan only when it permits good facades".

This connection between the composition of plan and facades applies rather more significantly to detached edifices erected on an open site than to buildings which are enclosed by party walls and therefore show only one or two visible facades. Assume a rectangular building erected on an open site. It will be enclosed by four facades. One facade marks the front of the building; it will be the principal facade; two others, the sides, will be identical or quite similar in design; while the rear will be composed according to its own importance. This system is logical since it is rare that the program either of the building or of the site permits facades or approaches of equal importance. The architect, therefore, has the liberty, within the limitations of the plan, to give to each facade the degree of accentuation that he considers proper. But in exercising this freedom he will be influenced, as in every architectural problem great or small, by compositions which have already been tried many times.

It is evident that the facades of complex buildings permit great diversity of treatment. Nevertheless it is possible to reduce them to three principal cases.

1 Facades composed with a middle projection and uniform wings.

2 Facades composed with two end pavilions and a uniform middle portion.

3 Facades combining these two systems.

Broadly these distinctions correspond in plan to the ⊥-shaped buildings; the TT-shaped building; and these two forms combined (See Figs. 125, 126). In some very complex buildings each individual combination may be employed more than once.

The first case accents the entrance by localizing in the central projection features of greater architectural interest (See Figs. 123, 124, 125).

The second is the usual case of lateral facades; also of build-

ings in a group which are to be followed in a parallel direction rather than entered; and of buildings with two separate entrances of equal importance (See Figs. 202, 204).

Fig. 137.—Perspective, American Academy in Rome.

The edifices of Place de la Concorde, Paris, are examples of the several cases of facades just mentioned—associated here in a highly monumental composition. The importance of the grand axis is emphasized, as it nearly always is, by the placing at its extremity of a significant point of interest—in this case, the Madeleine.

The design of varied facades—made up as they often are of many diverse elements, pavilions, porticos, wings, and so forth, calls for the exercise of the sense of harmony and proportion rather than for the application of rules (Figures 137, 137-A). It is enough to say, for example, that heights ought not to be equally divided, or that subordinate masses ought not to compete in

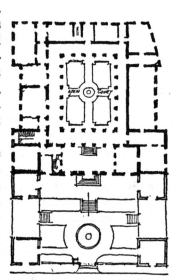

Fig. 137-A. — Plan, American Academy in Rome.—McKim, Mead & White, Architects.

interest with the principal mass, and the like. The precise adjustment of such and innumerable other variations must be left to the artistic sense of the composer. "There is no facade so small", says Guadet, "that does not have for its program the beauty of the edifice, even the beauty of the city."

TOWER-LIKE BUILDINGS

The composition of tower-like buildings, campaniles, clock-towers, office buildings and the like, where the verticality of the mass is greatly emphasized depends upon the artistic accentuation of certain conditions of program. These are briefly, the pur-

Fig. 138.—Bankers' Trust Company Building, New York.

pose of the building, the materials and mode of construction and the style of architecture. In buildings of ordinary height, the horizontal lines marking the stories are very important in determining the pro-

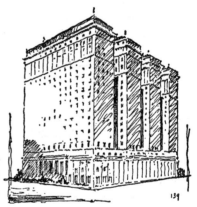

Fig. 139.—The Hotel Pennsylvania, New York.—McKim, Mead & White, Architects.

portions of the motives of which the facades are composed. In very high multi-storied buildings the ordinary floor levels are wholly suppressed in the effort to avoid monotony and to emphasize the verticality of the composition. The design of the roof is another factor which is of little importance compared to buildings of ordinary height.

Of the different factors, then, which are held to control the composition of facades, the most important in connection with tall buildings are the style of architecture and an accentuation of the structural system. In tall buildings classically composed there results the usual division in vertical proportion of base, shaft and capital (Figures 138, 139, 140, 141). In the tower-like structure of Gothic configuration, whether it be an office building or a campanile, we easily recognize the outstanding characteristic of the Gothic system which always tends to render vertical lines more evident than horizontal (Fig. 142). Besides the two styles above mentioned we have the later Italian styles from

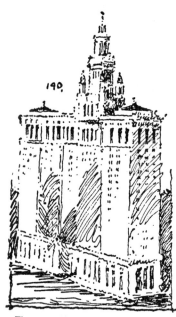

Fig. 140.—The New York Municipal Building.—McKim, Mead & White, Architects.

which to draw inspiration—especially t h e Lombardic and the Renaissance.

The composition of the facades of an office building follows naturally the plan and functions of the building. The first story will be high and monumentally treated, with an entrance corresponding to the importance of the edifice;

Fig. 141.—The Hotel Commodore, New York. Warren & Wetmore, Architects.

above this a secondary story forming a transition between the monumental ground story and many tiers of office floors "all treated alike because they are all alike." The top stories will be richly treated for the satisfaction of the eye which demands that the edifice be crowned and adequately terminated.

The reduction of the heights of buildings proportionately in the narrower streets of New York "in order to protect the rights and equities of property owners in sanitation and light and air" involves a new principle in the design of tall buildings. The city has been divided into five types of Height Districts called the "one and one-quarter, one and one-half, two, and two and one-half times" districts.

Taking the one and one-half districts as an example, this means "that if a street on which a building is to be built is 100 feet wide, taking the width between building lines, the building height will be one and one-half

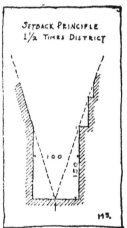

Fig. 142.—The Woolworth Building, New York.—Cass Gilbert, Architect.

Fig. 143.—High buildings in New York on narrow streets. Set-back principle.

times 100 feet or 150 feet. This refers to the height of the building at the building line. Above that height the building may go higher, provided the wall of the building is set back in the same proportion, that is set back one foot for every one and one-half feet of height that the wall is carried up. Several set-backs may be built, all conforming to the angle formed by drawing a line from

Fig. 144.—L. W. L. Building, New York.
Carrere and Hastings, Architects.
R. H. Shreve, Consulting Architect.

the center of the street through a point on the top of the wall of the first set back of the building line (Figures 143, 144, 145, 146). The plans may be built solid, concentrating service features such as corridors, lobbies, elevators, stairs, toilets, and so forth, in the center. This arrangement facilitates the set backs in towers and terraces (Fig. 147).

The plan of the ordinary office building is controlled in a large degree by the bay interval, which is usually taken at about eighteen feet. Eighteen by twenty-four feet is a good average size for offices as this area permits a subdivision into two nine foot offices with a public space adjacent to the corridor. With the ceiling heights generally employed it is not considered good practice to set the corridor partition further than twenty-four feet from the exterior windows.

It seems logical to assume that in general facades under a square in height should be horizontally accented; those over a square in height vertically accented, and combinations where the two proportions merge; but this cannot be asserted as a principle.

In many buildings of varying heights the use of the ground story requires that the wall shall be treated as continuous glass show-window. In such instances the most satisfactory treatment appears to be where the plane of the glass is slightly in advance of the wall-plane, thus giving the effect of a great case applied to the wall which is felt to be behind the whole. The apparent stability of the building is disturbed where there are only piers at the ends of the facades in combination with a recessed area of glass set into the stone frame.

The genius of Saarinen as disclosed by his competition design for the Tribune Building in Chicago has done much to establish the manner in which a steel frame building can acquire a logical form. The direct evidence for this statement is found in several high buildings of excellent proportions erected in various cities of the United States which so far as their exteriors are concerned are in all essentials counterparts of his design for the Tribune Tower.

The manner in which a steel frame building can logically acquire form has been clearly stated by B. J. S. Cahill. "It is in the main twofold. By articulation: in which the upper plan is a symmetrical group of unit pavilions growing up and out of the often amorphous lower portion as delineated by the lot lines: or 'form' is achieved by regression: by which the outer steel columns are stepped off and the face of the building made to recede as it ascends. It is at once obvious that a well planned unit pavilion of a commercial building of two rooms and corridor between, with an eccentrically placed column, will not

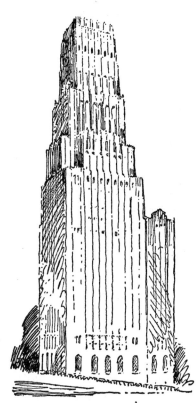

Fig. 144-A.—Competition design for the Tribune Building.—Eliel Saarinen, Architect.

stand a treatment of regression except at the ends. An extra wide pavilion can be reduced by about a third of the outer span without spoiling the floor above; in which case, however, the regressed columns and wall above must be carried on special beams over a void. It is also clear that where two typical pavilions meet and miter at right angles a regression of the corner panel is possible. This eliminates the usual inaccessible corner room and gives a maximum effect of regression at a minimum sacrifice of space, more especially when the building is seen diagonally."

BAYS

As previously indicated, the first consideration in the design of facades will be for the general form or silhouette of the entirety; the second will be for perspective effects, for the play of light and shade produced by massive projections and recessions. The third consideration in order will be for the treatment of the bays. It is perhaps unnecessary to repeat that bays, in common with complete facades, cannot be studied by themselves, but the individual treatment given them must be derived from the development of the program as a whole.

Fig. 145.—Park Madison Building, New York. Carrere and Hastings, Architects.

The determination of spacing of bays depends directly upon the study and correlation of the following factors; the arrangement of rooms and halls and the resulting partitions; the structural system which locates internal points of support recalled in the outer walls as piers be-

Fig. 146.—Project for a Hotel Building in New York.

tween the windows and doors; the symmetrical arrangement of the elements of internal architecture — especially the wall and ceiling treatment of the different rooms, whether flat ceilings or vaulted; the style of architecture sought, which directly affects the proportions of the bay ex-

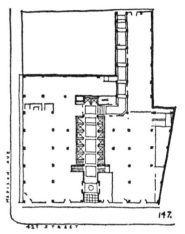

Fig. 147.—L. W. L. Building, New York—showing central location of service.—Carrere and Hastings, Architects.—R. H. Shreve, Consulting Architect.

ternally. If one of these factors may be said to control the others, it will be the character and proportions sought for in elevation. The most difficult thing to do in the study of the problem of the bay will be to correlate the treatment of the facade as a whole with the treatment of the ceiling internally.

The relative proportion of window to wall area has a strong characterizing effect in elevation. This proportion is first dependent upon the purpose of the building, second upon the artistic effect sought. Facades with a large expanse of solid wall produce a solemn, monumental impression—an impression of security and closure—whereas large windows produce an impression of lightness and openness. Naturally blank wall surfaces result in buildings where top lighting is employed, and therefore the character of the wall is impressed upon art galleries and museums. Effects of this sort are further accentuated by the apparent thickness of the wall as shown in the jambs of the openings (the reveal). A large depth of reveal adds to the monumental impression by increasing the apparent solidity of the wall. Since offsets in the wall occur externally, the inner plane of the wall is usually a single vertical, and as it is usually desirable that the glazing of the sashes should all be on one plane, reveals are probably thicker at the base than toward the upper stories of a building.

In studying the composition of bays, even in primary sketches, the shadows should always be indicated and the openings darkened, while receding planes should be toned down. The fingertip is a most useful ally to the soft pencil in the indication of these values. The precise casting of shadows and the determination of relative values in washes, assume the greatest importance in the rendering of facades. Shades and shadows are part of the alphabet of architectural design and the student should master this fundamental subject in his preliminary studies. Without an accurate knowledge of conventional shades and shadows, the study of the external forms of architecture would be almost fruitless.

In facades composed of several stories, these will either be sensibly equal, or one or more will dominate in height and importance over the others. Such variations propose a multitude of problems for the bay to solve. The first group calls for the use of superposed orders or of simple, plane wall surfaces. To insure pleasing proportions in such compositions is most difficult, yet here we have again the inspiration of Italian models where the difficulties have been most admirably overcome. Well known examples in the United States are Tiffany's store and the Pittsburgh Athletic Club building.

When there is one story of greater importance than the others it will be emphasized in various ways—by columns, pilasters, arches, and so forth, or combined motives. Often for the sake of effect a single colossal order comprises several stories, but even here the apparent height of the included stories cannot be too nearly equal. This motive is perhaps a violation of the strictest purity in composition, but admirable examples excuse it, such as the monuments of Place de la Concorde, the Petit Trianon (Fig. 148) and the New York Public Library.

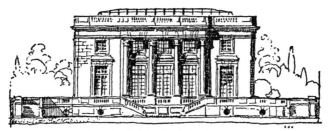

Fig. 148.—Palais de Petit Trianon.

BIBLIOGRAPHY

Guadet, J. Eléments et Théorie de l'Architecture. Book XV.

Durand, J. N. L. Recueil et Paralléle des Edifices en Tout Genre Anciens et Modernes.

Letarouilly, P. Edifices de Rome Moderne.

Strack, H. Baudenkmaler Roms nach Letarouilly Edifices de Rome.

Bühlmann, J. Architektur des Classischen Altertums und der Renaissance.

Gromort, G. Choix d'Eléments Empruntés a l'Architecture Classique.

L'Ecole Nationale des Beaux Arts. Les Médailles des Concours d'Architecture.

PART IV

PRIMARY RULES OF COMPOSITION

CHAPTER I

GENERAL PRINCIPLES OF COMPOSITION

All architectural composition begins with the study of the plan. In studying the plan the facades and interiors must be foreseen, but the arrangement and composition of the plan is the starting point from which all else results. Guadet remarks that "a beautiful plan" is one that "promises and permits beautiful interiors and facades. A plan is not beautiful as architecture simply because of a striking pictorial outline or arrangement on paper. Expression is quite legitimate and contributes to the beauty of plan, but plans are beautiful because of what they imply as architecture, just as books are beautiful by what is read therein, or a musical score, beautiful by its contents and not by the arabesque arrangements of the notes."

In the plan of every building, however complex, there is a separation of areas into two distinct divisions. One division includes those areas which are commonly called rooms, that is areas set for occupancy and use while the other division includes those parts giving access to the different rooms in the building, that is corridors, halls, vestibules, stairways, elevators; in a word communications—horizontal and vertical.

Besides these two divisions of occupied rooms and communications, it is also necessary, particularly in buildings of large extent, to arrange internal courts for the lighting and ventilation of spaces which are not in contact with the exterior walls of the buildings and would otherwise be dark. While the necessity for courts arises primarily from the requirements of light and aeration, courts may be designed solely for architectural effect. This is especially true in mass-plans of large extent where the open court is often employed in the fine arrangement known as the Court of Honor. In the monumental plan compositions of the French, the Court of Honor is a conspicuous and usual feature, and in such compositions it is regarded as practically indispensable. It would seem that its frequent occurrence as employed by them is amply justified by the superior architectural effect invariably secured. This practice contrasts forcibly with our American usage, since the American school of architecture accords the Court of Honor much less consideration in parti. A discussion of the reasons for such differing attitude toward what would seem to be a fundamental element of composition is not of importance here; it is a question of tradition and customary usage, combined in our case, with a lack of foresight in city-planning and the consequent absence of commanding sites.

In certain classes of buildings courts are unnecessary for lighting because top-light is to be preferred to side-light. Such are galleries for exhibition, in picture galleries and museums, monumental stair-halls ascending through two stories only, and in very large halls such as a hall of architectural monuments or the concourse of a railway station where the floor area is great and the ceiling high and vaulted, producing a feeling of spaciousness comparable to out-of-doors—consequently the necessity for windows in the side walls is not felt.

Although natural light and air have always been and should continue to be regarded as fundamental in plan compositions, it should not be forgotten that the inventions of mechanical ventilation and the electric light have had an increasing tendency to modify preconceived notions regarding the theory of planning. These inventions certainly permit us in many special cases to make our plans more compact than was formerly possible or desirable. More properly speaking, we may say, that by reason of them, convenient and habitable buildings are permitted in locations and under circumstances which would otherwise be impossible to utilize. No mechanical system can, however, be thought of as an equal substitute for natural light and air, particularly for monumental buildings on free sites. For such buildings, at least, the established principles of composition ought to remain in full force, while artificial light and air should be regarded as supplementary utilities to be reserved for the solution of special or exceptional difficulties.

Another consideration affecting good composition is the treatment of roofs. Here protection from the weather and the easy removal of rain-water are fundamental and any unnecessary complication is bad. A good plan always insures a rational plan of roofs, a poor plan makes the roof difficult if not impossible. In the search for the picturesque, roofs have sometimes been treated in a highly complex and irrational manner. Pinnacles, turrets, crestings, curved and straight mansards and like features have been a fruitful source of complication. All such devices should be avoided unless reasonably indicated by the program. This does not mean to say that roofs may not be treated in a picturesque or decorative manner, only that the question is as much one of detail as of general composition. Roofs may be steep or flat depending on the style of the architecture or the special character sought, but they should always be simply composed. Consider any of the best of our modern buildings, either public or private and it will be observed that straightforwardness and simplicity of roofs is an essential characteristic. The plan of the ground floor suffices always to indicate the character and composition of the roofs.

We have now indicated those elements which enter primarily into the composition of the plan, broadly considered. They are, briefly,—Rooms, Communications, Service, Light-courts and Roofs. Architecturally these correspond to the basic necessities of use, light, air and protection.

The first problem in planning is the proper arrangement and disposal of these grand divisions of composition. Equal importance should be accorded to each of them in the parti, yet it is a common fault and one to be avoided that the importance of the so-called useful areas, that is rooms, is magnified at the expense of the other divisions. Beginners especially labor under a false idea of economy, which leads them to strive to make plans too compact and condensed, thereby sacrificing the means of independent circulation, communication and free access to all parts of the plan. This does not mean to say that corridors should be expanded into halls, vestibules into lobbies, or that stairways be made more monumental than the program warrants; all these elements should be regulated by an intelligent comprehension of the character and purpose of the building, a question which reduces finally to the adjustment of proportions. Too great condensation in plan is a source of complication rather than of simplicity and for that reason should be avoided. Generally speaking, the simple, direct and adequate arrangement of circulation and services requires as much thought and study as the proper correlation, area and distribution of rooms. Figures 183, 184, 185, 228 are beautiful examples of well-composed circulations.

In this chapter on the Grand Rules of Composition, Guadet stresses the necessity for adequate lighting in all parts of a composition, referring here to the faulty ideas of composition prevailing among students and teachers in the early days of the architectural schools. "You invariably see then" he says "compact plans with at least three and often four or seven widths of adjacent buildings, all these only lighted by skylights in the roof; no aeration possible and suffocation assured." A comparison of Figures 148-A and 148-B which are two partis for the same project will serve to make this point clear. It must be remembered however, that here the separate rooms are enormous and therefore comparable to independent buildings grouped together. The point to remember is that there should be no crowding of the different elements in plan. Not only should a sufficiency of light and air be provided in the arrangement, but it is also desirable as a matter of expression that the plan as drawn should appear free and open and without complication. As an illustration of this see again Figures 183 to 228.

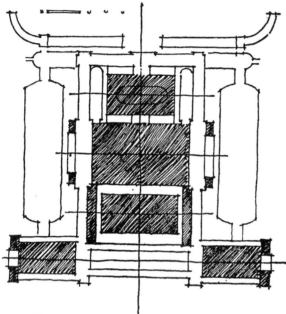

Fig. 148-A.—Block plan, Gymnase by Eustache.

"The first thing to learn in composition and the hardest thing to know is how to be simple," said Thomas Hastings. Composition proceeds by a series of sacrifices; the faculty of judgment is brought into play for appraising the relative importance of things, the tendency being always toward elimination and simplicity; another proof of the fact that to compose is to proportion.

It is impossible to be simple without first mastering the terms, requirements and intent of the program. One must comprehend thoroughly what he is expected to create, otherwise the imagination cannot work freely or in the right direction, and study becomes fruitless. This seems an obvious and therefore unnecessary recommendation, yet many compositions have been studied and developed whose chief faults are traceable to an initial failure to grasp the essential facts of the program in their proper relation. Before beginning to compose the floor plan it is necessary to re-

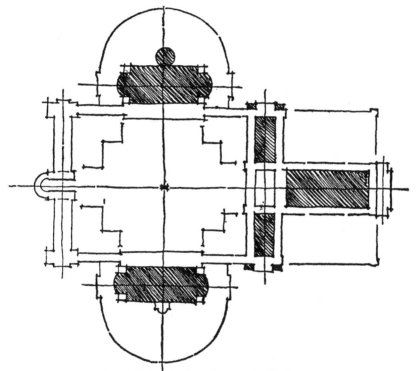

Fig. 148-B.—Block plan, Gymnase by Chedanne.

duce the problem to its simplest form, having regard merely for the requirements of use. Reasonable dimensions should be assigned to rooms, their relation to each other, their degree of separation or connection, and the means of access into the building and throughout all the divisions of the plan taken into account.

The question of site, the position of the building with reference to its surroundings, is also of fundamental importance. Nearly every building will have a principal facade and approach thereto which serves to give to that elevation more importance than to the sides or rear. Other factors such as the relation of the building to others in a group, the points of view from which the building may be seen to advantage, the inclination and other natural features of the site have a determining effect on the composition. Generally speaking a building should be placed on a site so that most of the grounds are to one side of it. In this position the maximum effect may be secured in the treatment of the approach and in the landscape architecture of the setting. A building ought never to be placed in the middle of a site unless its program indicates this position to be manifestly preferable. The topography of the site, the landscape, the surroundings or other existing factors will govern the general composition of the building in the beginning. After the building is completed it then controls the design of the immediate parts of the landscape which come in direct contact with it. In public buildings such surrounding features of the landscape are often treated in a highly architectural manner, their relation to the building then becoming so intimate that they are really part of the building and should be treated as such. The immediately surrounding frame of landscape, architecturally or informally treated, forms the setting for the building. It is called the "entourage". No plan is complete until the entourage is thoroughly studied and expressed.

Compositions are of three kinds—the symmetrical, the unsymmetrical and the informal or picturesque. A symmetrical composition is one which has uniformity and balance in all those corresponding parts that can be seen at one and the same time. Thus a symmetrical facade would necessarily recall on one side of the central axis all those corresponding features occurring on the other side of the axis. But it would be no violation of symmetry in the general plan if the rooms on one side of the building were of different sizes or shapes from those on the opposite side or if the facades were treated differently. Two opposite parallel facades can never be seen at the same time, and it is only where corresponding features can be seen from a single viewpoint that symmetry is demanded in the composition. In public and monumental architecture the majority of plans are of the symmetrical type, which is usually to be preferred. The unsymmetrical composition appears forced unless there is some evident reason for its use, such as irregularity of site or some exceptional requirement of the program rendering the balanced composition difficult or impossible

(See Figures 229, 245). Yet it often happens that an unsymmetrical parti promises a far more rational solution of the problem than a symmetrical parti, in which case the student should not hesitate to adopt it. The freedom of the imagination will be hindered if he permits himself to be governed by any previously conceived preference for one scheme over the other. There is a wide difference between unsymmetrical compositions and picturesque compositions and the two should never be confused. In the unsymmetrical composition the principal axes are just as important and evident as they are in the strictly symmetrical composition, except that in the first named the principal axis does not lie along the center line but off to one side of it. The balance of one is the balance of the steelyards, of the other the balance of the apothecary's scales. Symmetry and balance are as important in one case as in the other. In unsymmetrical compositions there is always strict symmetry in those parts which have a direct reference to the principal axis, and it will be seen that such compositions can always be subdivided into symmetrical elements by removal of the unbalanced parts. This is true for plan as well as elevation. The lateral facades of buildings are usually unsymmetrical.

The picturesque plan is also an adaptation to its surroundings, but it is a type of arrangement that is often very far removed, in effect at least, from conscious composition. Picturesqueness is the opposite of symmetry; essentially it is a quality which is not composed but freely results from time and the forces of nature. For our purposes, however, we may consider any plan as picturesque which, although not lacking coherence in its parts, is irregular and informal in arrangement. The variety of a purposely picturesque composition depends just as much on the architect and is just as much the result of study as any other, but it should never give the impression of that conscious intention which is permissible and often sought in symmetrical compositions. The picturesque composition is not a subject for systematic analysis, hence we shall confine our study of parti merely to compositions, symmetrical and unsymmetrical.

CHAPTER II

PROPORTION AND SCALE

The term proportion as a quality of architectural composition has previously been defined (Part 1). There proportions as a whole were separated for purposes of study into several groups, the distinction between them resulting directly from the consideration of the nature of architecture. Guadet defines proportion as "a propriety of ratios—the harmony that obtains between the different parts of an entirety." In sculpture and painting we have a direct criterion for proportions—Nature. It is not so with architecture whose proportions, although they may be powerfully inspired and affected by the animal and vegetable kingdoms and by environment, are not directly referable to them as units of measurement. Proportions in architecture—as will be explained more fully later—are only referable to Nature through the medium of "scale". Scale is a sort of imaginary yardstick which is used to bring all the essential details of a building into harmonious proportion. Scale is an adjustment of these elements to the requirements of human beings and to certain limitations in the nature of materials which are derived from usage, tradition and methods of construction and manufacture.

As the student advances in the study of composition it must become more and more evident to him that proportion, the relation of one part of a composition to another, constitutes very nearly all that is beautiful in any work of art. Form in the mass of a building—form even in the smallest detail of ornament—depends for its beauty upon proportion. The study of proportion is the study of all architecture.

Let us now consider more specifically the functions of proportion and scale in their relation to composition. We have seen that proportions result from the following considerations:

1 Proportions resulting from the mode of construction.

2 Proportions deduced from reasoning out the requirements of the program.

3 Traditional proportions—the result of usage and generally accepted taste.

This is the logical order in which the study of proportions should be pursued, for it is manifest that it is first necessary to have familiarity with the materials and processes used in constructions and the results of their combinations, before the mind is in a position to create anything constructible.

On the other hand from the standpoint of practical architecture,—that is to say, the point of view of the architect toward proportions—the natural sequence would be inverted; the designer engaging his mind, first with composition, second with proportion and finally with construction.

Before taking up any specific examples which will illustrate how construction modifies and determines proportions it is necessary to grasp clearly the different meanings in which the word construction may be used in its application to architecture. There is a meaning for construction as an art and a meaning for construction as a science—comprehended in the phrase "art and science of construction". Guadet makes this distinction intelligible in a few sentences. "Architecture," he says, "has constructions as its purpose, construction as its means." In art "science cannot create or rather science does not create, only lends its guarantee to the creations of art." In architectural designing this principle operates in the following manner: The designer originates or evolves by a process of free adaptation an element, such as a vault, pier-section, column or lintel, or other form necessitated by the requirements of the composition. The strength or stability of this form must be verified in either one of two ways —either by science or by comparison with similar or identical existing forms which have stood the test of actuality, a test which in most cases has extended over many centuries. The question then arises: how much certainty may be given by art—artistic proportions—to construction? In other words will the plan of the building construct well if the section of the piers, walls and columns are beautifully proportioned? To these questions it is safe to reply, that within the field of masonry architecture—the traditional manner of building monumentally, and excluding such comparatively recent systems of construction as the steel frame and reinforced concrete, the sections resulting from beautiful and artistic proportions in plan are invariably adequate, rendering scientific verifications superfluous. The sufficient reason for this statement rests on the fact that in the application of the principles of proportion to architectural composition the designer is governed by precedent rather than by theoretical considerations. The reliance on precedent frees the imagination from the restraints and economies that the mathematical frame of mind invariably imposes. Since architecture is the oldest art in the world its proportions are infinite and precedents therefore become many and varied. A trained sense of proportion will go very far toward overcoming the uncertainties of material elements in construction. Yet the architect should not be indifferent toward science. To be broadly trained he must have science at his command though lacking it he is still far from helpless as a constructor. Art has its part, which is to create beautiful forms and proportions—it remains for science to certify to their stability.

Specifically, the study of the plan from the point of view of construction consists in the study of "poché," of the points of support. That this is a matter essentially of proportions is evident from the following leading considerations: Given the same material and vertically acting loads, a high wall must be relatively thicker than a low one. The dimensions of rooms govern the thickness of walls because rooms of greater span have heavier roofs. Differences in material affect the thickness of walls and may be relatively and accurately expressed. The resultant thrust of a vault is a line inclined to the horizontal, the degree of its inclination depending on the curvature of the vault, the load imposed upon it and the weight of its buttress. Since for stability this line cannot fall without the base of the pier, wall or buttress against which the vault or arch abuts, necessarily such walls must be made thicker in the direction of the thrust, the amount of thickness being subject to proportionate adjustment.

These laws are very general but they are the starting points from which we proceed to a complete study of wall-section as shown in plan. Since vertical proportions depend very largely upon horizontal, within the building as well as without, the design of the poché—its silhouette—conveys, to those who are able to read it, a true indication and impression of the design and composition of the building in its entirety.

CHAPTER III

SPECIFIC PROPORTIONS RESULTING FROM CONSTRUCTION. VARIATIONS IN THE EFFECTIVE PROPORTIONS OF THE ORDERS OF ARCHITECTURE PROPORTIONS FOR ARCHES

In seeking to discover reasons for the diversity of proportions which exist in architectural elements, such as columnar orders, 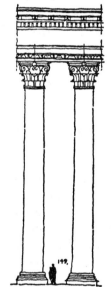 as they are generally used in design, we are confronted first with certain structural limitations resulting from the dimensions of the elements themselves. Thus in all classic architecture where the lintel is used to span an opening between columns, the maximum width of the opening was rigidly fixed by the length of lintel which it was possible to quarry and place safely in position. Consequently in free colonnades, the greater the height of columns, the narrower the proportion between height and width becomes (Fig. 149). The Portico of Octavius at Rome (Fig.

Fig. 149. — Temple of Jupiter S t a t o r. proportions of colonnade.

150) is a classic example of a small order placed next to a large one. In this example is clearly shown the general law

Fig. 150.—Portico of Octavius, Rome.

of proportions in its application to free-standing columnar orders. Here the small order is about two-thirds the height of the large one, yet the spacing is the same and the passage between the columns is actually greater in the lesser order. The same law naturally applies to the proportionate distance that a colonnade may be set away from a wall.

The most instructive examples of this law are drawn from classic Roman architecture, as the proportions found in the Greek temple are exceptional and have in general only a special application to modern work. Apparently the Greeks were very timid about the supporting power of a stone lintel, characteristically employing lintels of the densest marble, high proportions and correspondingly short length of span. The span was further diminished by the wide projection of the abacus, especially in the archaic style. The Parthenon establishes the ideal proportions for Greek Doric architecture (Fig. 151).

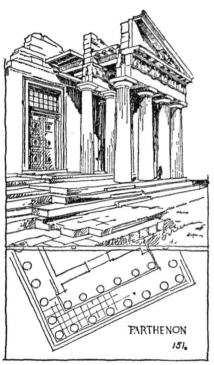

PARTHENON

151.

Fig. 151.—Section through the eastern portico of the Parthenon after a drawing by Riolet.

It is needless to say that this law is not inflexible. Always there is a wide latitude demanded by the arts for the expression of character and the artist is free to exercise this latitude whenever he may do so without violation of the limits established by precedent or of safe construction—both actually and in effect. The amount of variation permitted is a matter of taste, yet it should be remembered that when we wish to express the monumental most forcibly we should be guided by the proportions characteristically exhibited in Classic architecture.

Not only the actual dimensions of columns but the number of columns in a colonnade is a cause of variety in proportions. In general the greater the number of columns, the narrower the apparent proportions of the openings may be. The intercolumniation in a portico of four columns would, therefore, be relatively greater than in one of six or eight. The most obvious reason for this is that a greater number of passages is provided where there are more supports, but it is also a matter of impression or visual effect, since a narrow proportion is a function of the monumental which seeks to give dignity to an edifice by more numerous as well as by larger columns.

Fig. 152.—Bay composition colonnade of the Louvre.

The employment of coupled columns calls for proportions different from those appropriate to single columns. The two columns really form a single support and if spaced according to average proportions, the intercolumniation would then be too narrow in effect. The Colonnade of the Louvre is a fine example of noble proportions where the columns are coupled (Fig. 152).

In the case of columns placed against a wall or in combination with arches there is also demanded a variation in proportions which is a result of construction as well as tradition. The accepted proportions which are found here are derived from the study of the bay as a whole rather than from the consideration of the orders by themselves. Orders used in this sense are in effect purely decorative features, elements of wall-treatment. Such arrangements which take away from the column a large part of its prime function as a supporting element, appear to contradict the spirit of truth which is a basic principle of all architectural composition. Justification, however, is found in the great beauty and variety of combinations which have been handed down to us from antiquity. Since the wall actually and in effect carries the major part of the weight of the superstructure and may also support the lintel throughout its length, it is proper to give to engaged columns or pilasters a wider proportionate spacing than if they were free-standing. There are, however, no rules to follow here except those established by the masterworks of antiquity and the exercise of good taste. The motive of the arch and column permits great flexibility of proportions, a most advantageous characteristic, for by its study and adaptation the varied composition of the bay has been greatly extended. It must not be forgotten that engaged columns and pilasters act as buttresses, tending to stabilize the wall, but this constructive function although it affects the silhouette of the poché does not furnish us with any criterion for modifying external proportions.

Superposition: The mode of construction affects the proportions of superposed orders in a somewhat different sense than when single columns occupy the entire height of the edifice. Their proportions are rather a compromise between the effect they have on one another and the total effect which they have as a continuous single element of support. Considered singly, that is each range of columns by itself, the eye desires to see the wider proportions appropriate to the smaller orders; considered together the impression desired is that characteristic of single orders of an equivalent total height. In their relation to one another it is evident that the upper order should be smaller and lighter than the lower one, for the mind instinctively demands that a support should appear capable of carrying its load. This proportion is commonly adjusted by making the lower diameter of the supported column, equal to the upper diameter of the supporting column, thus securing a uniform taper from the bottom to the top of the entire combination. It also correspondingly follows that the more delicate orders should be placed over those of less slender proportions, as the Corinthian and Ionic over the Doric or the Corinthian over the Ionic. This rule does not apply so inflexibly to pilasters which have no taper and when used as elements of wall treatment are subject to extreme variations in proportion. Here again tradition and accepted taste play a leading part.

Fig. 153.—Grand Guardia, Verona. Domenico Curtoni, Architect.

Until recent years orders in superposition have been seldom employed in the public architecture of our time. Exceptions are the well known Tiffany store in New York and Pittsburgh Athletic Club, but for the proper study of this motive we must revert to the edifices of Rome and the Italian Renaissance period, where superposition was developed in its perfection. The most instructive examples are the Theatre of Marcellus (See Fig. 21) and the Farnese Palace (See Fig. 22).

Again the proportions of colonnades vary according to the positions assigned to them. Thus orders used over a high basement are properly given a different spacing than where orders are placed on a low pedestal course. Compare the colonnade of the Place de la Concorde (Fig. 152) with the Guardia Vecchia at Verona (Fig. 153). The spacing of the columns becomes wide when they are counted with the piers under them. (Compare also Figures 154, 21, 22, 24, 25).

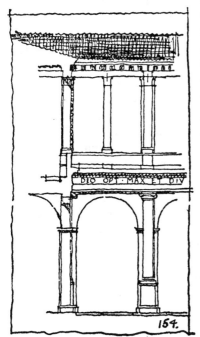

Fig. 154.—Angle Bay, Cloister of S.
M. Della Pace, Bramante

PROPORTIONS OF DOORS AND WINDOWS RESULTING FROM CONSTRUCTION

The proper function of a door is to provide passage in and out of a room or building—of a window, to admit light and air. Their dimensions are therefore primarily determined by human requirements. A door cannot have a height of less than six or seven feet, and the head of a window must be higher than the eye level of the average person standing before it. There must also be a certain minimum ratio of width to height based on use, convenience and good proportion. Between the ordinary and the highly monumental, proportions for rectangular openings vary greatly. At first determined by requirements of use, later as larger dimensions are assigned to them the proportions of openings are governed almost wholly by the desire to express character—especially the character of the monumental. This impression is arrived at by giving to doors dimensions approximating to those in the antique temples—as in the Erechtheum and Pantheon—where the effort was to impart to the edifice solemnity and dignity by proportioning the portal to the superior needs of a divinity.

As in the antique colonnade so in the case of rectangular openings the limit of width was fixed by the effective width of the lintel, which in the great door of the Pantheon reached a span of 20 feet. But the height is dependent on no such limitations; hence arises the law for rectangular openings which says that for a monumental impression the height shall be great in proportion to width.

The effect of construction on windows is equally apparent. As an element of architecture the window is closely related to the door and ordinarily receives the same decorative treatment. But windows have their independent function which is primarily to light interiors and their members and proportions must be based first on this consideration. The height of openings in general is governed by the design of the ceiling, its height and profile in section—whether flat or vaulted. Modern architects have ingeniously sought with more or less success to set aside this limitation even in monumental architecture; employing such devices as panels and recessed facias at the floor levels. (See almost any public building of multiple stories decorated with orders.) The width of openings is affected by the treatment and proportion of the bay as a whole; doors and windows can rarely be studied as isolated elements. They are subject to an almost infinite variety of treatment in design and perhaps it may be said, that in no other motive of architecture is the use and beauty of the edifice more clearly characterized.

PROPORTIONS FOR ARCHES

The arch was conceived through the desire or necessity for providing wider openings than can be spanned with a single stone. The arch is one of the oldest inventions of architecture, yet its inherent possibilities as an element capable of grand and varied effects were not appreciated by the ancients until the time of the Romans who made the arch and vault the most characterizing feature of their architecture.

Like rectangular openings, the proportions of arches were established primarily through their function in construction, these proportions being developed and fixed through the desire to achieve the monumental. In colonnades and rectangular openings the monumental impression is secured by height; for arches, on the other hand, the monumental impression is secured by width. Thus is established a law for proportions in arched openings inverse to that for rectangular openings. In both cases there is apparent the effect of construction on architecture. Between the niche, the smallest arch, and the masonry bridge, the largest arch, are many variations in proportion, yet everywhere is seen the invariable law, that as arches increase in size and grandeur their effective proportions become wider and not higher (Figs. 157, 160).

155.

Fig. 155.—Detail; Colonnade of the Educational Building, Albany. H. Hornbostel, Architect.

In height, arches are generally limited by the same considerations that apply to rectangular openings, but they have no such limitations in width. These considerations affect the proportions of arches in another way—that is in the ratio of the arched part of an opening to the height of its impost. Since in Classic architecture the majority of arches are semi-circular, it is evident that within the same limits of height as arches grow wider their imposts become shorter. An infinite variety is therefore produced in proportion between the curved and rectangular parts of arched openings which is always associated with the diversity of arches.

In proportioning arched openings the designer should never disregard the true structural function of the arch which lies in the direction of span rather than loftiness of effect. Generally in the composition of the same facade arches will be reserved for the large openings, while the smaller ones will be made rectangular. Many remarkable effects result from special combinations of arched and rectangular openings. In the Educational Building at Albany by Henry Hornbostel, Architect, we have a highly monumental colonnade backed up by an equally monumental arcade, each accentuating the

Fig. 156.—Portal of the Army War College, Washington.—McKim, Mead & White, Architects.

grandeur of the other (Fig. 155). So also the portal of the War College at Washington by McKim, Mead & White, (Fig. 156) and the Bridge from Chenevard (Fig. 157). Figures 158, 159 illustrate other and more usual combinations of proportions. The great Roman Basilica of Constantine and Maxentius is one of the most instructive examples of the monumental effect secured by a sequence of arched openings in different proportions at right angles to each other. Here it will be seen how indisputably were the Romans masters of the arch above all others (Fig. 160). The Church of Hagia Sophia Constantinople, is a n o t h e r unique example of the grand use of arches in varied proportions.

The arch is a flexible element susceptible of infinite modifications to correspond with the character of the edifice and the impression that is sought to be produced on the mind of the observer. Figure 161 illustrates a characteristic of arches that must be taken account of in composition, namely that in a motive composed of a series of concentric archivolts, the height is diminished by one while the width is diminished by two.

Fig. 157.—Detail from "Un Pont Triumphal" after M. Durand.

Fig. 158.—Corner of the Boston Public Library.— McKim, Mead & White, Architects.

Fig. 159.—Portal of the Brooklyn Trust Company Building.—York and Sawyer, Architects.

Fig. 160.—Lateral Vault, Basilica of Constantine.

Fig. 161.—Door from the Riccardi Palace, Florence—Michelozzi.

CHAPTER IV

PROPORTIONS RESULTING FROM THE REQUIREMENTS OF THE PROGRAM. PROPORTIONS RESULTING FROM LOCATION AND ENVIRONMENT. GEOMETRICAL THEORY OF PROPORTION

The satisfaction of material needs is the first law of architectural composition. In every composition, therefore, it is necessary to arrange all the divisions of the plan first from a utilitarian point of view. In respect to use the different rooms in a building will vary in importance according to a relative scale. This reduces the problem to a question of proportions. Usually some single division of the plan will be of more importance than all the rest—to it must be assigned the chief place in the composition; then there will be other rooms of equal importance, while still others will be subject to a varying scale which a thoughtful consideration of the special requirements of the problem will determine. This adjustment is a result of the direct application of the study of proportions to the utilitarian requirements of the plan. Before commencing to study the problem from this point of view it is necessary to reduce it to its simplest terms, so that its essential requirements may be easily grasped in their proper relation and carried in the mind at one time. The practical method of subdividing and arranging the program is fully treated in Part V.

In all architectural composition the greatest amount of study must be given to the plan, since it is most directly related to the program and controls and determines the entire design. Section and Elevation are reciprocal complements of the plan—they are necessarily parts of one and the same study, but they do not dominate. Although the plan is attacked first, neither plan, elevation nor section can be studied separately or successively through all stages of the problem's development. Mutual concessions soon become necessary in order that a rational and well proportioned composition of the whole edifice may result. The provisional order, however, is first the study of plan, second the study of section and finally the study of facades.

We have seen that every plan is made up of the three following grand divisions—occupied rooms, communications, and service, each division varying in relative importance according to the nature of the building. It is a question of utility and of proper proportioning of parts to ascertain and establish in the beginning of study just how much prominence should be given each of the above divisions. Thus in a hospital group a great amount of space would be assigned to the service functions, in a railway station great importance would be given to circulation, whereas in an office building both service and circulation are reduced to the minimum for efficiency. Corresponding to the essential divisions in plan, it frequently helps to clarify the intent of a program to subdivide its provisions into—principal parts, secondary parts, connecting parts and accessories.

When the student begins, then, to study and sketch a parti, his first thought will be for the location of the most important feature. Obviously this will be in the most conspicuous place, the most central place; in both symmetrical and unsymmetrical compositions it will be on the principal axis. Exactly where on that axis will be a matter for careful consideration. In French compositions where the plan is characterized by a Court of Honor the dominant place is easily marked (See Figures 129, 130, 131).

Guadet makes this point clear by a striking illustration. "Observe" he says "the Palace of Versailles. The chief place of honor is well marked in the center of the marble court, in the middle of the projection towards the lawn of the gardens. Mansard places there the royal chamber and the grand gallery for receptions; the chapel is placed in a wing, magnificent, but really sacrificed to the royal majesty. For Louis XIV was a very Christian king, yet first of all was the King. On the other hand see the Escurial; the chapel is there, the center and heart of the composition—all converging toward it. Yet Phillip II was the king of that realm on which the sun never set—but before all a Christian king."

The success of every parti vitally depends on the student's seizing on the dominating, characterizing motive of the program and its proper placement in the composition. This is true for all planning, but is doubly true for monumental planning. It is not easy to give to the dominating motive just the right degree of importance. In some types of buildings, especially buildings of a commemorative or religious nature, the controlling idea must be expressed with compelling force and power, in others it should be less forcibly indicated. Only by assiduous study and systematic analysis of the great architectural compositions of the world can the student fit himself to appraise the importance of this supreme element.

Conformable to the dual nature of architecture, there are clearly two ways of expressing the controlling idea of the composition. The material function, in a way, expresses itself, since it is a resultant of the logical analysis of the material requirements of the program. The expression of the moral and the esthetic is a far more subtle thing, involving all the taste, knowledge and imagination which the artist has at his command and all the search for character of which he is capable.

Turning to the secondary divisions of the plan, the mind naturally engages itself first with those parts which are of approximately equal size and proportions—in a sense balancing one another; next to those parts which are smaller and less vital to the composition, and so on down to the least conspicuous element of the service. Note that the term "importance" is not used here in its absolute sense, for every part is essential to the completion of the composition, but the idea that is sought to make clear is—that all parts of the composition are subject to a gradation of proportions which must be thoroughly grasped by the mind before the designer is ready to compose.

The proportionate areas and disposition of the different rooms—the vestibules, halls, corridors, stairways and light courts having been reasoned out and arranged in plan—the question of the proportionate height of these parts soon engages the attention. In buildings of several stories having continuous floors all rooms must necessarily have the same height, thus a limit of vertical proportions is established by the program. But in the majority of plans, especially those of considerable extent, neither floors nor roofs will be continuous throughout the entire composition. In this type of composition the principal parts are so related that each may be given a height proportionate to its area, and so the relative importance of these parts becomes clearly expressed in elevation and external mass. This is the only strictly logical method of composing which permits a monumental and truthful expression of character for the edifice. So far as the exterior composition is concerned there results the following four principal elements of mass—

Principal Mass, Subordinate Mass, Links and Appendages. These elments have their counterparts in the general composition of the plan as we have seen.

First the height of rooms must be in proportion to the character of the edifice. The rooms in a residence would not have the same height as those in a museum. Next the height of rooms is proportioned to their widths, rather than to their lengths. Proportions of this sort are infinite but are limited in practice by considerations of story-height, reason and artistic sense. Only in detached halls, called monumental or great halls, is the designer wholly free to proportion heights. The controlling motives here will be, as usual, material (that is constructive and utilitarian) and artistic (that is having regard for tradition and architectural character).

Such utilitarian considerations as lighting and aeration are of first importance. In large halls, in museums, theatres, lecture halls, court rooms and the like, extending from the ground, light is admitted often only through the roof. The height must therefore be great so that theoretically there is sufficiency of enclosed air to obviate stagnation. Practically in modern halls of this nature, mechanical ventilation renews the air in a much surer manner, but nevertheless the proportions imposed by tradition ought still to prevail. Usually monumental halls have some type of vaulted ceiling, the height in this case being proportioned to the width, and determined by the transverse section and proportions of the arch. Tradition and differences in style play a large part here in fixing proportions; the Halls of the Baths, the nave of a Christian Basilica and a Gothic Cathedral have quite different proportions, although each is a large hall for the assemblage of many persons.

Generally the wider a hall the less the proportionate height will be, that is for the Roman style. For other styles the chief causes that determine actual proportions are not identical. A Gothic nave is high because of a moral or spiritual reason, a gymnasium for hygienic reasons, the hall of a Roman bath for monumental or constructive reasons.

PROPORTIONS RESULTING FROM LOCATION AND ENVIRONMENT

The apparent size of an object is greatly influenced by its position with reference to the spectator and by comparison with nature and with contiguous objects not in the same scale. Statues, vases, the Orders, in fact all architectural objects, out of doors, lose in apparent size, whereas the same objects indoors appear to be much larger. A statue on top of a column appears smaller than when placed at its base. The greater distance at which objects are commonly viewed out of doors has something to do with their loss in apparent size, but more is due to the comparison of the object with the over-arching sky, surrounding atmosphere and extent of horizontal areas. This is one reason besides those of taste and tradition for making the orders used in interiors of slenderer proportions than those used on the exteriors of buildings.

The proportions of architectural features which are seen at an angle or from beneath projecting cornices have to be carefully studied for the positions they occupy; yet as Mr. Hastings remarks, "it is a great risk to lift features so much that they do not look well in elevation." This opinion is corroborated by M. Guadet who says that the results of perspective "cannot modify necessary dimensions, like the height of the steps of stairs or of a balustrade, neither of which depends on materials or the laws of construction, like the heights of cornices or combinations of stonework." This principle would eliminate balustrades six feet high or more, often indicated on drawings and even constructed. A balustrade is proportioned to human needs—to lean upon, and therefore cannot be more than four feet high. If the protection of a balustrade is necessary in some position where it cannot be seen it would be more logical to substitute some other feature of architecture, as a parapet wall, rather than to resort to absurd proportions in order to make it visible.

TRADITIONAL PROPORTIONS—THE RESULT OF USAGE AND GENERALLY ACCEPTED TASTE. GEOMETRICAL THEORY OF PROPORTIONS

Variety, that is diversity of character in buildings, is a resultant not only of difference in program but also of difference in style. In other words, individual character is the expression resulting from a combination of the special requirements of the program with a definite style of architecture. Moreover, within each style character is further impressed by the artistic handling of proportions. Every style or phase of a style is conditioned mainly on intrinsic proportions, producing in all variations and transitions characteristic differences easily recognizable.

The meaning of the terms "style" and "character" are often confused, while slightly different meanings are often given to the latter. Style may be said to be character, but character is not style. "Style is character expressive of definite conceptions, as of grandeur, gaiety or solemnity" is the definition given by Professor Hamlin. In modern architecture the effort to express the function of an edifice by the studied arrangement of mass and detail is that which imparts character to it. This configuration may be expressed in more than one style of architecture, although usually it will be found that certain styles are peculiarly adapted to certain programs, on account of traditions, usage or some other association. Thus a chapel may be designed as well in the Romanesque, Gothic or Renaissance styles, the purpose of the building—that is its character as a chapel—being clearly and definitely stated in each case.

Tradition and usage have impressed a more marked character on some types of buildings than on others. Especially has this been true for churches and religious architecture generally, to which tradition has given a very special character. In our own times we can point to many types of buildings which the increasingly complex requirements of our civilization have brought into being and to which a special character has been given in each case which will in turn become traditional. It is only necessary to mention—a type of State Capitol, a type of Terminal Railway Station, a type of Public Library, a type of high Office Building, a type of Armory, among others, in order to make this point clear.

Traditional architecture, the great body of the master works of past epochs of architecture, is the store house from which we ought to draw and in most cases do draw all the inspiration that goes to make for the greatness of our contemporary design. The greatest commentators are no uncertain advocates of this doctrine. Let us hear what M. Guadet has to say:

I know that to speak of tradition now passes far behind the times; the present tendency is to scorn tradition. That means to despise long efforts continued through centuries by the industrious generations preceding us; to seek generally to conceal ignorance by affecting to scorn the unknown in order to avoid the effort necessary to know it. Preserve yourselves from this error! Progress is slow and must be sure. Whoever proceeds slowly is sane, and whoever is sane goes far. Do you know what is very strong and original? It is to do very well what others have merely done well. The finest epochs are those in which tradition was most respected, when progress was continually perfecting, when there was evolution and not revolution. Never has there been spontaneous generation in art. Between the Parthenon and the temples preceding it are only shades of difference. Furthermore and especially for studies is tradition precious. To dare to become free from it one must judge it, and to do this it must be known. Tradition is a paternal patrimony; to dissipate it independently, one risks finding himself wandering at random and must at least know how to find himself another shelter."

Kenyon Cox voices this same point of view with equal force in the following paragraph:

"The Classic Spirit is the disinterested search for perfection, it is the love of clearness and reasonableness and self-control; it is, above all, the love of permanence and continuity. It asks of a work of art, not that it shall be novel or effective, but that it shall be fine and noble. It seeks not merely to express individuality or emotion, but to express disciplined emotion and individuality restrained by law. It strives for the essential rather than the accidental, the eternal rather than the momentary—loves impersonality more than personality, and feels more power in the orderly succession of the hours and the seasons than in the violence of earthquake or of storm. It loves to steep itself in tradition. It would have each new work connect itself in the mind of him who sees it with all the noble and lovely works of the past, bringing them to his memory and making their beauty and charm a part of the work before him. It does not deny originality and individuality—they are as welcome as inevitable. It does not consider tradition as immutable or set rigid bounds to invention. But it desires that each new presentation of truth and beauty shall show us the old truth and the old beauty, seen only from a different angle and colored by a different medium. It wishes to add link by link to the chain of tradition, but it does not wish to break the chain."

The elements of architecture are few and must of necessity be used over and over again, and yet an infinite variety exists in their applications. While this variety is due largely to the way they are combined, it is due more especially to intrinsic proportions. As an example of this compare the motive of the Basilica of Palladio with the motive of the Library of St. Mark (Figs. 24, 25). In both cases the architectural elements used are identical, but the effect is wholly different. What is the cause of this difference? Certainly the decoration has much to do with it, but chiefly it is in the proportions.

GEOMETRICAL THEORY OF PROPORTIONS

Professor Thiersch has sought to establish a law for traditional proportions based on geometry. There have also been other

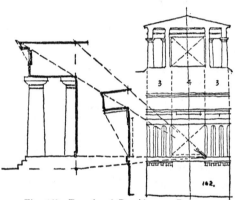

writers who believed that the harmony of proportions marking antique architecture was not wholly the result of artistic feeling, and to support this theory numerous examples have been selected from among the ancient edifices to prove that the basis for the proportions which we admire in them is to be found in the simple ratios of whole numbers or the similarity of figures in

Fig. 162.—Temple of Poseidon at Paestum; Geometrical relations.

geometry (Fig. 162). From their researches we are led to believe that simple numerical ratios "certainly participated in the proportions of ancient edifices." It is asserted that the following simple ratios were retained in the early Greek temples:

1 Width and height of the facade of the cella, so far as externally visible, are to each other as 3 to 2.

2 Width and height of the cella are equal, as well as the walls of the pronaos.

3 Height of the columns equals twice the distance between their axes.

4 Height of the architrave equals one-third the distance between the axes of columns, or of length of architrave blocks.

As buildings became more complex, however, such simple proportions were soon abandoned or disappeared. Certainly any serious attempt to apply them to the solution of modern problems would avail little, nor would it make designing any easier.

An examination of the geometrical theory based on the similarity of figures as a criterion for harmony in proportions seems to promise somewhat more fruitful results as some practical applications may be drawn from it (Fig. 162).

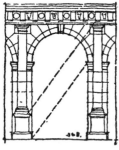

Fig. 163.—Proportions of an arcade after Palladio.

This theory to have any practical merit must have recourse only to such relations as may be readily perceived by the eye. A relation such as the "harmony arising from repetition of the primary form of the composition in its sub-divisions" would be easily visualized. In rectangular forms or outlines this harmony of proportion is readily perceived on account of the evident parallelism of the diagonals (Figs.163,164,165).

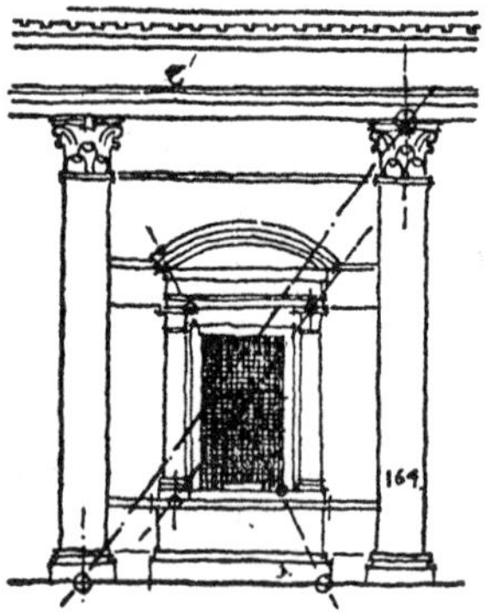

In conclusion it does not appear that any purely scientific theory can furnish a satisfactory explanation for the proportions inherent in the masterpieces of historic architecture. The sense of proportion—the feeling for correct proportion—is a question of refined taste. There can be no doubt that the ancient Greeks surpassed us in

Fig. 164.—Proportions of an interior bay of the Pantheon at Rome.

taste — in the appraisal of beauty—for their works show it and we acknowledge them as our masters. This is partly because the practice of the fine arts was with them a much more vital matter than with us.

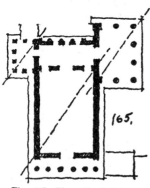

Fig. 165.—Plan, Erechtheion at Athens.

Fig. 166.—Plan of the Pantheon at Rome.

CHAPTER V

SCALE. THE RELATION BETWEEN SCALE AND PROPORTION

Scale is closely related to proportion. In fact we cannot study one without reference to the other. If a single work of architecture is a congeries of proportions mutually related, scale may be defined as the harmony in proportion common to all works of architecture. The unit of comparison or measurement is the human figure, and this is reasonable since buildings are intended primarily for human use. Beside the normal requirements of man, any material thing entering into the construction of a building whose dimensions have become fixed either as a result of the laws of Nature or through considerations of use, beauty or convenience, has a determining effect upon the scale of a building.

Since proportions are only referable to one another, it is obvious that a building may have good proportions and yet be entirely "out of scale". This idea may be made clearer by an illustration. Consider the human figure itself. If a man has abnormally large feet or hands, these members are out of proportion; if he is only four feet high, even though his members are in proportion to his height, he is out of scale. He may be perfectly proportioned and still be out of scale if he is a dwarf or a giant, or he may be both without scale or proportion—in other words, a monster.

So with buildings, which must conform to human requirements. A flight of steps, each of which is a foot high, would be out of scale, also a balustrade two feet high, a door four feet high, a seat three feet from the ground. All such illustrations are evident enough, but scale is a much more subtle thing than is indicated here. Indeed the mastery of scale depends upon the most highly cultivated taste and instinct for harmony in architecture.

Parts of buildings may be wholly out of scale and still be within reasonable dimensions so far as man is concerned, and in respect to such details it is obviously not easy to judge. Material requirements, as has been said, also affect scale. Examples are such things as height of stone courses, the size of bricks, the thickness of a mortar-joint, the dimensions of a lintel, and so forth.

From what has been said it is evident that a design may, besides being correct in scale, be either large or small in scale. A building which is large in scale appears to be designed for the use of human beings larger than man—inversely with buildings small in scale. Of these defects, bigness of scale is perhaps the least faulty since it implies a certain power and vigor of conception, excusable on that ground. A perfect building, however, will be in perfect scale; that is all its parts will seem to be as large as they really are. But there may be certain reasons inherent in the program demanding a modification of the natural scale in order that certain qualities may be better expressed. For example, the monumental impression may be often accentuated by introducing certain familiar elements at a different scale than that to which we are accustomed. And it is all right to do this, even though the harmony of the proportions is disturbed—provided always, that the license is justified by the result. This artifice, however, may easily be carried to absurd lengths, and it is the part of conservatism to avoid it. One of the great merits of the work of the late Charles F. McKim was his realization of correct scale and proportion. This may be said to result almost invariably when respect for tradition and precedent is evident.

Scale cannot be dissociated from proportion, since each is an essential quality of composition. Just as for proportion, scale is affected by location and environment. A different scale is demanded in exteriors and interiors, and for different styles of architecture. With the possible exception of Greek architecture, scale is a most marked characteristic in all epochs of architectural development. The quality of bigness of scale is the most outstanding characteristic of the Egyptian style, but that architecture was not subservient to human needs any more than the Greek. The Greek temple was designed to be the shelter for a god and before this ideal the requirements of man were merely incidental. In it perfect harmony of proportion was attained, whereas scale resulted solely from materials and construction. The Greek temple had about the same proportions whether it was large or small, although its scale varied immensely.

The Romans were certainly the first to seek to compose architecture in accordance with a fixed scale depending on the purpose and importance of the building, and in this idea which has been transmitted through the Gothic and Renaissance epochs down to us, we recognize one of the most important contributions to the systematic design of buildings in the history of artistic achievement.

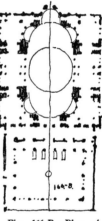

Fig. 166-A.—Michael Angelo's plan for St. Peter's.

In order to insure a correct impression of scale while designing it will be helpful to indicate a human figure at several places on the drawing, sketching it to the linear scale adopted. Or the figure of a man may be drawn without measurement, and if then it is found that he measures about six feet in height it is safe to assume that the scale is correct. This is at best but a trick, however; the trained artistic judgment is the only certain means for insuring harmony and consistency in scale as well as in proportion.

St. Peter's, Rome, is the edifice most frequently cited as an example of enormity in scale. Nevertheless, it is admirably proportioned, possessing two features of composition unrivalled in architecture — its plan (Fig. 166-A) and dome (Fig. 18). Compare St. Peter's with St. Sophia, Constantinople (Fig. 166-B) an edifice beautifully proportioned and noted for its absolute correctness of scale. The architects of the early period of the Italian Renaissance above all others knew how to design buildings correct in scale and their works, especially palace architecture, should be studied with this end in view. Among buildings of the United States the Boston Public Library should be cited on account of its distinguished beauty of scale and proportion (Fig. 158).

Fig. 166-B.—Plan of St. Sophia, Constantinople.

REFERENCES

Guadet, J. "Eléments et Théorie de l'Architecture"

    Book II, Chapter 3, "Les grandes régles de la composition"
         "   Chapter 4, "Les proportions générales"
         "   Chapter 5, "Les proportions spécifiques"
         "   Chapter 6, "Les proportions dans les salles"
         "   Chapter 7, "Corollaires de l'étude des proportions"

PART V

THE PROGRAM OF THE BUILDING

CHAPTER I

ESSENTIALS OF PROGRAMS IN GENERAL; REQUIREMENTS OF SPACE; SITE; LOCAL INFLUENCES; STYLE; IMPORTANCE OF PROPER INDICATION IN THE TECHNIQUE OF THE SKETCH

In the study of architectural design every program is a problem in composition. The program states the conditions of the problem; the answer or solution of the problem is the "parti" expressed and embodied in the preliminary sketch or esquisse. In every complete program certain clauses are of a general nature, embracing ideas common to all compositions; others are of a specific nature, having to do only with the particular problem under consideration.

Architectural problems as stated in programs group themselves naturally under the following heads—First, problems in specific proportions requiring a study of the elements, particularly the antique orders. Such problems are known as analytiques. Second, problems in the elements of composition—i. e., parts of buildings. The solution of these problems requires a combination of the elements of architecture with the elements of planning. The public lobby of a Court House would be an example of this class of programs; the stair hall of a theatre or a foyer in a theatre would be others. Third, problems in the planning and general composition of complete edifices. Programs for problems of this nature would be subdivided into three classes of compositions— plans for simple buildings; plans for complex buildings (known as mass-plans); group plans, i. e., a correlated group of several buildings.

The three classes of problems stated in the preceding paragraph comprise the largest part of what is most important in the study of composition, and a correspondingly varied list of programs may be catalogued under each head. Besides the programs in purely building composition, problems in decorative design—such as a stage setting; problems in the design of monuments and commemorative edifices—as a memorial bridge or a triumphal arch, or problems of a purely imaginative nature—such as an altar of peace—would have their place. Studies in archaeology to familiarize the student with historic styles of architecture together with measured drawing of existing masterpieces of architecture or of antique fragments would naturally also be given a place of importance.

For the purposes of this treatise the most important class of programs is that falling under group number three. The programs in group one do not concern us here, while fundamental arrangements under group two have already been considered in previous chapters (see Part III). Programs under these two groups are secondary to and included in the complete edifice and merely lead up to it. Consequently we shall consider only the formation and analysis of programs for simple buildings, mass-plans and group-plans. All that shall be said about the construction of the parti will then have the study of the complete composition for its ultimate aim.

A program for a student competition in architectural design naturally emphasizes only the essential requirements of the problem. All unimportant and incidental details should be omitted or merely indicated or reserved for the final study and development of the parti. The written statement should be as concise as is consistent with clearness and there should be no ambiguity or uncertainty as to what is required. It has often been remarked that "short programs are the best," and this is true, because if the intent is clear the essentials of a brief statement may be more readily grasped and retained in the mind.

There is no difference in the method of statement of the terms of programs for projets or esquisse-esquisses. The difference is in the presentation or rendering required. For a projet rendu more finished drawings are required and generally at a larger scale than is required for esquisses. It is no part of the purpose of this work to attempt to describe the various systems of delineation used in rendering projets, but our particular interest is with the technique of the sketch as this is the simplest and most direct method of indicating a parti.

All programs commence with a title—the name and subject of

the problem. Following the title there is a general statement giving the purpose of the building. Then its location is given, which will place it with respect to the topography of the site and its possible relation to other buildings and to such existing features as avenues, streets, parks or natural features of landscape. It will be stated whether the site is sloping or level, and the dimensions of the area—fixing the limits which may not be exceeded. Usually if the building is sufficiently important there will be an indication in this paragraph of the sort of landscape development that may be expected adjacent to it—that is the entourage. In a sentence, the opening paragraph locates the building and states its purpose.

In "Plan Problems" the student is as a rule not limited as to building materials or style of architecture, although these may be essential requirements of other sorts of programs, such as programs in archaeology.

After the general statement, the specific requirements of the problem are taken up. These are arranged in an orderly manner and are also as generalized as is consistent with clearness. Explanations are added where they are thought necessary in order to emphasize certain features of arrangement or to prevent the student going astray. The areas of all principal rooms are given in square feet, the floor heights are also established.

Finally there will be a list of the drawings required and the scales at which they are to be presented.

Since architecture has for its object the satisfaction of material and esthetic needs, the analysis of a problem in architecture must be directed toward those ends, and the process of reasoning must be guided by logic and expressed in terms of harmony and beauty. Philosophy lays down two primary rules for the analysis of any problem—to divide each difficulty under examination into as many parts as may be required for its solution, and to conduct the thoughts in order, commencing with the simplest objects and proceeding to the more complex. These rules apply directly to the solution of problems in architecture and it is well to bear them in mind.

A problem in architectural design is said to be solved when the graphical representation of the projected building is finally determined. This solution is not restricted to one parti only; many may be expected, from which there will be several good arrangements possible. But the fact that there are a variety of answers does not invalidate the logic of the analysis; it is only necessary for the solution of the program to be true, and reasonable.

The importance of a thorough understanding of the terms and intent of the program has been previously indicated. This is greatly facilitated by a systematic arrangement in writing of its essential requirements, as will be presently shown, bringing parts into their proper relation, giving prominence to the important, retiring that which is subordinate, and arranging and correlating everything in proper sequence and order. This may be done by reducing the program to the form of a brief or abstract which will serve to indicate more conveniently the proper relationship of the different parts. Obviously this cannot be done at all without considerable preliminary thought, but the true study of the composition begins with the sketch and by sketching only will the designer's creative ideas take form and advance toward a definite solution. To a certain extent a general image of the entire composition may be built up in the mind, this faculty naturally being in proportion to the artist's power of visualizing mentally—a power which is rapidly developed through the study of architecture.

The designer cannot proceed far without resorting to the pencil. Almost at the outset he must commence to analyze the program by reasoning graphically. This phrase (used for want of a better one) indicates the close coordination of brain and hand necessary to the proper study of an architectural composition.

The divisions of knowledge—science and art,—the creative impulse demanded of the designer of buildings and the paths to be followed by creative thought have been fully discussed in the foregoing chapters. To these intellectual resources must be added the ability to sketch—to indicate clearly, truthfully and skillfully the forms of architecture. The critical faculty, that is the faculty which enables one to master the conditions of the program, to classify its elements and to weigh that which is dominant, secondary or merely accessory, this belongs to the side of knowledge, thought and reason; the means of rendering a concrete and intelligible expression of the problem requires a mastery of graphic art —of technique. To all practical intents and purposes the student of composition is helpless and inarticulate unless he is able to interpret his conceptions by sketches and drawings.

If the ability to think in terms of architecture is the first requirement in designing, the ability to draw is certainly little short of it in importance. At least such is the case with present day school methods and the modern practice of architecture. There was a time when the creative artist worked directly in the stone; but that day is forever past—unfortunately, as some think, for the present and future state of the art. These are not the Middle Ages, however; we must be of our own times, and it is the place of the teacher to preach architecture as it is practiced.

It is not our purpose here to describe such accessories of architectural draftsmanship as drawing instruments and the straight edge. These implements have little place in the study of composition, although they find their place later when it becomes necessary to translate the original conception, through the system of divided labor under which work is now executed, into the eventual building.

The sketch is very far from a mechanical detail. The sketch is a freehand drawing and by its very nature it has or should have all the marks of a work of art, and a work of art has been declared to be the briefest possible expression of some fundamental idea.

The sketch as related to composition means the rapid delineation with a soft pencil usually on thin paper of an architectural conception; a quick study intelligently and economically presented; an esquisse embodying, it may be, the parti for the plan of a large building or group of buildings; the rational indication of poché, mosaic, entourage or other detail of plan, elevation or section. It is in itself an entirey, showing forth clearly by actual forms or suggestions all the salient features of the program. It has the capacity for transformation by the trained hand and eye into a fully developed design without essential violation of the original conception. The ability to make a beautiful sketch is only reached through years of industrious practice. In short this is a form of expression that may well measure up to the artistic ideal and is in every respect worthy of the best efforts of the student.

Viollet-le-Duc maintained that the perceptive faculties must be thoroughly developed and cultivated before it is possible to know whether or not the student possesses any creative power. "Drawing," he says, "is the best way to develop the mind and form the judgment; for thus one learns to see and to see is to know." Hear also what Guadet has to say about the practice of drawing. "Study drawing as much as possible. Drawing is the basis of the arts; without it there are no artists. Do not think that I recommend drawing, with rendered drawings as the special object in view. I say that you never can study architecture unless you are a good draftsman. Note the failure of those who, though wise and intelligent, yet lack this primary basis of artistic studies, and who thought to be able to study architecture with the sole aid of science and reason."

The implements used in the study of composition and the technical methods to be employed are surprisingly simple. A roll of tracing paper and a soft pencil comprise all that is essential. Primary studies are necessarily made at a small scale so that ideas may be expressed quickly and the composition easily grasped in its entirety. It is astonishing with what sureness and power the trained hand will be able to express the forms and details of architecture within the small compass allowable. Only by unremitting study and industry can this skill be acquired, there is no short cut to the "learned stroke."

CHAPTER II

ILLUSTRATIVE PROGRAMS FOR BUILDINGS

The following program is adapted from the program of the competition for the International Bureau of American Republics. It has been selected because it represents an unusually instructive type of program from the standpoint of the student of composition, and was the means of producing a beautiful and well known building.

PROGRAM

(Based on the competition for "An International Bureau of American Republics.")

General: This institution is to be built in Washington as the home of the twenty-one republics of America, supported by them for the purpose of promoting commerce and developing ties of friendship and peace. The peoples of the major portion of these republics are of Spanish or other Latin extraction, and it therefore may be desirable that the building have a character in harmony therewith. If the Spanish feature of a patio is included it should have a sliding or rolling glass roof capable of being opened in Summer. The site proposed is on one of the principal corners adjacent to the Mall in the park system of the District of Columbia. It comprises a level and approximately rectangular tract, 400'x500', open on all sides. One of the narrow sides facing the east is the principal frontage. Consideration must be given to the fact that the building will stand on a large square of ground, permitting space for driveways, approaches and landscape treatment.

The following principal divisions of space will be included in the building. These elements have been grouped under four headings but they may be combined or divided in the building as may be thought proper.

(1) Administration Section. For the Director of the Bureau and Staff.

Director's Office, including Private Secretary's room, vault and
lavatory   900 square feet
   General Waiting Room   600   "   "
Office of the Secretary of the Bureau with lava-
tory and room for stenographer   500   "   "
   Rooms for Archives and Accountants each about 250   "   "
Separate Rest rooms for men and women, toilets, etc.
   (2) Library Section.
Stack Room   2000   "   "
Reading Room   1200   "   "
Periodical and Map Rooms, each   800   "   "
Librarián's Office, Cataloguing Room, Acces-
sions, Study Rooms, etc., are to be provided.
   (3) Assembly Section.
A large Assembly Hall for Congresses and the
distinguished visitors   6000   "   "
   Board Room   1200   "   "
   3 Committee Rooms   1200   "   "
Caterer's Room, cloak rooms, etc.

Heating and mechanical plant, janitor's quarters, unpacking and
storage, etc., are to be located in the basement.

In general the plans and elevations should be conceived with due
regard for the specific purpose of the structure and not as an
average government office building.

Adequate provision should be made for ample stairways, halls,
corridors, courtyards, elevators, etc. There should be rest rooms
and toilets for both sexes on each floor.

Required for the esquisse:

Plan of the principal floor at the scale of 1/64″ to the foot.

Elevation of entrance facade and section perpendicular to the
elevation at the sale of 1/64″ to the foot.

ANALYSIS OF THE PROGRAM

The practical purpose of the building requires an active office
work and provision for a growing library. The expression of these
functions, however, should be subordinated to the impression that
should be conveyed by the requirement that the building is to
serve as the home of the American Republics. Hence the char-

acter of the building should be nearer that of a residence than
of an impersonal public building, but a residence infused with a
distinctly monumental and palatial character.

A great Hall of State, a place where representatives of the
American Republics might come together, seems the most suitable expression of the dominant theme. The subsidiary function,
represented by the office accommodation and the library, is provided in a subordinate story.

The superposition of the Hall of State over the Library is the
keynote of the winning parti (Fig. 167). This composition is

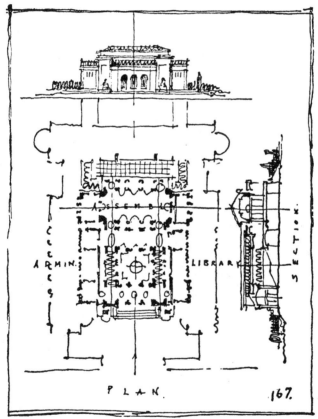

Fig. 167.—International Bureau of American Republics.
Albert Kelsey and Paul Cret, Architects.

strikingly organic in character, the elevation clearly expressing
the arrangement of the essential parts of the plan. The central

motive, the assembly hall, is expressed by the dominant mass
which rises above all subordinate masses (Fig. 168). The three

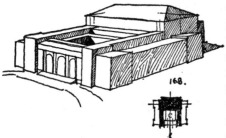

entrance arches between the
pylons express the vestibule
within, while the pylons themselves clearly indicate the ter-
minals of the staircases flanking the central court. Against
the main building, thus developed, are placed the two elements containing the working
offices and other adjuncts. In

Fig. 168.—Mass composition of the International Bureau of American Republics.—
Albert Kelsey and Paul Cret, Architects.

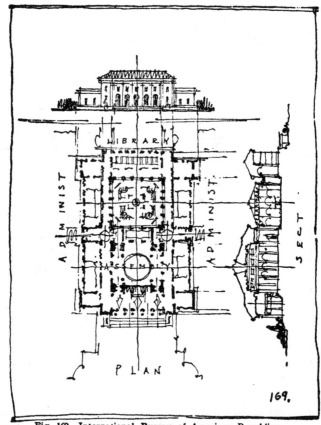

Fig. 169.—International Bureau of American Republics.
Parti of Carrere and Hastings, Architects.

plan, it should be noted, how the quality of spaciousness so desirable in a gathering place for assemblages, has been maintained. The stairways properly perform their function in the circulation as approaches to the great hall, while the patio or atrium, particularly called for in the program, naturally develops between the stairways as a logical incident to the central motive.

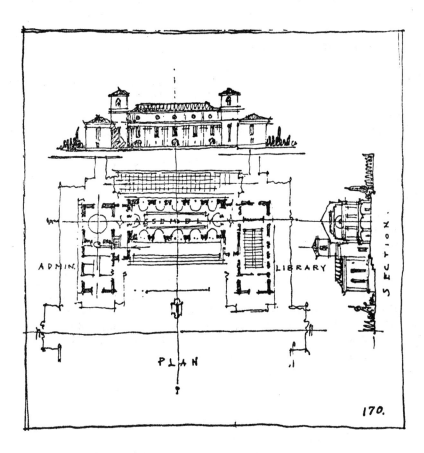

Fig. 170.—International Bureau of American Republics.
Parti of Haight and Githens, Architects.

Of the two other schemes shown, Figure 169 develops all the essential requirements on one level, while Figure 170 ignores the patio entirely and provides in its place, a shallow court of honor.

PROGRAM

A SEASIDE RESORT

It is proposed to erect on the shore of the Atlantic Ocean, about thirty miles distant from one of our large cities, a summer resort which will combine, within its confines, the requirements of a modern city hotel of the first class with the many attractions of the seashore. It will provide in the fullest measure for the needs and pleasures of guests assembled under its roofs by a community of summer interests. Here, if so minded, they will be able to enjoy the sports of boating and bathing, golf, tennis, etc., the pleasures of social intercourse, and all the mental and physical comforts of a well-ordered household.

The subject of this program is the planning of this resort in such a manner as to obtain a satisfactory architectural expression and a correct correlation of its various structures and elements. In this plan the following requirements shall be indicated:

A building in as many stories as desired, containing public rooms, i. e., lounges, lobbies, dining rooms, kitchen, reading and writing rooms, library, service rooms, etc. Connected with the above building by covered galleries three or four buildings, each three or four stories high, with a total capacity of 700 guest rooms, with baths, parlors, etc. The arrangement of the above buildings about an open plaza facing the sea shall be such as to provide a number of concessions for shops, tea rooms, etc.

A band stand, lounging and observation shelters, promenades and gardens.

A dance hall and casino.

A bathing beach and bath house with locker rooms, pool, turkish and shower baths.

A small yacht club house with pier, floats, gasoline and supply stations, and a small harbor for pleasure craft.

A garage for guests' and visitors' cars, with repair and supply departments.

A service buiding, accommodating 250 servants, three stories in height, with dormitories for male and female help, dining rooms, kitchens and living rooms.

A power plant for supplying heat, light and power to the resort.

Tennis courts with small locker house.

The golf course is without the scope of this plan.

The plan should indicate the consideration of the sea view and sea breezes, and of the approach, which is by a private road connecting with the public highway.

The limit of the indicated plan shall not exceed 1000 feet in its greatest dimension.

Required for the Esquisse-esquisse:

A general plan and main elevation at the scale of 1/64" to the foot.

The program clearly states the prime considerations that should be borne in mind in arranging the parti. The distinguishing characteristics of a seaside resort may be said to be, the bathing beach, sea view and sea breezes. The first consideration, then, should be that the beach be as wide as possible and not divided by any feature. The apartment building should be stretched out in a line facing the beach, not only on account of view and breezes, but also that guests may take a dip in the sea before dressing for breakfast. The service building may logically be placed behind the apartments. The central building containing the public rooms should be located in a position easily accessible to all the other elements, to the public way, to the boat landing, to the apartment buildings, the casino and the band stand. The approach from the land should lead directly to this building, while ample parking space for cars and garages should be adjacent. The place for the casino is near the central building, convenient to the sea and facing the open plaza. The yacht club house, pier, landings, etc., should also be on that side. The bath house may best be placed on the beach, convenient to the apartment buildings. Shops, tea rooms, shelters, gardens, the board walk, tennis courts, should be given due consideration so as to complete the scheme.

Of the various schemes indicated (Fig. 171 A B C D), the unsymmetrical partis appear most logical, for the following reasons: The widest possible bathing beach is thereby secured, the apartments are grouped together, as are also the public and recreational buildings, while a more picturesque general effect is secured.

The symmetrical arrangements have the advantage of locating the central building more conveniently to the apartments; but disadvantages, such as division of the bathing beach, separation of the recreational buildings and service units are practically unsurmountable.

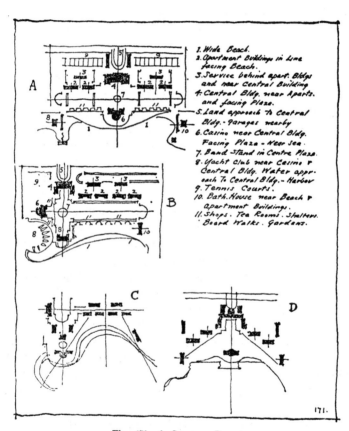

Fig. 171.—A Summer Resort.

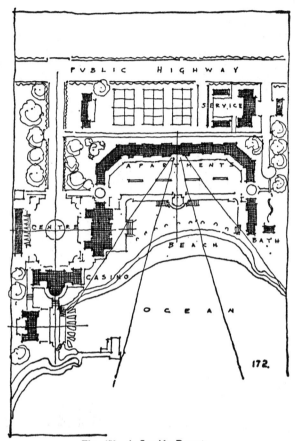

Fig. 172.—A Seaside Resort.

Figure 172 shows the parti as finally developed.

Figures 173, 174, 175, 176 represent four different partis in a student competition where the following specific requirements were to be considered:

"Un College de France"
1 Literature, etc.
2 History
3 Languages
4 Esthetics
5 Mathematics, etc.

6 Natural History
7 Chemistry
8 Library
9 Collections
10 Laboratories
11 Administration

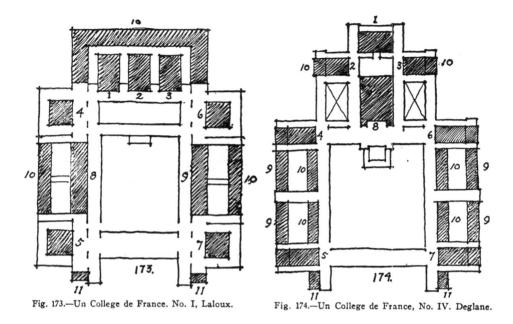

Fig. 173.—Un College de France. No. I, Laloux.

Fig. 174.—Un College de France, No. IV. Deglane.

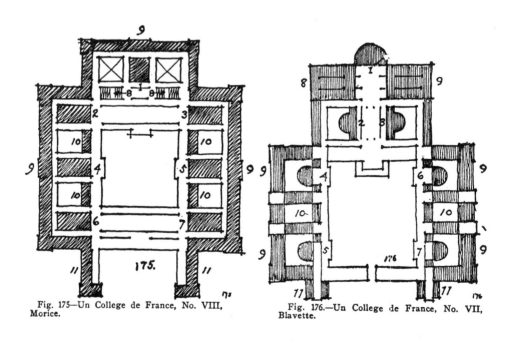

Fig. 175—Un College de France, No. VIII, Morice.

Fig. 176.—Un College de France, No. VII, Blavette.

PART VI

THE PARTI

CHAPTER I

GENERAL PRINCIPLES RELATING TO THE STUDY OF THE PARTI. ARRANGEMENT IN GENERAL

The function which the study of proportion has in the determination of the parti has already been shown. This connection appears in the early consideration which must be given to the utilitarian requirements of the program which find expression in the primary sketches in the indication of the relative importance of different rooms. To assign a definite shape, area and position to the several essential spaces called for is a study in proportions; to determine the general form of the structure and the style of architecture most appropriate to use is also a study in proportions.

The plan of the building is deduced from a study of its requirements and arrangements as stated in the program. This plan arrangement fixes the parti, and, as has been noted, its study logically precedes the study of elevation and section. To represent the composition in its entirety, however, requires the presentation of at least three drawings, which fundamentally are the principal plan, principal facade, and principal section.

Although the earliest study and the greatest amount of study is given to the principal plan this cannot be pursued independently of the study of sections and facades. After the scheme of the plan has been provisionally determined, sketches of sections and facades must soon be made in order that proportions both in mass and detail may be more correctly expressed. The controlling influence of sections is especially felt in giving proper proportion and scale to the poché. Sections also fix the heights of the stories, necessarily a preliminary to the composition of facades. Plan, sections, then facades is the logical order of study; but this order merely holds for the primary drawings, the interrelations between the different parts of the building soon becoming so intimate that consideration can then only be given to the structure as a whole. Nevertheless the order of study determines that the facade shall be a resultant of the plan and section.

This general procedure for artistic composition in architecture is both reasonable and necessary since it consists in solving the controlling requirements first, then taking up subordinate details, bringing all the elements in their proper order for systematic study.

Another consideration of a more or less general nature is the choice of a style of architecture appropriate to the program. In student competitions this choice is usually not so restricted as in actual practice, where such questions as the necessity for preserving the unity of a group, the predilections of the client, factors of cost and material are all elements which may easily assume more importance than the style or character inherent in or indicated by the program. Only in problems in archaeology, as a rule is the student restricted to a specific epoch of design, in all others he is free to choose. The question, whether or not student work should be more closely identified with the conditions of actual practice does not concern us here and is of doubtful importance. Definite style is one of the most powerful means for expressing character and purpose in a structure as well as being the source of individuality and distinction; hence the student should give this question thoughtful consideration at the outset.

In fixing on a parti the following general inquiries should be borne in mind:

1 Decide whether a symmetrical or an unsymmetrical parti is the most appropriate to use.

2 Decide on the style of architecture most characteristic of the program.

3 Decide on a parti whose proportions can be studied, modified and perfected without perpetuating initial defects.

As an example of the third inquiry, let us take the following case: Let us suppose that the program calls for a building, such as a hospital, in which the question of exposure of certain rooms is of great importance. If in your esquisse you have a bad distribution of rooms with respect to the points of the compass, it is obvious that you have settled an initial defect on your parti which can never be thrown off without rendering your projet "Hors Concours."

ARRANGEMENT IN GENERAL

Without reference to use or purpose, every organic plan arrangement may be subdivided or factored into a few elementary types of compositions. Conversely the combination of such types of compositions forms the parti of the building in its broadest sense. The familiar nomenclature of these types is derived from the several combinations of axes to which space enclosing elements are by nature subject. Thus when we speak of "the line," we ordinarily mean the simplest form of the building, placed either horizontally or vertically with respect to direction; the "T," either upright or inverted, indicates a combination of two or more simple buildings at right angles whose masses are of equal or unequal heights; the "U," also either upright or inverted, is an elementary composition formed of three buildings; while the defini-

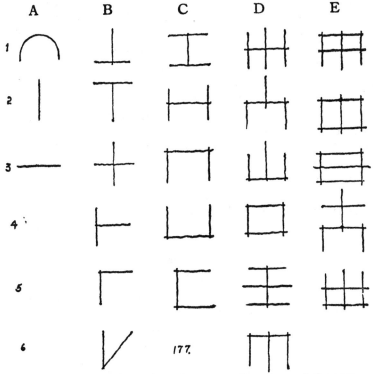

Fig. 177.—Planning—Combinations of one, two, three, four and five axes.

tion given above for the "T" will also serve for the "Cross." Finally, there are the unsymmetrical compositions on two axes, the "L" and the ⊢.

As a general rule axes are straight, but the curved axis occasionally enters into compositions where a special effect is sought or special conditions are imposed on the program, as in amphitheatres and colonnades.

Figure 177, A B C D and E indicate the more common arrangements and combinations of one, two, three, four and five axes.

The nomenclature given above broadly indicates the form of plan of buildings, simple or complex. One other thing is of decisive importance in determining the general form of the structure —that is the plan and shape of the roof. The importance of this results not only from the fact that the elementary masses of which the building is composed are ordinarily placed at right angles to each other, but also because they are not necessarily all of the same height. Such variations in the relative heights of the masses of a structure are simply those natural characteristics which distinguish any work of architecture; the configuration that results from the effort to express in the entirety the "triad of ideas summarized in fulfillment of purpose, truth of thought and beauty of form."

Having indicated the usual axial arrangement, let us now consider the elementary types of plan and their combinations in block which is the next step in the development of parti. The specific arrangement of parts will be reserved for a still further development of the subject.

Whether the building is to serve a useful purpose or is to be purely monumental makes very little difference so far as the study of the elementary silhouette of the block plan is concerned. In one case the external form is dependent upon the arrangement of the various space enclosing elements—wall, partitions, floors and ceilings; in the other the external form is dependent as well upon some ideal conception translated into terms of architecture by the transferral to it of certain forms otherwise purely ornamental, such as fountains, statuary, vases, or the larger decorative forms. It will be noted, however, that highly monumental structures usually partake in silhouette of the nature of the buildings of simple form, or at most a combination of simple forms (compare the plan of St. Peter's, Rome. Figure 166-A and the

Pantheon, Figure 166, among many others equally in point).

First, let us consider buildings of simple form. Buildings of simple form are primarily those which contain a single room undivided in plan or section, and having a single roof. The regular type forms which are suitable here are—the Square; the Normal Rectangle (a rectangle somewhere between one and two squares in proportions) ; the Elongated Rectangle, either vertically or horizontally placed; the Circle; the Annular Segment; and the Octagon (Fig. 178, A B C D E F G and H).

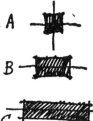

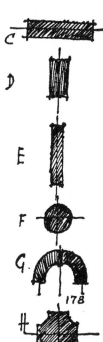

Of these forms, those which have symmetry with respect to a central point only are to be preferred for purely monumental edifices.

Simple and regular type forms of buildings, often of colossal dimensions, have been employed in all ages to embody purely idealistic concepts, or other ideals removed from the merely useful or material. Such are the temples, mausoleums and monuments of antiquity and the great cathedrals and churches of Christian epochs. It is sufficient to recall the pyramids of Egypt, the Parthenon, the Roman Pantheon and Halls of the Baths, St. Peter's and Hagia Sophia, all of which partake closely of the simple form of regular stereometic solids. In monumental buildings containing a single room latitude for the subdivision of space is permitted without destroying the unity of the interior. Such space-dividing elements must, however, be of a very open nature, colonnades, arcades and the like. A fine example of this composition is afforded by the great Lincoln Memorial in Washington by Henry Bacon (See Fig. 59).

Fig. 178.—Planning—
The Elementary Form.

ELEMENTARY COMBINATIONS

The foregoing classification of simple forms of buildings may be properly extended to include "T", the H, and the + (Fig. 179, A B C D E), since the characteristic partis of compound buildings are evolved through combinations of these forms with one another and with the strictly elementary forms already treated rather than through the invention of any new, complex types.

The universality of the adaptation of the "T" and "⌐" forms to plan composition is particularly noteworthy and must already have been marked by the student. If a reason is sought for this it is perhaps sufficient to say that it will be found in the nature of architecture. In almost every plan composition except such as are symmetrically composed around a central, vertical axis, one side is of greater importance than the others—that is the front, the entrance side. Symmetry becomes then from the viewpoint of the observer as he faces the building, a matter of right and left rather than front and rear. Hence there results in plan a longitudinal axis indicating the direction of the building; this is crossed at right angles by a vertical axis—the axis of symmetry. Thus originate the forms of the "T" and the +. Plan composition is completed by the "⌐"—the characteristic form of closure (See Figs. 125, 126).

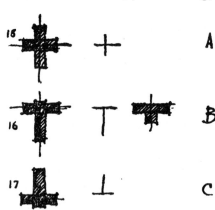

COMPLEX COMBINATIONS

With the foregoing elementary forms in mind, let us now consider some of the more usual combinations of these forms as they occur in the planning of compound buildings — proceeding from the simpler to the more complex.

Since the simple rectangle is the leading motive in the treatment of all forms of plan composition, combinations of rectangles are to be preferred for

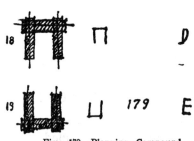

Fig. 179.—Planning—Compound Buildings.

the ground forms of extended buildings. It is reasonable, therefore, to begin with the simple linear composition, previously re-

ferred to as the line (Figs. 180, 180-A). A to N illustrate the
compositions that result where one direction only is emphasized.
Axially, it will be noted, that all these arrangements are analogous
to the type combinations already classified, the difference being in
the matter of elongation only. Compositions of this sort are largely
characterized by the treatment of the r o o f s, depending on whether t h e

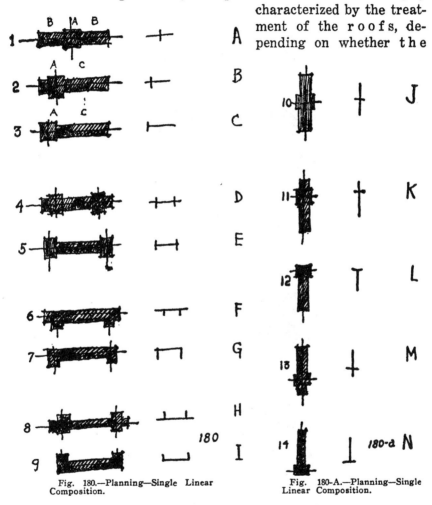

Fig. 180.—Planning—Single Linear
Composition.

Fig. 180-A.—Planning—Single
Linear Composition.

ridge is level or one part raised above another. As indicated,
either the long or the short side of the rectangle may be the principal front.

Next taking up compositions based on the "T", and + and

the "H" it will be seen that these naturally result from an extension of the short axes of the strictly linear compositions (Fig.
179, A B C D E). These compositions are also characterized by

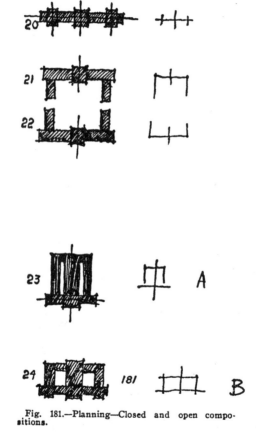

Fig. 181.—Planning—Closed and open compositions.

their roofs; that is to say their rectangular masses may be the
same in height, or one part may be larger and higher than another
part. Analogous to the "H" is the Closed Court, this being generally speaking, a combination of the former with the line. Next

in order comes the arrangement formed by either a close or open combination of the $\bot$ and the $\sqcap$. In the close composition we arrive at the plan shown in Figure 181-A and in the open composition we arrive at the plan with two courts (Fig. 181-B). Both arrangements are shown in block perspective in Figures 124, 125.

The extensive application of the combination indicated by Figure 181-B to forms of compound buildings in general is a fact

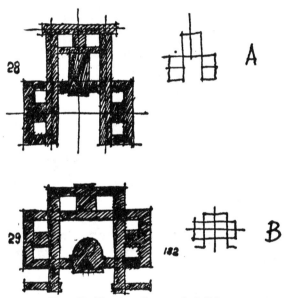

Fig. 182.—Planning—Compound Buildings.

worth remembering. As an illustration of this see Figures 182 A and B and 183, 184, 185.

Coming finally to the combinations of forms typical of highly complex buildings, it will suffice to indicate a few partis which are particularly well known, and where the compositions are clearly and distinctly characterized (Figs. 75, 223, 228, 245).

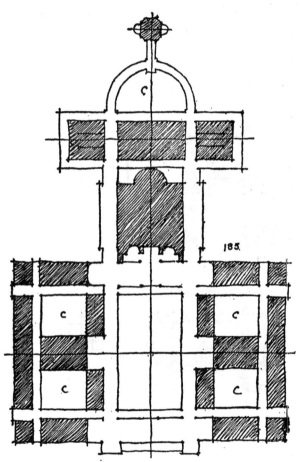

Fig. 183.—After Grand Prix Plan of M. Recoura
"Un Palais des Sociétés Savantes".

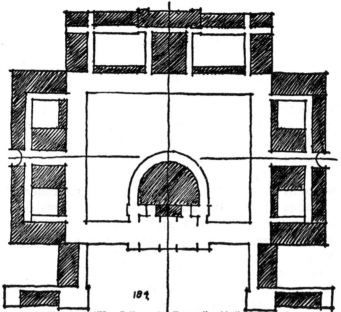

Fig. 184.—"Un College de France", Abella; General
arrangement and circulation.

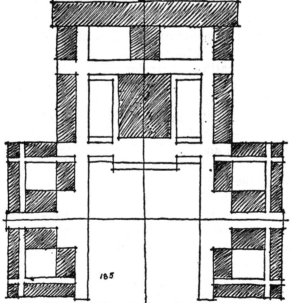

Fig. 185.—"Un College de France", Bonnet; General
arrangement and circulation indicated.

CHAPTER II.

SPECIFIC ARRANGEMENT

Up to this point we have considered plans only in block form. This is a valuable and necessary study and it is essential for the student to become familiar with all the more usual types of partis from this general point of view. The logical order of composition in planning buildings is to pass from general sketches to details; to commence by designing the structure as a single coherent whole. The knowledge of how the large, essential elements of the plan should be grouped, so as to form an organic sequence of parts, may best be gained through the study of great buildings, either actually constructed or merely projected. Methods of study will be treated more fully in Part VII, Chapter I. The documentary sources for study are numerous. First of all in importance should be mentioned Durand's great work, a monumental folio containing all the great historic masterpieces of architecture drawn to the same scale. Then there are the publications of student work in the Ecole des Beaux Arts, particularly the Grand Prix projets, the Concours Chenavard, Les Esquisses de 24 Heures in the Medailles series—all valuable for the study of parti. There are many works treating particular styles or phases of architectural development in a graphic manner which should be consulted with the same object in view. Of these Letarouilly's Edifies de Rome is easily the most valuable. For the study of group planning special mention may be made of Grands Compositions Executées, the inexpensive and readily obtainable folio of Gromort.

The first important consideration having reference to specific arrangement is the question of corridors, passages, and means of access—of circulations. In simple plans a mere vestibule often suffices, but in extensive plans of buildings the halls and circulations are necessarily spacious. The construction of the parti, in fact, often begins here, for in their combinations passages for communication throughout the building form the skeleton around which the rooms and courts are grouped in orderly sequence.

Reference to the plans indicated in Figures 183, 184, 185, where the circulations have been purposely accented for the sake of clearness, will serve to make the following principles more intelligible.

Generally speaking the width of corridors varies with their purpose. Whenever permitted by the program they should be placed along an external wall, usually a court wall, since otherwise they are difficult to light adequately. Corridors should be straight and direct; offsets or other complications are bad. In his excellent work "The Essentials of Composition Applied to Art", Van Pelt has briefly but adequately expressed the requirements of circulation in plan. To quote: "In a plan where the public is to enter, or in one where a crowd may have to pass at a given moment, do not be afraid of ample corridors. Such circulations should pass from group to group without interruption, yet not cut off part of a group." The plans of M. Chaussemiche, Deglane and Tournaire (Figs. 223, 228) are cited for well arranged circulations. The

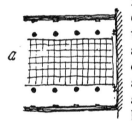

recommendation not to break any circulation extends even to the introduction of passages that have only an indirect use. In (Fig. 186) a suite of rooms runs up to a party wall, the corridor which connects them should continue around the fourth unused side of the court. a of Figure 186, shows a broken circulation, b, an unbroken one.

186

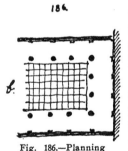

Fig. 186.—Planning
—Corridor.

"A circulation can be faultily broken by one of another class, i. e., the passages reserved for the public might be severed by a crossing of carriages or by a service hall (as from kitchen to dining-room ."

"Circulation and passages are among the most important factors in tying together different parts of a plan. The carrying, or tying through of walls, a requirement of sensible planning, indeed of good construction, is another means. Also, most important, is the preservation of the axes of avenues, openings, rooms, or other elements to be connected."

With the following series of examples the question of parti is brought practically toward the point of completion; that is so far as the graphical expression of formal composition in plan is concerned. The figures here shown represent freehand tracings made over the finished rendus of thoroughly studied projects; hence each drawing may be taken to represent the final study of the plan as indicated by its poché. In all cases features of decoration, such as mosaic and entourage have been purposely omitted. These examples have been selected with the view of illustrating varied arrangements of principal axes, diverse proportions of rectangular elements, circulations, the tying through of walls, and finally, the relative proportions given to the weights of the different points of poché. They should be studied with all these essentials in mind. The student will find it a profitable exercise to sketch eleva-

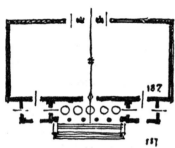

Fig. 187.—Simplest form of enclosed rectangular building with vestibule and two service rooms.

tions corresponding to certain of the following plans, especially t h o s e examples w h e r e the composition is evidently complete in itself.

The simple form of building extended along a horizontal axis recurs frequently in composi-

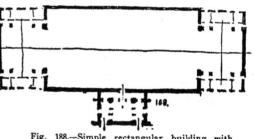

Fig. 188.—Simple rectangular building with lateral extension and connecting link.

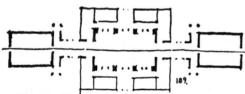

Fig. 189.—Three rectangular units of unequal height and importance linked horizontally on a long axis.

tions either singly or in combinations. Figure 187 represents the plan of a complete building with a vestibule and two service rooms. Figure 188 shows two l a t e r a l extensions slightly separated f r o m

the main part. In Figure 189 the lateral buildings are connected by links. Unequal heights are here clearly indicated by the weight of the poché. The above examples are of the type A3 (Fig. 177).

The inverted T of the type B1 is the axial basis for Figures 190, 191. Figure 192, which is the central portion of the Grand Prix plan of M. Chaussemiche, is a beautiful example of commodious and direct circulations. Here the two principal elements are placed one behind the other on the central axis (See also Figs. 127, 127A, 223). Note how varying proportions of parts in elevation and section are expressed by the plan. Figures 193 and 194 are examples of the T, type B2 (Fig. 177). The first represents a highly monumental parti involving four main elements, together with the most imposing of all stair arrangements, only permitted when, as here, the stairway leads to the central motive of the composition. In both examples the circulation proceeds from a center of radiation—characteristic always of the T.

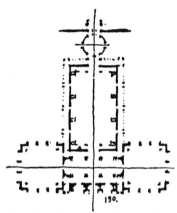

Fig. 190.—A parti similar but less compact.

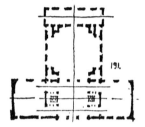

Fig. 191.—Three elements closely connected, the circulation divided.

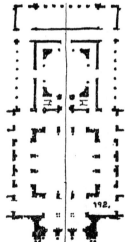

Fig. 192.—A vertical sequence of rooms analogous to the ⊥ two principal elements of axes with circulation around them.

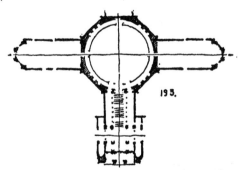

Fig. 193.—A highly monumental parti in oblong form, main elements, the most imposing arrangements of a stairway possible. Only permitted where the stairway leads as here to the focal point of the scheme.

The cruciform plan is of frequent occurrence in monumental architecture. (See Figs 195, 195-A and 196.) The example selected here (Fig. 195) is after the plan of the great Church of S. M. degli Angeli, established by Michael Angelo on the ruins of the baths of Diocletian. In Figure 196 the vertical axis is

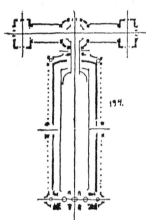

Fig. 104.—Arrangment of 3 elements.—One very large and important in proportion to the other two. The circulation is adapted to a center of radiation.

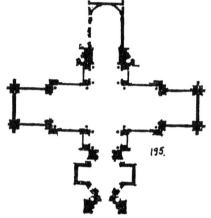

Fig. 195.—Church of S. M. degli Angeli; Michael Angelo.

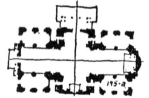

Fig. 195-A.—Cruciform Plan—church of the Sorbonne—Paris.

Fig. 197.—Unsymmetrical plan showing the balance of the steel yards. Here the fulcrum is the focal point "or principal axis", the subordinate mass balances the principal mass on account of the link.

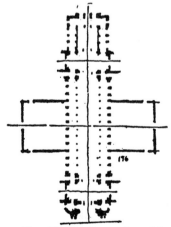

Fig. 196.—Cruciform plan with side elements loosely tied in a vertical axis highly accented. Top and bottom extension compose by themselves as well as with the central figure.

strongly accented, while the side elements are loosely tied in. It will be noted that the extensions at top and bottom compose by themselves as well as with the central portion of the plan.

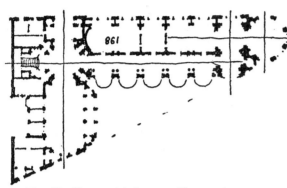

Fig. 198.—Unsymmetrical composition on two axes.

As previously stated, the unsymmetrical parti should never be forced upon the program unless there is some special imperative of site or arrangement which renders it the more desirable. It adapts itself particularly to o d d or unbalanced elements as in Figure 197. It conforms usually to the lateral facades of large buildings. Its balance is that of the steelyards, the principal axis coinciding with the fulcrum. In nearly all unsymmetrical partis the unbalanced elements may be removed without disturbing the symmetry of the principal mass. The L shaped plan (Type B5, Fig. 177) is a special case of the unsymmetrical composition on two axes. The space dividing elements of Figure 198 will repay careful study.

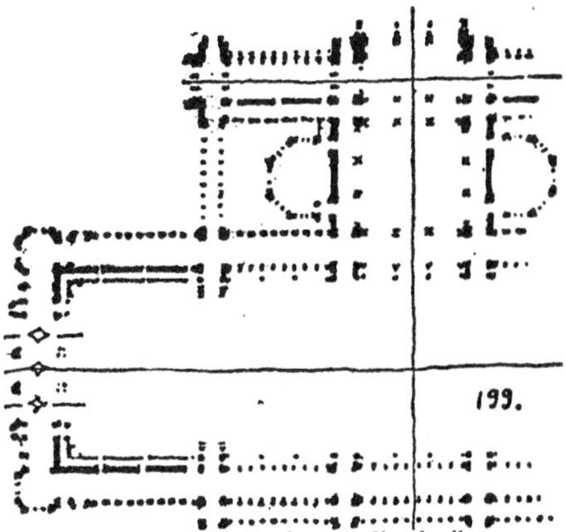

The composition exhibited by the beautiful plan, Figure 199, is adapted to many programs. It is of the type C1 (Fig. 177). Note here the perfect symmetry.

Fig. 199.—Note here the recall of all axes of points of poche. Great spaciousness is indicated by the proportional weight of poche. This is a highly organic plan.

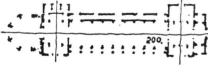

Fig. 200.—Horizontal extended building with terminal pavilions, indication of service and unsymmetrical extension.

Fig. 201.—Symmetrical parti with unequal extension. Note grouping of services.

recall of points of poché, general effect of scale, spaciousness, direct and ample circulations.

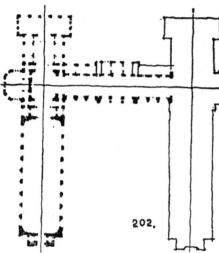

Figures 200, 201 are horizontally extended H shaped plans. This is the scheme for the building with two equal entrances, sometimes called the composition in two parts. See also Figures 202, 203, 204. Axially these partis belong to the types C2, C3, and C4 (Fig. 177). Figure 205 is a case analogous to the foregoing, the court in this case being closed and often covered. Two quite unusual arrangements of the building with two entrances are illustrated by Figures 206, 207.

Fig. 202.—This parti often adapts itself to the composition in two parts.

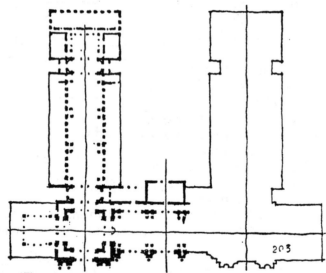

Fig. 203.—Analogous to the preceeding. Adapted to the composition in two parts.

Note in the latter plan how the sub-elements are interrupted by the main element, yet are tied in by their axes. In Figure 206 a plan of the type E4, (Fig. 177) we have the court of honor adapted to a small monumental plan of museum character.

We come now to several partis combining the ⊓ with the ⊥, (B1 plus C3, Fig. 177). As has been said this combination re-

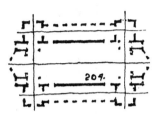

Fig. 204.—A building with two entrances, H shaped plan with pavilions linked. This arrangement may be clearly expressed externally.

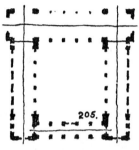

Fig. 205.—The open court closed and roofed.

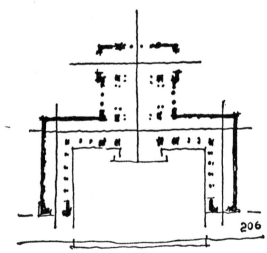

Fig. 206.—Accented Court of Honor.

curs very often in planning. Figures 208, 209, 210 are of the closed type, adapted to small museums, art galleries and lecture halls. Notice the location of stairways in Figure 209. Extended horizontally these partis result in the plan with two courts, (Figs. 211, 212). Figure 212, the plan of the St. Louis Public Library, is especially valuable for study in connection with its program. The functions of the architectural organism are here clearly expressed.

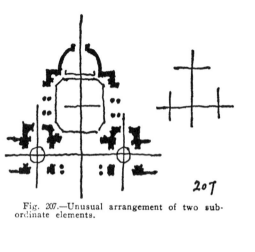

Fig. 207.—Unusual arrangement of two subordinate elements.

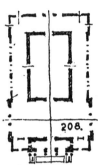

Fig. 208. — Combination of T and ∩ (greatest concentration) typical gallery arrangement.

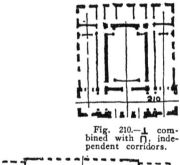

Fig. 210.—⊥ combined with ∩, independent corridors.

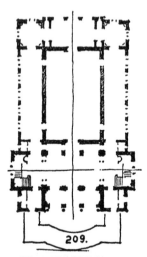

Fig. 209.—Slightly more extended combination of the ⊥ and the ∩ Note — staircases, vestibules, service rooms and galleries.

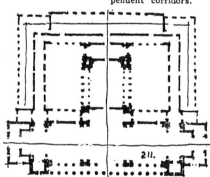

Fig. 211.—Extended arrangement of the ⊥ and ∩ giving the plan with two courts.

Figures 213 and 214 illustrate the use of the curved axis as a frame for the focal point. This arrangement lends itself particularly to pictorial and decorative compositions where a maximum effect is sought to be expressed. Raphael's Sistine Madonna is an

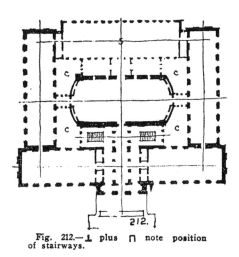

Fig. 212.—⌐ plus ⋂ note position of stairways.

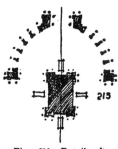

Fig. 213.—Detail after M. Pontremoli — Monument to Joan of Arc.

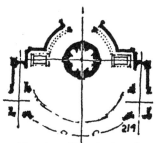

Fig. 214.—The focal point framed. A composition analogous pictorially to that of Raphael's "Sistine Madonna." Architectural the open court, combined with ⋂ framing the edifice.

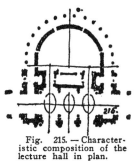

Fig. 215. — Characteristic composition of the lecture hall in plan.

analogous arrangement. The detail of Figure 213 is from M. Pontremoli's strikingly beautiful design for a monument to Joan of Arc (See Fig. 226). This plan is especially full of suggestion. Curved plans are also adapted to auditoriums and theatres, both large and small, since this arrangement permits an equal distribution of seats about a common center (Figs. 215, 216, 217). The external form of Figure 216 would unmistakably declare the func-

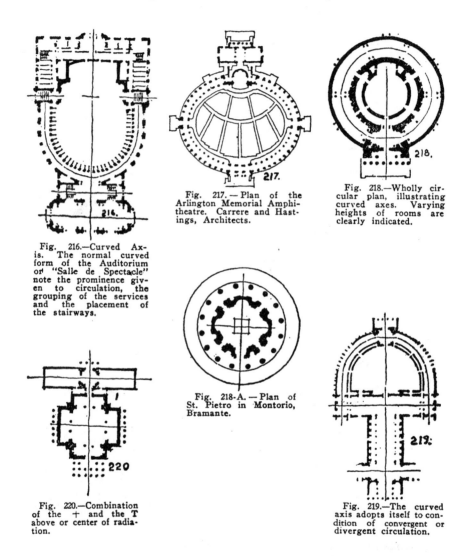

Fig. 216.—Curved Axis. The normal curved form of the Auditorium or "Salle de Spectacle" note the prominence given to circulation, the grouping of the services and the placement of the stairways.

Fig. 217.—Plan of the Arlington Memorial Amphitheatre. Carrere and Hastings, Architects.

Fig. 218.—Wholly circular plan, illustrating curved axes. Varying heights of rooms are clearly indicated.

Fig. 218-A.—Plan of St. Pietro in Montorio, Bramante.

Fig. 220.—Combination of the + and the T above or center of radiation.

Fig. 219.—The curved axis adopts itself to condition of convergent or divergent circulation.

tion of the building. Figure 218 is a rather novel parti based on circular axes. The wholly circular building risks giving the impression of revolving on its center (Fig. 218-A) hence is apt to lack repose unless it is solidly anchored by a projecting mass, as in the Pantheon. This observation does not apply to circular temples or pavilions of a purely decorative nature.

Note in Figure 219 how curved axes adapt the plan to conditions of convergent or divergent circulations.

Figures 220, 221 are analogous partis based on the form of the T. Both occur very often in planning. Axes easily compose when at right angles to each other (Fig. 222). The composition of parallel axes is the more difficult case.

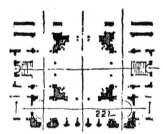

Fig. 221.—Entrance details from a large plan, note position of stairways.

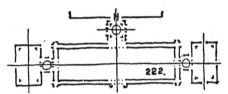

Fig. 222.—Arrangement of three elements on a horizontal line. Axis of smaller rectangles perpendicular to large one. Frequently an alternative parti.

CHAPTER III

THE ENTOURAGE

According to the generally accepted usage of the atelier, the term entourage embraces all features of landscape architecture immediately surrounding the building. From this close proximity there naturally results a correspondingly close relationship of the building to its setting, and the same general principles of composition are taken to apply to the one as to the other.

Landscape architecture may be either formal or informal, varying in character from balanced and highly symmetrical schemes of layout to the purely naturalistic garden plot or wooded park. Compared to building architecture the latter compositions may be said to be analogous to informal and picturesque types of building plans, which although they are possibly as much arranged as the more regular types of symmetrical and unsymmetrical partis, are by nature of their programs and the special effects sought not subject to strictly formal rules.

Practically every feature of what may be termed the architectural entourage is the result of intention. On the other hand in picturesque gardening the effort usually is to conceal intention or to bring about accidental effects. The academic rendu of formal architecture falls almost altogether within the first class, and this is right because the chief value of the academic study of architecture is in doing things by intention and making that intention as evident as possible. This does not mean that informal features are excluded but that they are only introduced in places where a strong contrast of effects will serve to enhance the impression which the dominant idea of the program seeks to produce. Thus there is seen a characteristic rendering of mysterious and gloomy wooded spaces in the upper corners of a drawing; purely artificial, it may be said, but highly purposeful nevertheless. The usual and accepted system of rendering the entourage of plans goes back to the composition of the setting of the Italian Renaissance villa on a sloping site, where the upper part of the slope was wooded to form a background for the picture, the middle part was the level on which stood the casino, while the lower part was treated as a formal garden.

Bearing in mind what has been said in previous chapters concerning composition in general, let us see how these principles apply to the special case of the entourage.

In respect to the elements of architecture and of decoration as applied to the entourage, there must be a selection of certain motives, forms and materials which have an appropriate application and are not subject to injury through exposure. Such elements then as walls, the orders, arches, gateways and portals, fountains, statuary, vases, pedestals and balustrades and other decorative features in marble, stone and bronze are peculiarly appropriate.

Certain of the elements of composition, specifically treated with reference to their location have also an essential bearing on the solution of all problems of external arrangement. Thus we find the counterparts to corridors, passages, galleries and staircases, in driveways, walks, boulevards and promenades, as well as stairs and ramps— all external circulations of varying importance. Large halls, courts, atriums and vestibules are recalled by external courts, partly enclosed or entirely open, by secondary courts for access to the building or retirement from it; while certain elements of facade and bay treatment are frequently called into requisition to complete such features as rise above the ground. Of the latter, constructions like retaining walls supporting elevated plateaus correspond to the basement and foundation parts of buildings; many types of freestanding buildings secondary to the edifice like exedras, loggias and belvideres have special programs which may be considered often as well by themselves as in connection with entourage composition as a whole.

In comparing the composition of the entourage to the composition of the building plan one essential difference should be borne in mind, namely, the question of roofs and ceilings which, of course, have no application to landscape design.

Finally in the decoration of the more architectural elements of the entourage, the indication of mosaic and poché will find an application equally as important as in the case of the building itself.

In our study of entourage, then, it will be seen that such accessories as trees, shrubbery, flowers, turf and the like are the only features necessary to render it complete which are not indigenous to purely architectural design.

It has been said that in the beginning questions of site dominate over the design of the building, whereas after the building is complete it in turn controls the site. This is only another way of saying that the entourage must be designed with direct reference to the design of the building, the latter having received its placement and direction in accordance with certain previous imperatives of site. It has been noted, furthermore, that as a rule a building will not be placed in the middle of a site, but closer rather to one side. This is logical for most types of buildings in order that the most may be made of the entourage. The exceptions will be found chiefly in connection with monumental architecture and for edifices where all sides and approaches are of equal importance. The question of how much relative space to give to the different areas constituting the entourage is one of proportions which must be solved by reference to those essentials of the program which direct and control it. It is obvious that questions of slope, view and orientation have a strong influence in determining the location of buildings in actuality; sometimes such conditions are intentionally imposed upon academic problems. They should be regarded, however, as special elements of the program rather than elements of the general case. The ground form of the building cannot of course be regarded as thoroughly studied until it has been studied with direct reference to its surroundings.

The only one of these questions which is general enough to consider here is that of slope, but since the limitations imposed by the sloping site are more evident in relation to a group of buildings than to a single building, a discussion of it will be reserved for the next chapter where the group-plan is considered.

In our study of entourage arrangements the site will be considered to be level, while only the two most important cases of orientation will be noticed, namely, the case of the edifice with a principal access on the principal facade only, and the case where there is also an access of primary importance on the opposite facade.

Let us suppose that all due provision has been made for the imperatives of site. The point arrives when the study of the composition is so far advanced that the building may be said to control its surroundings; in other words its plan is practically finished. The student is now ready to design the entourage—to give to it such an indication as will serve to complete the composition and bring the site into harmony with the controlling ideas which have already been expressed in the plan.

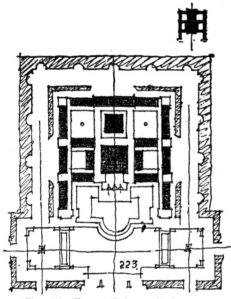

The first general principle then, is to compose the entourage with reference to the plan of the building. To do this the principal axes of the plan must be recalled, establishing vistas which will be terminated on axis by suitable motives, architectural or naturalistic.

The proper arrangement of the entourage will serve to intensify the impression which is sought to be conveyed by the exterior of the building, by the prolongation of axes and the directing of sight lines to focal points on the facade. Of no less importance is the outlook from within the building; but it must be remembered that the relative importance of outlook to external view varies immensely with the architectural character and purpose of the edifice. Besides axes which coincide with those of the building itself, the entourage will also have certain independent axes. The first will be those perpendicular to the facades, the second will be those parallel to them. Identically as in the plan of the edifice, the plan of the entourage will compose about certain basic combinations of axes. Thus there are evolved simple forms of the ⌐, the + and the ⊓ with their combinations, which of all arrangements perhaps are the most monumental (Figs. 223, 224, 226, 227). It is unnecessary to repeat, that in every arrangement the plan of the building as indicated by its silhouette, poché and mosaic will form an integral part of the whole composition.

Fig. 223.—Characteristic academic entourage framing the building. Chaussemiche.

Coincidently with the consideration of axes of the entourage there must be a consideration of those spaces—courts, driveways, walks, garden plots and the like, which give it form and meaning. The outline of the plan of the building, especially if it is a complex building with numerous projections and recessions, must be framed by a line which simplifies and regularizes its silhouette.

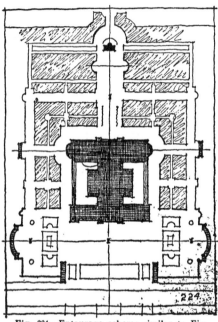

Next it will be essential to give emphasis to the entrance. Thus if there is a paved court in front of the building, this means of access is often treated with a wide flight of steps leading from the public way to a raised plateau. Walks and driveways at the sides and rear should be proportioned to the requirements of circulation and effect, while more or less emphasis should be given to the indication of service depending upon its importance in the program.

An examination of any collection of formal projets will show that, on approximately level sites, the amount of paved areas is in direct proportion to the degree of prominence given to monumental effect. Grass plots and wooded areas will usually occur at the sides and rear, while formal gardens will be situated on some important sub-axis, or on the main axis front or rear in special programs. Re-entrant courts on the sides of a plan unless of great width are commonly closed by the entourage —that is cut-across. Finally it seems to be a fairly fixed general principle that the regularized silhouette of the plan shall be recalled by the circulations and plots which frame it (Fig. 226).

Fig. 224.—Entourage scheme similar to Fig. 195. Great importance given to tthe fore-court plateau. By Nenot.

Passing to more specific details of arrangement, let us consider several entourage partis which may be considered typical. First examine the case of the monumental building with one principal access. Figures 223, 224 adapted from the well-known projets of M. Chaussemiche and Nenot are beautiful examples of the inverted "T", where established principles of design, proportion and indication are given great prominence. Figure 225 is an example of the same parti in which the forecourt is greatly extended horizontally. Figure 226 adapted from M. Pontremoli's "Monument

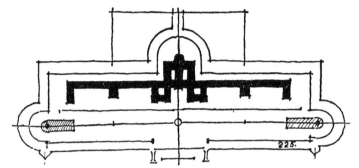

Fig. 225.—Horizontally extended composition analogous to "the line".

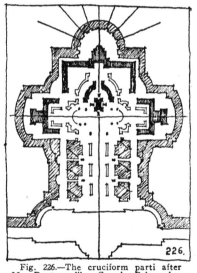

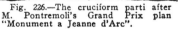

Fig. 226.—The cruciform parti after M. Pontremoli's Grand Prix plan "Monument a Jeanne d'Arc".

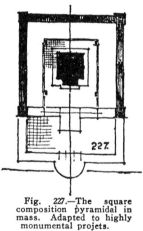

Fig. 227.—The square composition pyramidal in mass. Adapted to highly monumental projets.

a Jeanne d'Arc", is based on the form of the cross, a configuration, which by reason of its solemnity and spiritual meaning, must always appeal to the highest emotions. Figure 227, the square, is perhaps the entourage composition in its greatest simplicity. Here the entourage is simply a great base for the edifice, where every line of sight leads up to and centers on the focal point. All these examples illustrate an evident intention to avoid complication by a search for a mass that will tend to bring all parts of the composition into complete unity. The importance of the edifice is clearly emphasized by its placement, which will be either behind the principal court or in the center of it, while the frame which surrounds the plan ties it in and secures unity of effect.

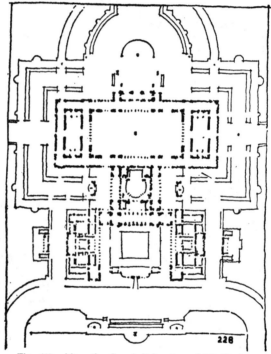

Fig. 228.—After the Grand Prix plan of M. Deglane.
A complete plan with two principal entrances.

The case of the building with two main entrances—front and rear—often occurs in large programs. The entourage will clearly indicate this by its approaches. Compare the adaptation of M. Deglane's Grand Prix plan (Fig. 228).

As for the entourage of unsymmetrical parti, it will be composed according to the general principles just referred to in connection with the strictly symmetrical arrangement. This type approaches the informal and consequently, gardens and decorative planting, often assume an importance in the scheme almost equal to that of the edifice itself. The entourage will naturally take account of this—a question of program and site. Figure 229

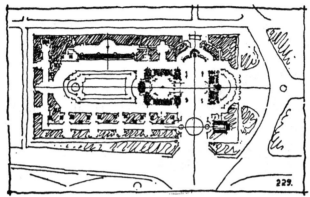

Fig. 229.—Unsymmetrical group plan, composition on two axes after the Grand Prix plan of M. Hulot.

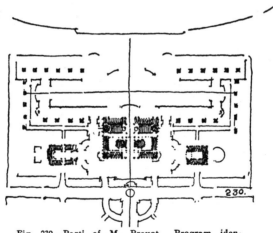

Fig. 230.—Parti of M. Prevot. Program identical with Fig. 201.

illustrates a rather typical scheme of the unsymmetrical entourage on a level site. Figure 230 also illustrates the basis for a composition in which the site is largely occupied with gardens. But note in this instance, as in all, that the simplest means for securing the desired result are adopted. Figure 231 represents a formal garden treated after the manner of an elaborate architectural entourage.

Having now considered the entourage as to its general character, we are ready to take up some of its lesser elements, especially as they affect the rendering or presentation of drawings.

In the decoration of the entourage the same principles of indication apply as to the plans of buildings. Architectural features

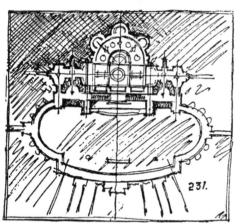

which arise above the ground, such as pedestals, exedras and monuments are all given their proper degree of accentuation by means of poché—usually either black, grey or red. A judicious placement of these features gives the required emphasis to the termination of vistas or intersection of axes. This emphasis is properly made more evident by a variety in gradation or tone in the poché. All of which will

Fig. 231.—Monumental entourage adapted to the formal garden after M. Tonlie.

be controlled by taste and the sense of proportion. Important courts are treated with borders and all-over patterns derived from antique Roman pavements. These patterns are generally indicated at a larger scale and more lightly than interior mosaics. The same pattern should not be repeated everywhere but should be judiciously varied—rich and decorative in important courts and around focal points, simpler elsewhere. Ordinarily walks and driveways are sufficiently decorated by the indication of grass strips, trees and lamp posts. A pattern of inlay wauld obviously be out of place there. Minor circulations are sometimes interrupted by major circulations or by the projection of architectural features of the edifice itself, as porticos or flights of steps. An added accentuation is given to the entrance by the projection of a flight of steps into a court. This is often recalled in the treatment of the mosaic (see the plan of M. Chaussemiche Fig. 223).

Finally, washes or other gradations in tone will complete the external scheme of indication. The chief purpose of the wash is to emphasize the configuration of the entourage and to accentuate the center of attraction. The general effect should be that of a grade from the top to the bottom of the drawing. This effect should be sought in the esquisse as well as in the rendu. Washes are lighter in the central parts of the drawing, lightest around centers of attraction, darkest at the sides and top, especially in the upper corners. Walks and driveways disappear into the general gradation toward the margins of the drawing. In regard to the tone of the wash it should be remembered that the diluted lines of mosaic are often equivalent in effect. The indication of shadows from raised objects which are sometimes cast, should extend down toward the right, because a drawing hung on a wall is normally lighted from the top.

To excel in the treatment of entourage requires a development of taste equally as high as that required for excellence in building composition. Skill in one will not be gained without skill in the other, for each is merely a part of the study of all architecture. In the field of art there are no fences.

CHAPTER IV

THE GROUP PLAN

SYMMETRICAL AND UNSYMMETRICAL PARTIS; SLOPING SITES

As regards composition the group plan may be conceived as a more or less extended mass plan. There is a close analogy between the two cases in the application of the essential elements of planning. Fundamentally everything that has been said about axes, scale and the proportionate relation of parts applies as well to the group plan as to any plan composition. Wherein the problem differs from the building plan is rather in the degree of emphasis placed on certain of the elements than in the way these elements may be combined. Such differences result in the main from the extended nature of group plans. It may easily happen that one part of a group plan may be on a level site and another part on a slope; or one building of a group may be quite remote from another so that it is impossible to connect them except by an axis, yet the entire arrangement must be brought into harmony. Such conditions of placement of course do not happen in the planning of compact buildings, at least not in the same degree.

In group plans the space between and around buildings becomes very important, whether the ground be level or sloping; in fact it will be found that the composition of these spaces must be as carefully considered as the arrangement of the buildings themselves.

Regardless of any special requirements of program, group plans, just as in the case of mass plans, may be separated into a few fixed types of compositions. These will be, for example, the simple rectangle (generally referred to as the line), the closed square, the open square or ⊓, and compositions on two axes like the ⊥ and + either symmetrical or unsymmetrical. Already it has been noted how great a variety of partis result merely from varying the proportions of these simple combinations.

In his discussion of the theory of the group plan, Alfred Morton Githens gives the following definition of a composition which serves to make its relation to the group very clear. "A composition" he says "is an arrangement of several buildings and perhaps open spaces in such a way that all produce a single architectural effect. A composition must be complete in itself. All buildings or natural objects necessary to this effect form part of the composition. Any outlying parts of the buildings themselves or any surrounding buildings that may be removed without hurting the effects are not parts of the composition, and it is generally possible from at least one point of view to see to advantage all buildings, open spaces, courts, trees or other objects included in the composition."

For the purpose of this chapter it is hardly necessary to draw a sharp line of distinction between types of symmetrical and unsymmetrical partis. The effects of sloping site, however, are more special and may profitably be considered separately. Only the block plans of buildings will be taken into consideration and special attention will be given to the treatment of corners and to problems of oblique connection.

In previous chapters we have considered the elementary types of compositions which either singly or in combination form the more usual arrangements of mass plans. Let us see how these same types apply to group plan arrangements. It has been noted that there are perhaps no more than eight types, and having now in mind the open nature of the group plan parti let us take them up in order, with a view to their application to any general problem.

THE CLOSED COURT

The closed court has characterized the planning of buildings from the earliest times. It is the simplest of all arrangements and is adapted to any degree of separation or concentration of its elements. Historically the closed court may be traced through all phases of architectural development; from the Egyptian temples, through the Assyrian palaces, the antique houses of Greece and Rome, the churches and mosques of Byzantine and Saracenic architecture, the cloistered enclosures of mediaeval times, the arcaded courts of the Renaissance, on down to the varied edifices of modern times. It may be noted that closed courts as the integral element of the plan of single buildings are usually actually closed on all sides, as in the Farnese Palace, Figure 62, whereas in group plans the buildings themselves define the court and are often quite detached from one another. This is clearly exempli-

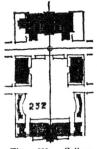

fied by the M. Bénard plan for the College Square of the University of California (Fig. 232). Here, it will be noted that the circulation does not terminate in the square, but is carried through — an arrangement which also characterizes the i d e a l type of city square (Fig.

Fig. 232. — College Square, University of California, Bénard.

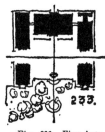

Fig. 233.—Fine Arts Square, University of California, Bénard.

233). In the Railway Station plaza the arteries of travel are continued, but by a different form of circulation, namely that of the railway tracks themselves (See Fig. 69).

THE OPEN COURT

In modern times the open court finds a more extensive application to problems of grouping than the closed court. This is for the reason that the open court naturally and effectively terminates a vista, while the buildings in front of a closed court obstruct the

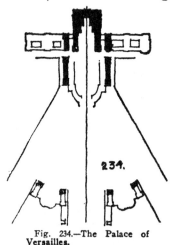

view. Moreover the open court adapts itself to buildings of all degrees of importance, from highly monumental Courts of Honor such as those of the Louvre and Versailles to the modest garden plot between three cottages. It will also be noted that the open court is equally justified for reasons of outlook or view, to which its own importance as a focal point may be subordinated (Figs. 234, 235, 236).

In discussing the open court, Mr. Githens calls attention to a peculiarity of many American compositions namely "an entire indifference to the corners

Fig. 234.—The Palace of Versailles.

of a court, important as the sides and far more difficult to compose." The following instructive examples offering a solution of the problem are cited. Corners connected by low arches, as in the "Palais d'Enfance" (Fig. 237); wings placed on axis before the

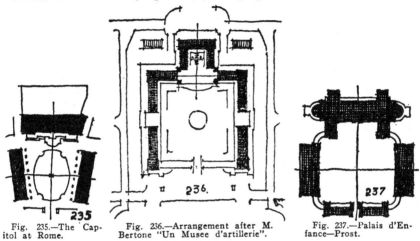

Fig. 235.—The Capitol at Rome.

Fig. 236.—Arrangement after M. Bertone "Un Musee d'artillerie".

Fig. 237.—Palais d'Enfance—Prost.

pavilions of the central buildings as in M. Eustache's "Un Gare Centrale" (Fig. 238); or on axis with them laterally as in M. Prost's "Imprimerie Nationale" (Fig. 239); or finally the wings flanking the main building as in the Fine Arts Square of the University of California (Fig. 233). In Figures 238, 239 it will be seen that the wings partially mask the central building from certain points of view.

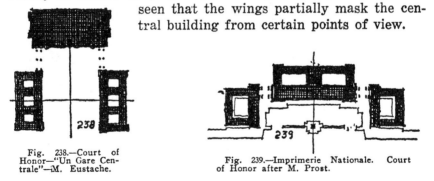

Fig. 238.—Court of Honor—"Un Gare Centrale"—M. Eustache.

Fig. 239.—Imprimerie Nationale. Court of Honor after M. Prost.

THE TELESCOPE

The telescope is produced by a recession of courts of diminishing widths. The effect is to increase the apparent depth. The

Cour de Carrousel of the Louvre (Fig. 240) and the Champs de Mars of the Paris Exposition (Fig. 241) are examples.

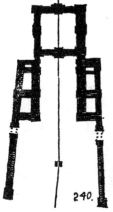

Fig. 240.—Palace of Louvre.

THE "T", THE CROSS AND THE UNSYMMETRICAL COMPOSITIONS ON TWO AXES

Fig. 241. — Champ de Mars, Paris Exposition, 1900.

These are among the most usual arrangements for large groups of buildings as they are readily adaptable to programs of varied requirements and proportions. Extended horizontally they are analogous to the open avenue, extended vertically they approach the "telescope" or closed avenue. Examples showing diversity of proportions are given in Figures 242, 243. The unsymmetrical composition on two axes almost invariably has its approach on the short axis, the long axis being ordinarily closed (Fig. 229).

Fig. 242. — Palace for a Conclave of Monarchs. M. Bigot.

THE AVENUE

Open or closed, the avenue is merely a long, narrow court. The closed avenue finds a frequent analogy in the thoroughfares of a great city where the vista is closed by some important edifice—the open avenue in a facade fronting an open view, such as a boulevard along a river front. In the latter case the group tends naturally to stretch out longitudinally, forming the composition known as the "Line" (Fig. 225). The "Line" is often placed on axis of its court as well as behind its court.

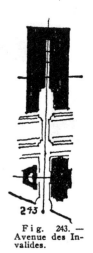

Fig. 243. — Avenue des Invalides.

THE PYRAMID

The pyramid composition is usually reserved for highly monumental programs. Merely placing the edifice in the middle of a court, so that the general silhouette will build up toward the center, is the strikingly simple arrangement for this type of composition. The Library of Columbia University with its surrounding courts is a well known example. Others equally impressive may be found among the academic compositions for the Prix de Rome (Fig. 227).

OBLIQUE CONNECTIONS

The group plan for the Carnegie Technical Schools, Pittsburgh, by Henry Hornbostel (Fig. 224) is an instructive example of two unsymmetrical compositions connected by a skew junction. In the case of the principal group, to quote from Mr. Githens, "one axis along the ridge of the hill passes through the entrance and is terminated or closed by the School of Applied Arts; the other starts at the great tower between the museum and the auditorium, extends down the campus and is closed by the tower for physical experiments at the power house. Both ends of both axes are closed by buildings of the group; in neither case does the vista along an axis extend between the buildings to distant objects. The composition would be open along one axis if for instance the power house and its tower were removed or placed to one side, so that from the museum auditorium at the top of the hill the central vista swept beyond the campus, across the valley with its railroad, to the parks or buildings on the hillside beyond and so entirely outside the group. Though the School for Women and Athletic Field were never built, with very little change this central group would seem complete. This is also true of the School for Women, like the first an unsymmetrical composition on two axes."

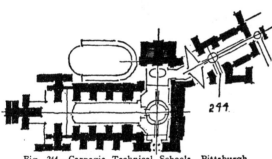

Fig. 244.—Carnegie Technical Schools, Pittsburgh.
Henry Hornbostel, Architect.

ADAPTATION TO SLOPING SITES

The formal court or plateau so characteristic of group planning in general is not easily or logically adaptable to slopes of marked inclination. In order to compose a plateau on a hillside it is necessary to grade and terrace the surface which then loses most of its landscape character as a slope; consequently an informal land-scape treatment is the most natural one to adopt where the terrain is undulating or sharply inclined. Moreover unless the program compels the opposite arrangement, it is logical to place buildings so that their long axes are perpendicular to the slopes. Adjacent buildings will then be parallel to one another, the horizontal distance between them depending upon the angle of slope and upon the fact that it is desirable that a building should not unduly mask its neighbor. This simple rule should be borne in mind in studying the plan composition.

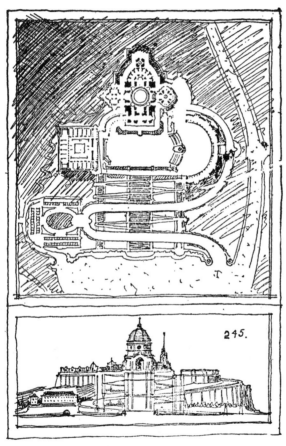

Fig. 245.—Grand Prix Composition of M. Duquesne.

The principle governing the laying out of driveways is equally simple. In order to make the ascent easy for vehicles it is only necessary in the case of any roadway or other circulation to lengthen the travel line. Architecturally there are two ways of accomplishing this, either by curved or broken lines of travel. The Grand Prix projet of M. Duquesne furnishes a beautiful example of the sinuous driveway ascending a steep slope (Fig. 245)

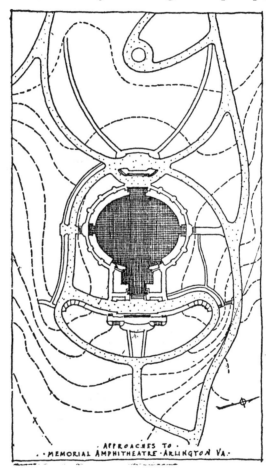

Fig. 245-A.—Approaches to Memorial Amphitheatre, Arlington, Va. Carrere & Hastings, Architects.

also "Approaches to Memorial Amphitheatre" Arlington, Va. by Carrere and Hastings (Fig. 245-A). Two things will be noted in this connection. Axes retain their importance, and the two branches of the "S" curve are quite unequal. Figures 246, 247,

248 illustrate methods of ascent by broken lines of travel; in these cases symmetrical with respect to the central axis. The projets from which these details are taken are also highly instructive for their arrangements of monumental stairways.

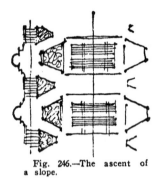

Fig. 246.—The ascent of a slope.

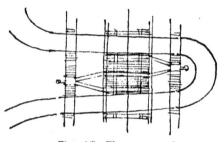

Fig. 247.—The ascent of a slope.

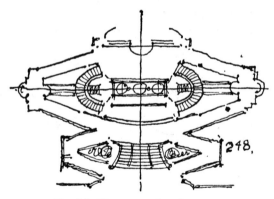

Fig. 248.—The ascent of a slope.

Figure 249 which indicates a part of the winning parti submitted by Henry Hornbostel in the competition for the Western University of Pennsylvania, illustrates about all that needs to be told about the arrangement of buildings on an irregular site. It will repay careful study. The arrows indicate the directions of slope. The composition is primarily an unsymmetrical one on two axes. The central building which occupies the highest and most commanding place is the focal point of the whole group. Its importance is logically accented by placing its long axis at right angles to the normal position, thus bringing the gable to the front and further accenting the pyramidal silhouette of the entirety.

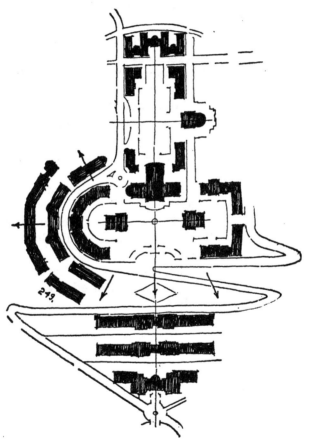

Fig. 249.—Part of competition plan for the Western University of Pennsylvania.—H. Hornbostel, Architect. (Arrows indicate direction of slopes).

REFERENCES—PARTI

Ecole des Beaux Arts. "Les Grands Prix de Rome d'Architecture"
Ecole des Beaux Arts. "Les Médailles des Concours d'Architecture"
Durand, J. N. L.   "Recueil et Parallèle des Edifices en Tout Genre, Anciens et Modernes"

REFERENCES—GROUP PLAN

Gromort, G.   "Choix de Plans de Grandes Compositions Exécutées"
Githens, A. M.   "The Group Plan" (Brickbuilder) 1906, 1907, 1912.
Hegemann W. and Peets, Elbert   The American Vitruvius. A Manual of Civic Art, N. Y. 1922

REFERENCES—ENTOURAGE

Gromort, G.   "Choix de Plans de Grandes Compositions Exécutées"
Triggs, H. I.   "The Art of Garden Design in Italy"
Triggs, H. I.   "Formal Gardens in England and Scotland"
Du Cerceau, J. A.   "French Chateaux and Gardens in the XVI Century". Edited by W. H. Ward, M. A.

PART VII

THE DEVELOPMENT OF THE PARTI

CHAPTER I

CRITICISMS BY INSTRUCTORS; STUDY OF BUILDINGS IN ACTUALITY

Methods of teaching design in the schools and ateliers of America are almost without exception based upon the system originated and developed in the ateliers of Paris. The remarkable vitality and success of this system may be said to be largely due to the spirit of emulation and competition which it fosters and upon which it rests. Rewards for success are merely of a relative value and simply insure merited advancement according to a standard which can never sink below the level of the average capacity of all the competitors. From this system there undoubtedly results a healthy struggle for individual progress in the whole art of architecture—the thing most to be desired. A highly methodical, formal and impersonal method of procedure eliminates any possibility of favoritism. Anonymity of all the problems submitted to judgment is rigidly enforced, while the juries are selected from groups of high professional standing.

The essentials of the system are broadly—a submission of the program of the building to the students on a specified date; the working out of original partis simultaneously and en loge by the students, who will return them to the instructor on the hour stated in the form of a preliminary sketch or esquisse; the development of the parti through the usual resources of personal study, research and criticism (as will be presently discussed in detail); the completion of the drawings and simultaneous submission of the rendered projects (projet rendu); finally the formal judgment by the jury, publication of awards and exhibition of premiated drawings.

It will be seen that strong points of the system are its formal impersonality and strict adherence to a time schedule. Extensions of the period of charette beyond the hour when the problem is due are permitted for no reason whatever, and any design adjudged Hors Concours receives nothing in credit.

Most important factors in the system are the program and its complement, the parti. It is perhaps unnecessary to recall that the program will permit many varied solutions, each of which, if a true and correct expression of it, will be an admissible parti. This variety is a resultant of the nature of problems in design, which may be composed of a diverse character of elements, combined in the light of the varying tastes and individualities of the designers. The arrangement of forms and elements broadly constituting the designer's parti is shown in the esquisse, and it follows that the rendu shall in all essentials be the scheme as stated in the esquisse, and in order that this condition be fulfilled, it is reasonable to require, that no essential feature not shown in the esquisse shall appear in the rendu, neither shall any essential feature be omitted in the rendu. The relative positions of the parts judged to be essential to the parti shall not be changed to constitute another parti, although no addition nor subtraction has been made. The relative area of essential parts is usually fixed by the program, but no restriction is placed upon the development of proportions—which is in itself the essence of the study of composition.

Once the student has embarked upon the development of his parti, numerous external sources of information and suggestion lie before him. These may be stated in the following order of importance:

1 Criticisms by instructors.
2 Study of buildings in actuality.
3 Documents.

Assuming that the student has recorded his conception of the terms of the program, in other words has "handed in his preliminary sketch", it then devolves upon the instructor to assume the direction of the development of the parti chiefly through a course of constructive criticisms.

This he has to do largely by suggestion, making as direct and stimulating an appeal to the student's imagination as their reciprocal states of mind permit. Taking a soft pencil and a roll of tracing paper which he places over the original sketch, he proceeds to tell the student by means of a highly personal system of graphical indication some of the things he should do to develop his ideas and bring the elements of his parti into correct proportionate relation with one another. It is manifest that the depth and refinement of his criticism must be in proportion to the depth and refinement permitted by the work before him. He may not change the parti in any essential way; hence it goes without saying that a conception that is fundamentally wrong or inferior cannot be brought finally to the same state of perfection as a conception that is fundamentally right. Nevertheless it is possible for the student to get valuable experience from the working up of a poor parti. On the other hand, if his parti is impossible or absurd, as sometimes happens, he should abandon it and assume one that is possible, taking the inevitable Hors Concours and the corresponding penalty for "change from esquisse." Then at least he will not have wasted his time. All this emphasizes the importance of the preliminary sketch, of assiduous study and an intelligent analysis of the program. At the very least, as has been said, a parti should be selected whose proportions can be studied without perpetuating initial defects.

In the atelier the instructor gives his criticisms at intervals, usually one a week, while during the interim the student studies and works out the suggestions for improvement. As the problem progresses toward completion, these suggestions, passing as they must from general to particular points, become more and more decided, and there is a gradual progression toward a certain degree of finish and perfection, which, however capable and inspiring the critic may be, is after all only proportional to the student's intelligence, skill and diligence.

It has been said that criticism destroys originality and makes mere imitators and copyists, but this would appear to be an extreme view, and one hardly justified by results. Students in design learn far more rapidly by observing what others can do who possess more knowledge and ability than themselves; exactly as a student of chess, for example, develops ability in the game more rapidly by playing with adversaries of greater skill than himself. Discrimination and understanding are developed by criticism and observation and these faculties are precisely what are needed in as large a measure as possible in order to guard against imitation.

In his criticisms the instructor concerns himself at the outset with the larger elements of the composition, such as proportion between areas in plan and masses in elevation; features that are out of scale or not intelligently combined are worked over and brought into harmony with each other. He sees that the climax or focal center of the composition is sufficiently accented, rightly placed, and given due prominence over subordinate features. He takes care that there is no undue crowding in any of the parts of the plan, that the circulation is direct and adequate and that light and air, being free and desirable, are not excluded. Throughout his preliminary analysis his chief concern is with the plan, although he will not hesitate to sketch possible sections and elevations whenever needful. This graphical analysis is reinforced by a running commentary of explanations and suggestions, at one moment referring to a certain book or plate, at another to some building or bit of well known historic detail. In order to make his criticisms stimulating and effective, the instructor has to assume on the part of the student a considerable degree of architectural information, and will no doubt give him credit for more competence than he possesses. It is up to the latter, then, to take pains to elaborate to the very best of his ability all the hints and suggestions given him, being assured that his parti will develop exactly in proportion to the amount of time and study put upon it. He should not be discouraged if he is slow in "arriving", never being satisfied with a faulty arrangement if there is a chance of improving it by further study. The critic will single out these faults and will be able to cite references in the documents which will enable blunders to be rectified.

Research and careful study of the masterworks of architectural art are most essential factors in training. By strengthening taste, discrimination is thereby made more sure and the novice will have the right to feel that he has climbed many steps when he is able to select the good from the inferior. It is well to remember that in the study of design it is far better to copy something that is really good than to try to create out of a limited imagination. After all imagination is rather largely a matter of memory, if it is not all that. In architecture the sort of originality that consists in the new use of old materials is quite satisfactory for all purposes. It was good enough for the Greeks, why not for us?

Furthermore in order to become a first rate designer of buildings it is necessary to become a first rate critic and, it may be added, a first rate draftsman. This is said with a full realization of the fact that there are good critics who are neither designers nor delineators and clever delineators who are neither designers nor critics. The art of architectural design has some points of difference. in this respect from the art of painting; for painters who are highly skilled draftsmen seem to be more seldom the best painters, nor are the best painters always the best critics —at least of their own work. The distinction is due in part to the evident fact that painting is an end in itself, whereas architectural drafting is not an end in itself but a means to an end.

These convictions strengthen still further the importance of the sketch. Designs for buildings cannot be developed merely by thinking about them. It is necessary to study by repeated sketches, tested by severe criticisms; in other words to draw and to draw skillfully, combining cleverness with knowledge.

THE STUDY OF BUILDINGS IN ACTUALITY

The study of architectural design logically falls into three general subdivisions. First must come the study of the Elements of Architecture; next the study of the Elements of Composition; finally the study of Composition itself. Since the plan of this book is based on the above system of progression, to enter into any further explanation of it would be merely to repeat what has already been said.

In view of the nature of these subdivisions of education, it seems reasonable to reaffirm what seems to be the generally accepted belief among teachers, namely, that the Elements of Architecture may best be studied through actual contact with buildings themselves, while Composition may best be studied from documents. Taking the student to architecture in actually is the essence of what has been called the "Direct Method". It consists in observing all that can be seen of an edifice; that is to say, the externals of the building—wall treatment, doors, windows, columns, cornices, vaulting—the elements in fact; concentrating the attention upon these forms in their full size, measuring them, making sketches and viewing them from different angles and points of view.

There is no doubt that this method greatly facilitates the study of the Elements and is therefore superior to the indirect methods of the atelier. That the observation of reality must make a more powerful and lasting impression than the observation of plaster casts or documentary representations seems incontestable. But this is true only for those objects whose forms, meaning and relations are such as the eye can perceive. Obviously there are many things that cannot be seen or studied in their existing relations, such, for example, as the relative areas and configurations of pier sections, of the proportionate space assigned to circulations and to rooms of varying importance. Such facts can only be compared and realized through the documentary study of plan, section and elevation. The direct observation of architecture develops a feeling for scale and proportion in the elements; focusing the attention upon documentary representations develops a feeling for scale and proportion in the entirety.

The atelier and the library are the laboratories in which the student must acquire the greater part of his preparatory experiences in architecture. To these experiences "field work" must be regarded as chiefly supplementary, valuable and necessary, it is true, but not always to be pursued concurrently in the course. There is reason to believe that travel and the direct observation of architecture may best come after a certain period of preparation. It is especially true in architectural education that the mind of the novice is not fitted to observe. The beginner cannot focus his attention with much discrimination upon details about which he knows little. If there is an art of observing at all it is an art that must be cultivated by serious instruction and industrious self-education for the preparation of the mind, for putting it into the state in which it will be more fitted to observe. The same is true for invention. Education does not necessarily teach how to do a thing, but how to make us capable of doing it.

CHAPTER II
DOCUMENTS; THE EARLY LITERATURE OF
ARCHITECTURE

In his lecture on the study of architecture, Mr. Reginald Blomfield makes the following remark: "The reading of books will not make an architect; his proper study must always be buildings." By this statement we may take him to mean—the reading of books alone, or not reading them in the right way. Now it must be remembered that the lecturer is an Englishman and that his observation was addressed to students of the Royal Academy. In every part of England, as in every other European country, there are to be found historic buildings which exemplify every phase of architectural development; edifices which we speak of as "the monuments", and about which architectural history has been written and countless monographs made. They are, in fact, the solid foundations of historical research. Here in America our case is different. Much as we may value and admire what we have inherited in the way of architecture from our Colonial forefathers—English, Dutch, French and Spanish,—we cannot think of these possessions as being architecturally comparable to the historic monuments of the Old World; at least not in the same sense of independent style. The distinction is at once apparent. Over there architectural students have their material ready at hand; they are surrounded by the great buildings of the past and may see all and know all at small expense in money and comparatively little in time. Over here many of us will never be able to contemplate those great ideas of genius except through the eyes of a transcriber. How shall we see otherwise then, except we surround ourselves with books, pictures, measured drawings and descriptions?

This being the case—how to know those books and how to use them—how to make the most of them—become important questions.

The oldest book on architecture handed down to us from antiquity is the Architecture of Vitruvius. This book was held in great veneration by Renaissance architects; doubtless for the following reasons:—It was the only text-book then in existence;

it treated of Roman architecture, and it appealed to the literary predilections of early scholars. Its contents certainly do not justify its reputation and it may be doubted whether its teachings really ever have influenced architecture very much. Vitruvius is said to have died probably before the first century B. C.; although there is a well-founded belief that he lived several centuries later; but was merely a dilettante amusing himself by writing about architecture which he actually knew little about. If the first is true, he never actually saw Roman architecture at its grandest phase—that of imperial Rome. In either case his interpretation of Roman architecture fell far short of what it actually was or came to be. His Architecture is a book of technical and constructive details—hard and fast rules of proportion—just the sort of things, in fact, that artists have always chosen to disregard. Read the translations of Vitruvius if you will, but do not spend time studying him as you will profit little by it. There are several renditions, probably the best known that of M. H. Morgan.

A more remarkable work is Alberti's "De Re Edificatoria," the first printed book of the long series on architecture that has continued without a break up to the present day. It appeared in 1485, some years after his death.

Printing presses were set up in Rome in 1467, in Venice in 1469, in Florence and other north Italian cities in 1471. At first only the classics were printed. Vitruvius' famous work, known to the early Renaissance architects in manuscript was also printed for the first time shortly after Alberti's. The translation into Italian did not appear until 1521. This was made by Calvo at the expense of Raphael, to aid the latter, it is said, in his architectural work. The original translated manuscript has been preserved and is now in the Munich Library.

It is stated that of all books on architecture published at this time, the one that had the greatest reputation was Palladio's best known literary effort, "I quattro libri dell' architectura", printed in Venice in 1570. He also published other works. In 1554, "Le Antichita di Roma," the result of studies made by himself. Many of the other leading architects of the sixteenth century also published books on architecture; Serlio in 1540 and 1547; Vignola in 1563; Scamozzi in 1615. Vignola was the author of "Regola delli cinque ordini d'architectura." Peace to his ashes! Let us not hold him responsible for the many architectural transgressions that have been committed in his name. He has kept many students from straying far from the truth, but countless others have been led into the delusion that orders of all sizes may have the same proportions. Filarete wrote a work that was never printed and only portions of the original have been preserved—"Il trattato d'architectura," illustrated it is said, by 250 drawings, beside his own designs; drawings of the Colosseum, Mole of Hadrian, and other old buildings of Rome.

All these books show the enthusiasm for scholarship as well as for the antique that animated the Renaissance artists; but with the possible exception of Palladio it is doubtful whether any of them approached their subject from the standpoint of the architect—being, as they were, too much influenced by the method of Vitruvius. It remained for the pensioners of the French Academy at Rome to show the world how the results of the study of antique architecture should be recorded so that these investigations might be made of practical use to architects and students everywhere.

The Renaissance achitects knew how to make use of the knowledge and inspiration they had gained for themselves by the contemplation and study of the antique, and if this genius does not show forth so much in their books, it assuredly shows forth brilliantly in their works. With moderns exactly the reverse seems to be true. We have wonderful treatises on architecture,—measured drawings and restorations of antique art, such as were never dreamt of in the sixteenth century; but instead of our imaginations being kindled as theirs were kindled, the spirit of free adaptation, if not wholly extinguished, appears to lie dormant before the power of our masters.

The question is likely to be asked—have we no literary legacy from the Gothic period? The best known original source is Villard de Honecourt's sketch book—an album of details principally, with one or two sketches of plans. This book is said to have had rather a disastrous influence upon the architects of the Gothic Revival, who regarded it as confirming their own habit of looking at architecture as a matter of detail. The difference between this point of view and that of the Renaissance architects is evident; the latter seeking to analyze buildings by measurement and not by mere sketches of external features. The practice of making sketches is, of course, a good one for students; but it must be remembered that mere sketches of detail without some methodical attempt at analysis of the architecture, such as measurements, profiles and the like, are only of value in developing skill in free-hand drawing, and will be of very little service to the designer. We say this without thought of discouraging what is in itself a very necessary practice. Students do far too little independent sketching of any sort.

All of the books so far touched upon, being primarily of antiquarian interest, make their appeal chiefly to the bibliophile; consequently it is not to be expected that the average undergraduate student will be inclined to bestow much attention on them—unless he happens to have an unusual literary turn. The list of books consulted by students in the course of a year on such subjects as design and history is not large or varied as a rule, and few of them date prior to the nineteenth century. But such works as are consulted are referred to over and over again and hardly ever repose in their designated places on the shelves. The plates in these books have to be mounted on cloth, otherwise they are shortly thumbed out of existence. The student's attitude toward specified titles is very much influenced by the opinion and direction of the instructor, who finds that leading a student to a book and showing him a reference in it is much more effective than printed instructions or lists. And it has been noticed that instructors vary in a corresponding degree in their own predilections, which is but natural, since design is so largely a matter of taste and temperament.

It has been said that the books most used are those which have been published during the last century. There is one great exception—Piranesi. After speaking of his work and its value in the study of design, I shall take occasion to mention a few other books which students of architecture ought to know about, if not to put to practical use in their daily work.

At once the inspiration and despair of young draughtsmen, probably no book of architecture composition holds a more secure place in their estimation than the collection of Piranesi's, "Oeuvres Choisies." It would be a sterile year that did not witness several attempts by students to render their drawings after the manner of Piranesi, and besides delineation there is an immense amount to be learned, too, about architectural composition from his wonderful etchings. Piranesi was born in 1720 and died in 1778.

From a paper by Russell Sturgis, I extract the following estimate of this great genius. After commenting on his work as an architect, which is of little account—he says: "Piranesi is known now in one way only, and in that way is not half so well known as he should be. . . The prints from his large etchings bind up in twenty-four folio volumes, more or less, according to the fancies of the owner. . . It is true that a hundred plates selected out of the mass contain all that is best in his work, and that twice as many would furnish the student with all that he need study. . . It is not, the present writer believes, because he himself is an enthusiastic student of architecture that Piranesi's work seems attractive. . . The thing to look for in Piranesi is not so much architecture (there is something to say on that side of him too) as fine and masterly engraving of original subject. He was one of the last of the great painter-etchers and painter-engravers of old times, and by no means the least of them. It may be extravagant to say, as some have said, that his work would be gathered as eagerly as Rembrandt's if it were not so bulky; but it is not extravagant to say that no man has seen all that the engraver's art is capable of until he has seen and studied nearly everything that Piranesi has left."

For the purposes of this chapter architectural books may be broadly classified as follows: Books of purely antiquarian interest; books embodying the results of archaeological research; books of reference for the study of design. As I have indicated, most of the works hitherto mentioned may be relegated to the first class. As for histories of architecture, it will suffice to place them in the second group, although in its primary meaning archaeology deals specifically with interpretation of fragments dug up out of the ground. All works such as topographical studies, monographs, books of measured drawings and photographs, the theory of architecture and the like, may be grouped together under the general head of reference books. Although these distinctions are not very scientific or accurate, from the viewpoint of the undergraduate student they are perhaps sufficiently definite. Classifications by themselves do not mean very much anyway, and you will soon discover that it is futile to try to fence off one part of the field of art from another part.

There are a dozen or more famous works, which in the light of fuller and more exhaustive research or by reason of more up-to-date reproductive processes, have been superseded and pushed back from the third to the second class, and are now thought of as, at least archaeological if not antiquarian. These books in their day exerted a profound influence on building design, but are now infrequently consulted by students of architectural design. I refer to such publications as those of the "Society of Dilettanti."

This was an association of English scholars, travellers, and collectors, founded in London in 1733 for the purpose of lending aid to the study of Roman and Greek art and for the purchase of antiquities. The Society subsidized the publication of a number of volumes during the latter part of the eighteenth century. James Dawkins' and Robert Wood's researches—better known as Wood's "Ruins of Baalbec" and "Ruins of Palmyra" appeared about 1750. The greatest work published at this time was "Antiquities of Athens" by Stuart and Revett. The painter James Stuart and the architect Nicholas Revett reached Athens in 1751 and remained there three years; their enterprise being accounted the most important so far undertaken. The plates in their work are beautifully engraved. The Society later undertook the survey and publication, at their own expense, of the "Antiquities of Ionia" and "Antiquities of Attica".

"The Architectural Antiquities of Rome," measured and delineated by Taylor and Cresy, Architects and Fellows of the Society of Antiquarians, is a fine work in two volumes, published in London, 1821. The methods pursued by the authors of this work more nearly approach the modern mode of reproduction, inasmuch as the line drawings have been scaled with scientific accuracy and these are frequently supplemented by details of ornament and decoration rendered in light and shade. This was accomplished by elegant line engravings and well-composed lithographs, which are an inspiration to the student.

An earlier work in which the drawings are also engraved to simulate relief, is that of Desgodetz. A well known edition is the translation and revision of G. Marshall, architect; printed in London in 1795. Up to that time Desgodetz' work was the most accurate and complete of any that had been offered to the world on the subject of Roman architecture; but, although as Marshall says, the book "was constantly in request as the standard of ancient and modern art," the originals were scarce and until his adaptation was issued were hardly to be consulted by students. The dedication of the original, which was issued by Desgodetz in 1682, was addressed to Colbert, minister of Louis XIV, and is sufficiently fulsome. After blessing heaven for his birth in an age so full of wonders, "wherein the monuments of antiquity reared by the Augustuses, the Trajans and the Antonines have yielded the first place in the temple of glory to the invincible, the great, and the magnanimous Louis", he concludes his epistle by requesting his lordship's permission to thank him "a thousand times for casting eyes upon me, so as to deign me any share in the execution of those admirable designs which you daily meditate for the glory of the greatest king upon earth." Marshall's apostrophe, directed to his own monarch, is hardly less adulatory. "Be pleased, Sir, therefore", he says, "to favor this representative of Roman art and Roman power, exerted in edifices on which succeeding ages have gazed with wonder, and which are likely to stand unrivaled, unless your Majesty's influence should enable us to excel them." "Edifices Ancienne de Rome" by Desgodetz, Paris 1779, was one of the architectural books in the library of Thomas Jefferson which was doubtless frequently consulted by him. Latrobe, in a letter to the President, suggests that he verify a matter of proportions by reference to this authority.

While on the subject of Classic architecture, Gibbs' book of Orders should not be passed over without mention. This work still holds its own among many others of later date treating of the details and proportions of the elements, and is a safe and useful guide for students. It was published in 1724. James Gibbs was a famous architect of his day whose name has been often coupled with that of Wren. He was the architect of S. Mary-le-Strand, S. Martin-in-the-Fields—London churches—and of the Radcliffe Library, Oxford—his master work.

It must not be thought that architectural commentators of this age were wholly pre-occupied with ancient Greece and Rome. There was some architecture nearer home, as well, worth writing about; as Desgodetz took occasion to state in his dedicatory epistle. "To turn over the pages of seventeenth and eighteenth century books on architecture", says Simpson, "is in itself a liberal education. Marot, Le Pautre, Blondel, Mariette, and so forth, take one back to the days of the fine gentleman and full-bottomed wigs, to the stateliness of the time of the later Louis."

The most famous of these works is Blondel's "Architecture Francoise", a treasure for any library fortunate enough to possess it. Eight volumes were contemplated, but four only were published (1752-6). The plan of the Tuileries as designed by de l'Orme, Bernini's gigantic scheme for reconstructing the Louvre, together with Perrault's design for a similar rebuilding, are all reproduced in Blondel's work. It is interesting to recall that there were three Francois Blondels, who were noted architects. The beautiful arch of S. Denis, Paris, which as a composition is in many respects superior to the triumphal arches of the Romans, was designed by Francois Blondel the elder, born in Picardy in 1618. The author of "Architecture Francoise" was a native of Rouen, born in 1705.

"Les plus Excellent Bastiments de France" published in 1579, is especially valuable for its records of many buildings of the period; buildings which have since disappeared or suffered mutilation. It is a work of exquisite draftsmanship excelling, in this quality, the works of the Italians. The writer and engraver was the architect Du Cerceau. Many of Du Cerceau's most beautiful original drawings are reproduced in Ward's "French Chateaux and Gardens in the XVIth Century". Concerning the work of Du Cerceau this author says: "No other country can boast so complete a picture of its Renaissance architecture as seen by a contemporary, still less one by the trained and sympathetic hand of a great architect. It is a picture full of suggestion for architects and designers of today, to whom French influence makes so strong an appeal, illustrating as it does the works, not only of Du Cerceau, Jean Bullant but other less known or unknown names."

CHAPTER III

MODERN ARCHITECTURAL BOOKS

The nineteenth century is rich in the fruits of research in all phases of architectural art. The student of archaeology may yet have something more to say to us about the external life of the ancients; but in the field of architecture, so far as the searching observation and re-integration of the monuments of the past, there seems little left to do. It has been noticed that: "Scientific archaeology has done much to help us to understand the art of the past, but it sometimes seems to forget that details which are vital to the archaeologist may, on occasion, have no value for the artist." In a large measure this seems to be true of the sort of critical interpretation that is to be found in the majority of the German archaeological works. There are some notable exceptions—as the works of Durm and Bühlmann—but in the main the books produced by the Germans that are useful in the daily study of design are not numerous. On the contrary this is the field in which the French excel and it is pre-eminently their domain. A clear grasp of essentials and a sure instinct for selection; an ability to conceive and construct through the power of the creative imagination working in space, often from only a few remains, a brilliant and convincing restoration that will speak to us in terms of lofty architecture; all this embodied in terms of lucid statement and perfect illustration; such characteristics place the publications of the French artist-architects above those of the workers in the same field in every other country. Their works far outnumber the learned treatises of the Renaissance masters to which your attention has already been directed.

The complete architectural library of today will contain all sorts of sumptuous volumes on topics both varied and similar and will combine methods of printing and photogravure not even imagined by the early writers. Then it was a slow, tedious undertaking to engrave on steel or copper every plate by hand; whereas now the mechanical processes of reproduction have practically done away with the laborious ways of handicraft. Your simon-pure bibliophile may regret this, but students of design do not. The usefulness of books has not been impaired but greatly extended. It is true that there is a certain satisfaction resulting from the contemplation of an engraved plate that is not afforded by a photo-etching or reprint; but that satisfaction should be reserved for those whose preoccupation is with books for their own sake, rather than for what they may teach us.

Books of pictorial illustration abound, such as collections of large photographs of individual buildings—like the chateaux and cathedrals of France and the palaces of Italy. Others, perhaps the most beautiful and inspiring for us, are the collections of rendered restorations made by the pensioners of the French Academy in Rome—the winners of the Grand Prix. These comprise the collections familiarly known as d'Espouy, and such brilliant monographs as Epidaure, Pergame, Selinonte and the Parthenon. Still others are the folios of drawings carefully made in line of certain styles and periods of architecture; studies representing years of unremitting labor and painstaking measurement, like Letarouilly, Durand and Bühlmann. Then we have those much dog-eared folios of designs—dear to the eyes of our own students —produced by the students in the Ecole des Beaux Arts. It is unnecessary to enlarge further on the evident fact that the scope of modern works depicting architecture and architectural decoration is immense and that reproductions are innumerable.

Among all the noble books relating to our art it seems to me that there are two which deserve to be placed on a pedestal by themselves. I mean—Letarouilly—"Les Edifices de Rome Moderne" and Durand—"Recueil et Paralléle des Edifices en Tout Genre, Anciens et Modernes". A companion work to Letarouilly's is Strack's "Baudenkmaler Roms des XV—XIX Jahrhunderts"; a folio of photographic illustrations of the same subjects as are delineated in the former and a valuable supplement to it.

For inspiration in design I believe Letarouilly's to be the most useful and beautiful work ever offered either to student or practician; the work that in modern practice he would most frequently have occasion to consult. And I do not believe that I am assuming too much in making this recommendation, conceiving it to be one that the majority would support. There is a good reprint of "Les Edifices de Rome Moderne", the plates reproduced unfortunately at a smaller scale than the original. Letarouilly's work is so well known that it is unnecessary to describe it in any detail.

It is in three large folios, published in 1840—the dedication addressed to his majesty Louis Philippe. There is also a volume of descriptive text. At the beginning of the first volume you will find that inimitable plan of the "Eternal City"; a marvelous expression of the engraver's art and an instance of the perfect expression of a transcendent subject. Letarouilly was also the author of the equally beautiful monographs of St. Peter's and the Vatican; a work in two volumes, entitled "Le Vatican."

The other work which I have chosen to specially single out (I believe with as good reason as the one just mentioned) is the grand folio of Durand; one of the largest in size of plates of any in the library. The superficial dimensions of this book are governed by the fact that all the different plans, elevations and sections throughout the work are drawn to the same scale. Moreover as its field is the whole field of historic architecture, the dimensions of the plates are more or less determined by the largest edifices ever constructed, such as the Circus Maximus—a vast stadium reputed to have seated some 250,000 spectators, and other large buildings. When we stop to consider the immense advantage that accrues to the study of design from having all the important buildings of all ages of architecture drawn to a uniform scale, it is no exaggeration to say that if instructors in architecture were so circumstanced that they might retain only one work for reference, the majority would prefer to retain this one. Durand, who was a professor in l'Ecole Polytechnique, first published his work in Paris in Anno IX (1800). It was re-issued at a later date in an augmented form by a firm of editors in Liege. Reprints are also obtainable. In addition to drawings of constructed edifices, "Durand" also contains famous projects never put into execution and many plates of detail and other architectural elements.

The chief value of "Durand" to students of design is not the study of architectural monuments from the viewpoint of history —although it is valuable for that too—but the sudy of parti from the viewpoint of composition. Such is also the particular value of the premiated design in the competitions for the Grand Prix de Rome and in a lesser degree of the volumes of Croquis and Medailles. The publication of "Croquis d'Architecture" was discontinued about 1900 after twenty-five volumes had been issued.

Some instructors prefer it to the folios of Grand Prix, but just at this juncture it does not appear to be much favored by students.

There is a right way and a wrong way to use these books for study, the wrong way consisting in slavishly copying the conceptions of others—a habit far too prevalent.

As an example of what I consider to be the right method of study, let us examine for a moment one of the projets in Part II of "Grand Prix"—the fine conception of M. Chaussemiche—"Un Palais des Sociétés Savants". A familiarity with the principal requirements of the program is first essential; there will not be many. The problem should then be thought of as one of proportions—proportions and relations between the principal elements of the plan. Make a pencil tracing of the plan, drawing first the principal axes, indicating rooms simply by shaded rectangles and leaving communications white. This will fix in your mind the essential facts of the composition—the "parti"—and the proportions of the chief elements, the relative area devoted to corridors, light-courts, halls and rooms. Similar tracings may be made of elevations and sections. In the latter care should be taken for the interior silhouette, while in the former it will usually be sufficient to indicate broadly the proportions between voids and solids. Next you should make a study of "poché" by tracing with black ink certain typical parts of the plan. Finally, for comparative study, trace or sketch the alternate schemes.

Studies such as I have indicated above consume only a minimum of time. By forcing you to analyze they serve to greatly extend your knowledge of the large facts of plan composition, and consequently your ability to reason in terms of architecture and to solve programs becomes more competent. Mere aimless tracing of detail from books is of little value. Have some purpose and method. Keep in mind always the broad plan of your course in design. First to study elements; Second to combine elements, to compose; Third to combine proportions, to design.

It would appear that undue emphasis had been placed in this discussion on the literature of classicism and that mediaeval architecture had been inexcusably neglected. This might be taken by some to imply a negation of the importance of Gothic architecture, and I would not have it thought that it has not been realized that Gothic architecture is equally valuable for study, or that there is any superiority in one over the other. A course in design would certainly be incomplete if it did not include programs outside the Classic and Renaissance periods, and for the solution of such programs it is essential that the student apply himself most assiduously to the documents. But there are several reasons why the Gothic cannot and, as I believe, ought not to occupy so large a space in our thoughts as students of design. In the first place it is almost impossible to conceive of our contemporary life, outside of our religious life, being lived in an environment of Gothic architecture. In the second place, although there are many splendid monographs on Gothic buildings, the literature of Mediaeval architecture is by no means so extensive or voluminous as that of the Classic and analogous styles. Without entering further into the merits of the controversy that has been waged between the advocates of these two great divisions of architecture as they affect the study of design in the schools, I will close my remarks with a quotation from Professor Blomfield's lecture on Rome, which seems to me expresses a rational view of the matter. "We might" he says "by a process of mental abstraction, imagine ourselves back in mediaeval life, and by a sustained effort of mental histrionics, express ourselves in terms of mediaeval art. But the natural man, the actual conditions of life, will surely reassert themselves. We shall only feel at home in the broad spaces and serener atmosphere of classic art. I do not say that Roman architecture was perfect and impeccable. That architecture had its faults. It had lost the sensitive refinement of Greek art, it was given to accepting the details of architecture without much thought, possibly even with contemptuous indifference to minute refinements of form. But where it is forever memorable is in the splendid courage of its constructions, in its capacity for ordered thought dealing with vast conceptions. It is because of its superb resource, of its masterful method of conquering any and every problem set it, that Roman architecture remains the greatest and most profitable study for the serious architect."

Among works treating of Gothic architecture which are especially useful for the study of design, may be mentioned: Viollet-le-Duc's "Dictionnaire Raisonné de l'Architecture", a justly celebrated work embodying the results of profound research. C. H. Moore's "Gothic Architecture", and the second volume of Simpson's "History of Architectural Development"; both emphasizing the details of structure. Pugin's "Gothic Architecture", a five-volume work containing details, of which a reprint is available. Another work especially good for the study of detail is "An Analysis of Gothic Architecture" by R. and J. A. Brandon. Two very modern books on the style are F. Bond's, "Gothic Architecture in England" and "English Church Architecture"; up-to-date pieces of scholarship which are regarded by authorities as being probably the most valuable works on English church architecture. "Church Building", by Ralph Adams Cram explains many things about church planning not generally understood. Finally I will mention the third part of Guadet's "Eléments et Théorie de l'Architecture", which treats in an exhaustive fashion the whole subject of Catholic churches.

Guadet's work on the theory of architecture is certainly in a class by itself. Perhaps it may be of more value to the instructor than to the average student, but no one could study this work carefully without being immensely the gainer thereby. Treatises have been written in other languages on the general theory of architectural esthetics by thoughtful teachers, notably the discourses of Thiersch, Wagner and others in the German Handbuch series, but none of them approach Guadet in rationality of method and clarity of statement. Guadet bases his theory of proportions in architecture on construction, whereas the German writers incline toward the recondite analogies discoverable in the human and other organisms, and such geometrical analogies as are found in the similarity of rectangles.

One cannot study Guadet without being profoundly influenced by his teachings, whereas the German theories do not carry with them the same degree of conviction.

Two very fine and useful works are Bühlmann—"Die Architectur des Classischen Altertums und der Renaissance", and Gromort —"Elements d'Architecture Classique". The former obtainable in a good, translated reprint, and the latter in an inexpensive folio. For beginners there is perhaps no more useful work than Gromort's—the plates showing a close correspondence with the examples cited by Guadet. Bühlmann's work is equally valuable, the fact that it is one of the most used folios in the library speaking for itself.

Of contemporary publications it is deservedly fitting that special mention be made of the Monograph on the Work of McKim, Mead and White. The uniformly high character of the work of this firm places it on an equal footing with much of the best work of the Italian Renaissance architects. McKim himself has been often spoken of as the greatest English-speaking architect since Sir Christopher Wren.

The reading of books for inspiration in design is a comprehensive undertaking and one not likely to find a limit in your lifetime. My object in this chapter has been to confine myself in the main to reference works, since your study of design partakes so largely of the nature of research among books. But I also have another purpose which is to stimulate you to form the habit of reading the best books dealing with our art, whether they be philosophical, romantic or descriptive. With this end in view the following are among the most stimulating that I am acquainted with:

A work which is worthy of great admiration is Hippolyte Adolphe Taine's "Lectures on Art"—translated by J. Durand— consisting of a course of lectures delivered before the students of art of the Ecole des Beaux Arts, Paris, during the winter of 1864. This is an accomplishment of the highest genius—the thought being clothed in a style as perfectly artistic as any I know. The style of Ruskin is regarded in the field of letters as being particularly distinguished, but to my mind it does not surpass that of Taine; besides the esthetic opinions of the former critic have many of them fallen into disrepute. Nevertheless read "Modern Painters", "Stones of Venice" and "Seven Lamps of Architecture". Taine undertakes to apply to art the same theory he has applied to literature in his "Histoire de la Literature Anglaise"; that is, to explain art by social influences; humanity at different times and places, climate and other conditions, furnishing the facts on which the theory rests. You would also be delighted with his "Voyage en Italie". Theophile Gautier was another elegant writer, who—while not dealing specially with esthetics—had an uncommon knowledge and appreciation of architecture. This is especially evident in his "Romance of a Mummy", "Constantinople" and "A Winter in Russia". Read also "The Alhambra" by Washington Irving.

The vain glory and outrageous effrontery of one of the world's greatest artists has been admirably recorded by himself in a most remarkable recital of personal experience—"The Autobiography of Benevenuto Cellini". Read that and also Vasari's "Lives of the Most Eminent Painters, Sculptors and Architects".

In the preceding pages I have sought to emphasize as forcibly as I was able what seems undeniably true, that books on art exist primarily for what they may teach. At least that is their relation to us. What we may learn from them is, on our part, our chief interest. Furthermore our desire to understand what these books may interpret to us about the art of the past is only of importance in the sense that the art of the present may be vivified and a reasonable development of the art of the future assured. A book may be immensely interesting in itself—just as drawings are immensely interesting in themselves, and it is very easy to drift into the pleasurable belief that neither exists for anything except the satisfaction of contemplation and possession. Never forget that you are studying to be architects and that books and drawings are only an important means to an end—the acquisition of power in design. Next to the study of great buildings, the study of great books about them is the most powerful stimulant to the creative faculty—not less powerful for the student of architecture, I should say, than the consideration of nature is for the painter. I am only paraphrasing the words of Sir Joshua Reynolds, when he said: "The habit of contemplating and brooding over the ideas of great geniuses 'till you find yourself warmed by the contact, is the sure method of an artist-like mind."

GENERAL REFERENCE LIST OF WORKS IN CLASSIC AND RENAISSANCE ARCHITECTURE

Documents especially valuable for research and reference in the study and development of the parti and for the rendu.

(This list includes principally atlases of drawings and photographs.)

Durand, J. N. L.	Recueil et Paralléle des Edifices. Paris 1800.
Esquié, P.	The Five Orders of Architecture.
Gromort, G.	Choix D'Élements Empruntés L'Architecture Classique. Paris 1907.
Gromort, F.	Choix de Plans de Grands Compositions Exécutées. Paris 1910.
Guadet, J.	Éléments et Théorie de L'Architecture. Paris 1902. 4 vol.
Reynaud, F. L.	Traité D'Architecture. Paris 1850, 4 vol.
Viollet-le-Duc, E.	Lectures on Architecture. London 1877-8, 2 vol. Translated by Benjamin Bucknall.
Viollet-le-Duc, E.	Dictionnaire Raisonné de l'Architecture Française. Paris 1834-68, 10 vol.
Bühlmann, J.	Die Architektur des Classischen Altertums und der Renaissance. Stuttgart 1893.
d'Espouy, H.	Fragments D'Architecture du Moyen Age et de la Renaissance. Paris, no date.
Gailhabaud, J.	Monuments Anciens et Modernes. Paris 1850, 4 vol.

GENERAL REFERENCE LIST

Macartney, M. E. - - - - - Practical Exemplar of Architecture. Westminster, no date, 6 vol.

Strack, H. - - - - - - Ziegelbauwerke des Mittelalters und der Renaissance in Italien. Berlin, 1889.

Collignon, L. M. - - - - Le Parthénon. Paris 1912, 2 vol.

Defrasse, A. and Lechat, H. - - Épidaure. Paris 1895.

d'Espouy, H. - - - - - Fragments D'Architecture Antique. Paris 1905, 2 vol.

d'Espouy, H. - - - - - Monuments Antiques. Paris No date, 3 vol.

Hulot, J. and Fougeres, G. - - Sélinonte. Paris 1910.

Laloux, V. and Monceaux, P. - Restauration D'Olympie. Paris 1889.

Pontremoli, E. and Collignon, M. Pergame. Paris, 1900.

Biagi, G. - - - - - - La Renaissance en Italie. Paris 1913.

Blondel, J. F. - - - - - Réimpression de L'Architecture Francaise. Paris 1752-56. 4 vol.

Briere, G. - - - - - - Le Château de Versailles. Paris 1907, 2 vol. in 4.

Briere, G. - - - - - - Le Parc de Versailles. Paris 1909. 1 vol. in 2.

Dimier, L. - - - - - - Fontainebleau. Paris. No date 2 vol.

Haupt, A. - - - - - - Palast Architektur von Ober Italien und Toscana. Berlin 1911-23. 6 vol.

Letarouilly, P. M. - - - - Les Édifices de Rome Moderne Paris 1868-74. 3 vol.

Letarouilly, P. M. - - - - Le Vatican. Paris 1882. 3 vol.

Schütz, A. von - - - - - Die Renaissance in Italien. Hamburg 1882. 4 vol.

Strack, H. - - - - - - Baudenkmaeler Roms.... Zu Letarouilly, "Édifices de Rome Moderne." Berlin 1891.

McKim, Mead and White - - Work of, New York 1913. 4 vol.

Piranesi, J. B. - - - - - Oeuvres Choisies. Paris 1913. Reprint 2 vol.

Racinet, M. A. de. - - - - L'Ornament Polychrome. Paris 1873-86. 2 series.

Hegemann, W., and Peets, Elbert- The American Vitruvius. An Architects Handbook of Civic Art. New York, 1922.

L'ARCHITECTURE ET LA DECORATION AUX PALAIS DE LOUVRE ET DES TUILERIES
Photo-engravings. Paris. No date, 2 vol.

BRITISH COMPETITIONS
Alexander Koch, (Ed.) London, 1905—on. 4 vol.

CONCOURS CHENAVARD
École Nationale des Beaux Arts. Paris 1909

CONCOURS ROUGEVIN ET GODEBOEUF
École Nationale des Beaux Arts. Paris. No date.

CROQUIS D'ARCHITECTURE
Intime Club. Paris. 1866-98. 25 vol.

LES GRANDS PRIX DE ROME D'ARCHITECTURE
École Nationale des Beaux Arts. Paris, Continuation. 5 vol.

LES MEDAILLES DES CONCOURS D'ARCHITECTURE
École Nationale des Beaux Arts. Paris 1898—on. 15 vol.

A CATALOG OF SELECTED DOVER
BOOKS IN ALL FIELDS OF INTEREST

100 BEST-LOVED POEMS, Edited by Philip Smith. "The Passionate Shepherd to His Love," "Shall I compare thee to a summer's day?" "Death, be not proud," "The Raven," "The Road Not Taken," plus works by Blake, Wordsworth, Byron, Shelley, Keats, many others. 96pp. 5³⁄₁₆ x 8¼. 0-486-28553-7

100 SMALL HOUSES OF THE THIRTIES, Brown-Blodgett Company. Exterior photographs and floor plans for 100 charming structures. Illustrations of models accompanied by descriptions of interiors, color schemes, closet space, and other amenities. 200 illustrations. 112pp. 8⅜ x 11. 0-486-44131-8

1000 TURN-OF-THE-CENTURY HOUSES: With Illustrations and Floor Plans, Herbert C. Chivers. Reproduced from a rare edition, this showcase of homes ranges from cottages and bungalows to sprawling mansions. Each house is meticulously illustrated and accompanied by complete floor plans. 256pp. 9⅜ x 12¼.

0-486-45596-3

101 GREAT AMERICAN POEMS, Edited by The American Poetry & Literacy Project. Rich treasury of verse from the 19th and 20th centuries includes works by Edgar Allan Poe, Robert Frost, Walt Whitman, Langston Hughes, Emily Dickinson, T. S. Eliot, other notables. 96pp. 5³⁄₁₆ x 8¼. 0-486-40158-8

101 GREAT SAMURAI PRINTS, Utagawa Kuniyoshi. Kuniyoshi was a master of the warrior woodblock print — and these 18th-century illustrations represent the pinnacle of his craft. Full-color portraits of renowned Japanese samurais pulse with movement, passion, and remarkably fine detail. 112pp. 8⅜ x 11. 0-486-46523-3

ABC OF BALLET, Janet Grosser. Clearly worded, abundantly illustrated little guide defines basic ballet-related terms: arabesque, battement, pas de chat, relevé, sissonne, many others. Pronunciation guide included. Excellent primer. 48pp. 4³⁄₁₆ x 5¾.

0-486-40871-X

ACCESSORIES OF DRESS: An Illustrated Encyclopedia, Katherine Lester and Bess Viola Oerke. Illustrations of hats, veils, wigs, cravats, shawls, shoes, gloves, and other accessories enhance an engaging commentary that reveals the humor and charm of the many-sided story of accessorized apparel. 644 figures and 59 plates. 608pp. 6⅛ x 9¼.

0-486-43378-1

ADVENTURES OF HUCKLEBERRY FINN, Mark Twain. Join Huck and Jim as their boyhood adventures along the Mississippi River lead them into a world of excitement, danger, and self-discovery. Humorous narrative, lyrical descriptions of the Mississippi valley, and memorable characters. 224pp. 5³⁄₁₆ x 8¼. 0-486-28061-6

ALICE STARMORE'S BOOK OF FAIR ISLE KNITTING, Alice Starmore. A noted designer from the region of Scotland's Fair Isle explores the history and techniques of this distinctive, stranded-color knitting style and provides copious illustrated instructions for 14 original knitwear designs. 208pp. 8⅜ x 10⅞. 0-486-47218-3

CATALOG OF DOVER BOOKS

ALICE'S ADVENTURES IN WONDERLAND, Lewis Carroll. Beloved classic about a little girl lost in a topsy-turvy land and her encounters with the White Rabbit, March Hare, Mad Hatter, Cheshire Cat, and other delightfully improbable characters. 42 illustrations by Sir John Tenniel. 96pp. 5⅜₆ x 8¼. 0-486-27543-4

AMERICA'S LIGHTHOUSES: An Illustrated History, Francis Ross Holland. Profusely illustrated fact-filled survey of American lighthouses since 1716. Over 200 stations — East, Gulf, and West coasts, Great Lakes, Hawaii, Alaska, Puerto Rico, the Virgin Islands, and the Mississippi and St. Lawrence Rivers. 240pp. 8 x 10¾. 0-486-25576-X

AN ENCYCLOPEDIA OF THE VIOLIN, Alberto Bachmann. Translated by Frederick H. Martens. Introduction by Eugene Ysaye. First published in 1925, this renowned reference remains unsurpassed as a source of essential information, from construction and evolution to repertoire and technique. Includes a glossary and 73 illustrations. 496pp. 6½ x 9¼. 0-486-46618-3

ANIMALS: 1,419 Copyright-Free Illustrations of Mammals, Birds, Fish, Insects, etc., Selected by Jim Harter. Selected for its visual impact and ease of use, this outstanding collection of wood engravings presents over 1,000 species of animals in extremely lifelike poses. Includes mammals, birds, reptiles, amphibians, fish, insects, and other invertebrates. 284pp. 9 x 12. 0-486-23766-4

THE ANNALS, Tacitus. Translated by Alfred John Church and William Jackson Brodribb. This vital chronicle of Imperial Rome, written by the era's great historian, spans A.D. 14-68 and paints incisive psychological portraits of major figures, from Tiberius to Nero. 416pp. 5⅜₆ x 8¼. 0-486-45236-0

ANTIGONE, Sophocles. Filled with passionate speeches and sensitive probing of moral and philosophical issues, this powerful and often-performed Greek drama reveals the grim fate that befalls the children of Oedipus. Footnotes. 64pp. 5⅜₆ x 8 ¼. 0-486-27804-2

ART DECO DECORATIVE PATTERNS IN FULL COLOR, Christian Stoll. Reprinted from a rare 1910 portfolio, 160 sensuous and exotic images depict a breathtaking array of florals, geometrics, and abstracts — all elegant in their stark simplicity. 64pp. 8⅜ x 11. 0-486-44862-2

THE ARTHUR RACKHAM TREASURY: 86 Full-Color Illustrations, Arthur Rackham. Selected and Edited by Jeff A. Menges. A stunning treasury of 86 full-page plates span the famed English artist's career, from *Rip Van Winkle* (1905) to masterworks such as *Undine, A Midsummer Night's Dream,* and *Wind in the Willows* (1939). 96pp. 8⅜ x 11. 0-486-44685-9

THE AUTHENTIC GILBERT & SULLIVAN SONGBOOK, W. S. Gilbert and A. S. Sullivan. The most comprehensive collection available, this songbook includes selections from every one of Gilbert and Sullivan's light operas. Ninety-two numbers are presented uncut and unedited, and in their original keys. 410pp. 9 x 12. 0-486-23482-7

THE AWAKENING, Kate Chopin. First published in 1899, this controversial novel of a New Orleans wife's search for love outside a stifling marriage shocked readers. Today, it remains a first-rate narrative with superb characterization. New introductory Note. 128pp. 5⅜₆ x 8¼. 0-486-27786-0

BASIC DRAWING, Louis Priscilla. Beginning with perspective, this commonsense manual progresses to the figure in movement, light and shade, anatomy, drapery, composition, trees and landscape, and outdoor sketching. Black-and-white illustrations throughout. 128pp. 8⅜ x 11. 0-486-45815-6

Browse over 9,000 books at www.doverpublications.com

CATALOG OF DOVER BOOKS

THE BATTLES THAT CHANGED HISTORY, Fletcher Pratt. Historian profiles 16 crucial conflicts, ancient to modern, that changed the course of Western civilization. Gripping accounts of battles led by Alexander the Great, Joan of Arc, Ulysses S. Grant, other commanders. 27 maps. 352pp. 5⅜ x 8½.　　　　0-486-41129-X

BEETHOVEN'S LETTERS, Ludwig van Beethoven. Edited by Dr. A. C. Kalischer. Features 457 letters to fellow musicians, friends, greats, patrons, and literary men. Reveals musical thoughts, quirks of personality, insights, and daily events. Includes 15 plates. 410pp. 5⅜ x 8½.　　　　0-486-22769-3

BERNICE BOBS HER HAIR AND OTHER STORIES, F. Scott Fitzgerald. This brilliant anthology includes 6 of Fitzgerald's most popular stories: "The Diamond as Big as the Ritz," the title tale, "The Offshore Pirate," "The Ice Palace," "The Jelly Bean," and "May Day." 176pp. 5⅜ x 8½.　　　　0-486-47049-0

BESLER'S BOOK OF FLOWERS AND PLANTS: 73 Full-Color Plates from Hortus Eystettensis, 1613, Basilius Besler. Here is a selection of magnificent plates from the *Hortus Eystettensis*, which vividly illustrated and identified the plants, flowers, and trees that thrived in the legendary German garden at Eichstätt. 80pp. 8⅜ x 11.
0-486-46005-3

THE BOOK OF KELLS, Edited by Blanche Cirker. Painstakingly reproduced from a rare facsimile edition, this volume contains full-page decorations, portraits, illustrations, plus a sampling of textual leaves with exquisite calligraphy and ornamentation. 32 full-color illustrations. 32pp. 9⅜ x 12¼.　　　　0-486-24345-1

THE BOOK OF THE CROSSBOW: With an Additional Section on Catapults and Other Siege Engines, Ralph Payne-Gallwey. Fascinating study traces history and use of crossbow as military and sporting weapon, from Middle Ages to modern times. Also covers related weapons: balistas, catapults, Turkish bows, more. Over 240 illustrations. 400pp. 7¼ x 10⅛.　　　　0-486-28720-3

THE BUNGALOW BOOK: Floor Plans and Photos of 112 Houses, 1910, Henry L. Wilson. Here are 112 of the most popular and economic blueprints of the early 20th century — plus an illustration or photograph of each completed house. A wonderful time capsule that still offers a wealth of valuable insights. 160pp. 8⅜ x 11.
0-486-45104-6

THE CALL OF THE WILD, Jack London. A classic novel of adventure, drawn from London's own experiences as a Klondike adventurer, relating the story of a heroic dog caught in the brutal life of the Alaska Gold Rush. Note. 64pp. 5³⁄₁₆ x 8¼.
0-486-26472-6

CANDIDE, Voltaire. Edited by Francois-Marie Arouet. One of the world's great satires since its first publication in 1759. Witty, caustic skewering of romance, science, philosophy, religion, government — nearly all human ideals and institutions. 112pp. 5³⁄₁₆ x 8¼.　　　　0-486-26689-3

CELEBRATED IN THEIR TIME: Photographic Portraits from the George Grantham Bain Collection, Edited by Amy Pastan. With an Introduction by Michael Carlebach. Remarkable portrait gallery features 112 rare images of Albert Einstein, Charlie Chaplin, the Wright Brothers, Henry Ford, and other luminaries from the worlds of politics, art, entertainment, and industry. 128pp. 8⅜ x 11.　　　　0-486-46754-6

CHARIOTS FOR APOLLO: The NASA History of Manned Lunar Spacecraft to 1969, Courtney G. Brooks, James M. Grimwood, and Loyd S. Swenson, Jr. This illustrated history by a trio of experts is the definitive reference on the Apollo spacecraft and lunar modules. It traces the vehicles' design, development, and operation in space. More than 100 photographs and illustrations. 576pp. 6¾ x 9¼. 0-486-46756-2

Browse over 9,000 books at www.doverpublications.com

Greek
Doric   Ionic   Roman
                          Corinthian
Parthenon   Acropolis
perfection of
 beauty

Tuscan   composite

Walls Cornices Windows Doorways

Vignoles   diameter of column   unit of meas
        Proportion w/o scale
TRIGLPH Interval metope